Praise for *Wedding Goddess*

"Rev. Laurie Sue Brockway has done it again! Her newest guide, *Wedding Goddess*, is a must-read for any bride-to-be who needs to recharge her own power, spirit, and capacity for love and calm. *Wedding Goddess* rescues the bride from wedding planning stress, bringing back her radiance, her higher wisdom, and her belief in her dreams coming true. Rev. Laurie Sue Brockway shares the ultimate wedding present . . . bliss for the bride."

—Sharon Naylor, author of *Your Special Wedding Vows* and twenty-one additional wedding books

"This magnificent book is a blessing to any bride and groom as they go through the sacred ritual of marriage. Rev. Laurie Sue Brockway is a compassionate, wise, intuitive guide. I highly recommend this book to every woman who wants to cross the threshold in the most divinely inspired way."

—Judith Orloff, M.D., author, *Positive Energy*

"If anyone has the wisdom, the heart and spirit to guide new brides across the finish line with ease, it's Rev. Laurie Sue! This book will revolutionize how it feels to say "*I do*"—after reading this book and before walking down the aisle. Fresh, breezy, like a fairy godmother in your pocket, *Wedding Goddess* is the perfect prep for that perfect day."

—Patti Britton, Ph.D., coauthor of *The Complete Idiot's Guide to Sensual Massage*, and sex coach

Wedding Goddess

A
DIVINE GUIDE
TO TRANSFORMING
WEDDING STRESS
INTO WEDDING BLISS

Laurie Sue Brockway

A PERIGEE BOOK

THE BERKLEY PUBLISHING GROUP
Published by the Penguin Group
Penguin Group (USA) Inc.
375 Hudson Street, New York, New York 10014, USA
Penguin Group (Canada), 10 Alcorn Avenue, Toronto, Ontario M4V 3B2, Canada
(a division of Pearson Penguin Canada Inc.)
Penguin Books Ltd., 80 Strand, London WC2R 0RL, England
Penguin Group Ireland, 25 St. Stephen's Green, Dublin 2, Ireland (a division of Penguin Books Ltd.)
Penguin Group (Australia), 250 Camberwell Road, Camberwell, Victoria 3124, Australia
(a division of Pearson Australia Group Pty. Ltd.)
Penguin Books India Pvt. Ltd., 11 Community Centre, Panchsheel Park, New Delhi—110 017, India
Penguin Group (NZ), Cnr. Airborne and Rosedale Roads, Albany, Auckland 1310, New Zealand
(a division of Pearson New Zealand Ltd.)
Penguin Books (South Africa) (Pty.) Ltd., 24 Sturdee Avenue, Rosebank, Johannesburg 2196,
South Africa
Penguin Books Ltd., Registered Offices:
80 Strand, London WC2R 0RL, England

Copyright © 2005 by Rev. Laurie Sue Brockway
Text design by Stephanie Huntwork
Cover design by Liz Sheehan
Interior photos by Arlene Sandler/Lensgirl.com except for "Mother and Child" in Chapter 16 and
"Bride and Groom" in Chapter 20 by Jason Groupp/jasongphoto.com

ISBN: 0-399-53099-1

PRINTING HISTORY
Perigee trade paperback edition / July 2005

PERIGEE is a registered trademark of Penguin Group (USA) Inc.
The "P" design is a trademark belonging to Penguin Group (USA) Inc.

This book has been cataloged by the Library of Congress

PRINTED IN THE UNITED STATES OF AMERICA

3   5   7   9   10   8   6   4

To all the brides who dare to take that journey down the aisle,
and to their beloveds, who await.

May your journeys be good.
May your marriages be blessed.
May you be kind and loving to each other for all time.

And . . .

To Rev. Vic Fuhrman, my new husband,
to whom I also dedicate this quote:

"Marriage is not a ritual or an end.
It is a long, intricate,
intimate dance together,
and nothing matters more
than your own sense of balance
and your choice of partner."
—AMY BLOOM

ACKNOWLEDGMENTS

Blessings to my agents, Arielle Ford and Brian Hilliard, whose love story inspired me to find my own true love and, ultimately, marry in my own unique way. Thank you for always being in my corner, as well as for being the poster couple for creative multiple wedding ceremonies.

Blessings to the Perigee Goddesses: My delightful editor, Christel Winkler, who has now seen me through two books and whose insights, great ideas, and long chats I value dearly! To senior editor Michelle Howry, a sweet and supportive presence in my life. And to PR Goddess Heather Connor, who has always gone beyond the call of duty on my behalf. I treasure the friendship I share with all of you and thank you all for your heartfelt support. What a gift!

Blessings and thanks to Arlene Sandler of Lensgirl.com whose beautiful photos bless these pages. She put great care into providing fabulous photo illustrations for this book.

Blessings to Rev. Charlotte Richards, of the famous Little White Chapel who inspired me with her spirit and love.

Blessings to Rev. Deb Steen Ross, now assistant director of The New Seminary, and to Rev. Judith Marcus, my former dean. You were both there for me in my early days as a wedding officiant, and I am truly grateful for your willingness to share your wisdom and expertise.

Blessings to Rev. Diane Berke, Spiritual Director of the One Spirit Interfaith Seminary, who has always been an inspiration to me.

Blessings and thanks to: Shelley Ackerman, Kathy Bishop, Barbara Biziou, Dr. Patti Britton, June Soyka Cook, Arlene and Randy Cronk and my friends at the New York Wedding Group, Phyllis Curott, Tracy Day, Judith Glaser, Rev. Joyce Liechenstein, Daphne Rose Kingma, Dr. Judy Kuriansky, Rev. Paul Michael, Gerard and Eileen Monaghan, Dr. Judith Orloff, Valerie Rickle, Carley Roney, Candida Royalle, Rabbi Roger Ross, and Rev. Susan Turchin.

Blessings to all the experts who shared their insights in this book. You will find them all listed in the Resource Directory.

Blessings to the brides and grooms who allowed me to share their stories. Many of the weddings mentioned in these pages are weddings that I had the honor to officiate. I am so grateful that these lovely couples selected me as their wedding officiant, and allowed me to play a role in their sacred experience. Marrying couples in love has been a great joy in my life. It is through their creative wedding planning and personalized ceremonies that I have gained the wisdom to share in this book, to help other brides and grooms.

Blessing to the brides who helped by filling out my massive Wedding Goddess Questionnaire, sharing their insights so generously: They included: Jane Abramson, Andrea Bergin, Elizabeth Brown, AnaMaria Correa, Jackie Cuscuna, Amy Cunningham, Monica Douglas-Clark, Jodi DiPetro, Ariel Ford, Randi Goetke, Patti Guest, Julie Hill, Lori Innella-Venne, Brooke Inman, Amy Kraft, Deborah Losardo, Patricia McCaffrey Rosa, Summer Moore, Katerina Muller, Anna Ng, Sharon Lynn Nelson-Borriello, Teresa Papanikolas, Sophia Rakowsky, Jodi Kate Sanders Calvert, Jessica Shatan, Jessica SeQuinot, Barry Singer, Laurie Smith, June Soyka Cook, Courtney Summer, Rev. Susan Turchin, Kelly White, Laura Ziv.

Blessings and thanks to the brides and grooms pictured in these pages in photos by Arlene Sandler of Lensgirl.com: Marie-Joëlle Brassard (introduction and also, along with hubby Mark Brightman and their wedding party, in Chapter 15); Elizabeth Schorn (Chapter 2); Jodie Sanders Calvert and Andrew Calvert (Chapters 4 and 12); Haya Brant, with friends Sandra McKenzie and Annette Perel (Chapter 5); Denise Cante-Tanz, with parents Diane and Richard Cante (Chapter 7) and Jason Tanz (Chapter 8); they're also pictured together with maid of honor Kelly Parisi (Chapter 19); Derek Mah and Erin Tang (Chapter 8); Jason Tanz (Chapter 9); Carla Sapsford and Hector Olásolo (Chapter 13); Nancy and Michael James (Chapter 14); Nicola and Troy Inglis, with bride's parents John Clark and Elizabeth Mercer Clark (Chapter 14); Dara Sicherman (Chapter 17). And Blessings to Bethan Williams-Velenosi and Michael Velenosi (Chapter 20) and Bethan and baby Max (Chapter 16), photos by Jason Groupp of jasongphoto.com. (Thanks, Jason!)

Blessings and a special *thank you* to Rabbi Joseph Gelberman, who brought me together with my true love and who married us seven years later in a charming ceremony on a Monday morning in September. And to our dear friends Barbara Biziou, who hosted our engagement ritual and later renewed our vows before friends and family; and H. P. Phyllis Curott for performing our spiritual marriage ceremony in her beautiful garden. And to Dee-Dee Duffy and the staff at the Graceland Chapel who helped us with our Elvis vow renewal, officiated by Rev. Norm Jones, the only ordained Elvis in Las Vegas. Thank you all for your blessings and love . . . and for helping us get hitched!

Blessings to my mom, Shirley, who always taught me marriage is a choice, not a necessity for women. And to my mother-in-law Mal, and my loving family of siblings and siblings-in-law, and many nieces and nephews—now expanded by our combined families. Thank you, all, for cheering us on as we followed our personal, somewhat off-beat path to the altar.

Blessings to my husband, Vic, and to our amazing kids, Alexander and Abby. It's so great to be a family . . . and so it is.

CONTENTS

PART SEVEN
After the Wedding:
Keeping the Sacred Alive As a Married Couple

What Is Your Bridal Personality?

As you begin the journey of planning your wedding, it will be so helpful to find out just what kind of bride you are most likely to be. This quiz will help you define your wedding priorities and style as it shines a spotlight on early warning signs of things that can get out of whack while planning a wedding—such as the places you might be focusing too much on the appearance of things or what people think. Answer honestly. There are no right or wrong answers here, just an opportunity to do a reality check on what will be most important to you on your journey to the altar.

1. **As little girls, many of us played bride or set up mock weddings with friends or siblings. What was your favorite way to play dress up?**
    A. You made your mother buy you a bride costume.
    B. You borrowed your mom's white slips and camisoles, and grandma's lace doilies.
    C. You took toilet paper from the bathroom and pinned it to your hair as a makeshift veil that flowed to the floor.
    D. You never liked to play bride.

2. **When you fantasized about your perfect wedding when you were little, how did you imagine your big day?**
    A. A wedding fit for royalty, huge and attended by dignitaries, where everyone you know is invited and each minute detail attended to by huge staffs of people who are there only to serve at your pleasure.

    B. A lovely family gathering; everyone who has touched your life would come to celebrate.

    C. Barefoot on a beach or on a mountaintop . . . someplace natural.

    D. A very romantic and intimate experience where you and your groom feel as though you are the only two people on the planet.

3. Now that you are a bride-to-be, what would you say is your dream wedding?

    A. A big, stylish black-tie affair, with all the trimmings and traditions.

    B. A beautiful wedding experience in a lovely place with just your closest friends and family members.

    C. A romantic or exotic setting, such as the beach or a gorgeous garden.

    D. Something simple, not too frilly and not too much to manage.

4. Now that you can get the wedding dress of your dreams, what kind of dress are you most likely to go for?

    A. The most stylish and breathtaking dress—something that will make people say *"Wow!"*

    B. The dress or gown that makes you feel most comfortable and most like yourself.

    C. Something that matches the mood, theme, or location and makes you feel beautiful inside and out.

    D. You want to look nice and feel good, but you would go for something un-bride-like . . . perhaps a nice suit or a new dress.

5. We all tend to obsess about our weddings. Which of the following do you find yourself obsessing about most?

    A. The way the wedding looks and comes off to others, and the way you look and are seen by others.

    B. How to have a wedding experience that includes everyone who is special to you, and also makes people feel welcome.

C. Creating a wedding that has your unique signature and marries you in a personal way that is very gratifying for you and your beloved.

D. That the wedding be low-key and un-wedding-like so that you do not have to deal with family issues, wedding drama, financial drain, and fuss.

6. **In terms of the rites of passage that lead up to your wedding day, what kind of shower would you love?**

A. A traditional shower, maybe more than one . . . and all the wonderful gifts.

B. A small shower with people you love most, and enjoying the spirit of their company.

C. A small gathering of girlfriends to bless your new life.

D. A coed shower with my beloved.

7. **Since planning a wedding can be like having another full-time job, how will you approach creating the wedding of your dreams?**

A. Hire a wedding planner.

B. Ask your best friends and family to help with specific tasks.

C. Do a lot of it on your own or with your groom, because you want to put your personal touch on it.

D. *Ugh!* I dread the idea of planning a wedding. It will feel easier, more like just making lunch reservations.

8. **In general, you see yourself as someone who tends to have a flair for being:**

A. Dramatic.

B. Accommodating and inclusive.

C. Uniquely self-expressive.

D. Very low-key or shy.

9. **Almost any place can accommodate a wedding these days. You see yourself getting married at:**

A. A big hotel or a huge, upscale wedding venue.

B. A more nontraditional venue, such as a loft or rooftop.

C. A destination, such as Mexico or Hawaii, or an unusual land-

mark, such as atop the Empire State Building or a favorite ski mountain.
  D. A park or a restaurant.

10. **When it comes to the ceremony, your options are unlimited. Which of these ceremonies seems right for you?**
  A. Religious and traditional.
  B. Nondenominational, with aspects of tradition, but not religious, per se.
  C. Personal, unique, offbeat, and possibly interfaith or intercultural.
  D. Simple, short, and sweet.

11. **For the bridal party, you'll want:**
  A. All of your best friends, your siblings, and his siblings.
  B. Just the people closest to you.
  C. Only the people you really want to stand for you—you wouldn't want to ask someone just because they'd expect it.
  D. You don't feel as though you need a bridal party.

12. **Since a bride is immortalized in her wedding photos, what kind of wedding album will you want to look at later?**
  A. State-of-the-art wedding photos, many of them, with posed pictures of the two of you with everyone, as well as many candid images that capture the fun and experience of the wedding.
  B. A photojournalistic approach, where you do less posing and more enjoying yourselves.
  C. Photos that capture the essence of the day as well as the more unique aspects, such as a beautiful altar table, the ocean, or the guests blowing bubbles on a mountaintop.
  D. One or two nice photos would make you happy, and you can just ask friends to take those.

13. **When it comes to the food at your wedding, you'd like to serve:**
  A. An elegant sit-down dinner, preceded by a cocktail hour featuring multiple grazing stations and numerous different hors d'oeuvres brought around by servers.

B. A fabulous buffet with delicious food, and a delightful Viennese table for dessert.

C. Yummy delectables local to the destination or that fit in with a cultural theme—such as a Chinese banquet or Mexican fair.

D. You'd just like to eat at your favorite restaurant.

13. **The kind of music you would like at your reception is:**

A. A live band or orchestra.

B. A DJ.

C. Something culturally unique, such as salsa or Celtic music.

D. A friend playing a boom box.

14. **If you could have one very special item at your wedding altar, what would it be?**

A. Flower arrangements with Austrian crystals in them.

B. Your grandmother's lace handkerchief.

C. A sacred item, to be blessed in the ceremony.

D. Just the two of you, simple and free.

15. **At the end of your ceremony, you can imagine:**

A. Everyone throwing rose petals from beautiful white organza bags.

B. Everyone blowing bubbles.

C. Everyone offering a blessing on your marriage.

D. Looking into your beloved's eyes, smiling, happy that you don't have many logistics or relatives to attend to.

18. **How do you see this event being paid for?**

A. Your parents will pay.

B. You and your beloved will pay with the help of your parents.

C. You'll pay for it yourselves.

D. You will ask friends to bring dishes to share.

17. **Your wedding will be an amazing event that will give you the opportunity to:**

A. Enjoy being the center of attention and the belle of the ball.

B. Celebrate loved ones as you declare before witnesses that you are marrying the man of your dreams.

C. Start your new life together in a way that is personally empowering and magical.

D. Marry the man you love without the frills.

18. **To you, marriage means:**

A. Growing up and becoming a woman in the eyes of your family.

B. Making a commitment to blend two lives and two families.

C. A promise to build a unique and loving union with your best friend.

D. Deepening your relationship and making it more official.

Scoring: What Is Your Bridal Personality?

*T*he Wedding Goddess embraces the best of all of the options above and turns them into a wedding experience with her own special stamp on it. Yet to become a Wedding Goddess, you need to know your starting point. These general assessments will help you see the path that is your starting point.

THE FORMAL BRIDE

If your answers were mostly A's you definitely see yourself as a bride who is looking forward to a formal, fancy, and stylish wedding experience. Your dream wedding is likely on the upper end of the wedding price scale, and it is a great thing if you have the financial wherewithal to afford the best of everything for your special day. But you are halfway there if you feel entitled to it. This will help you conduct yourself like a Goddess and will ensure that you truly get a chance to create your dream wedding. Of course, you will need help with a big wedding like this, and there will be many guests to greet and many thank-yous to write, but if this is what you have dreamed of and desire, what a wonderful experience it will be, and what a great memory you will have. The dark side is that if you become too demanding or too focused on how it all looks, you could lose sight of what your wedding is all about.

Warning sign: If you find yourself thinking of your big day as a series of impressive experiences and a fabulous, to-be-talked-about party—as opposed to the day you will marry the one you love—it is time to stop and remember what it's all about.

The Casual and Inclusive Bride

If your answers are mostly B's, you are a casual bride who seeks some tradition but looks more toward intimacy, sentiment, and inclusion of others. For you, the wedding experience is meant to be shared with those you love and celebrated in a way that is affordable and manageable. While you might want a midsized affair, that can take just as much planning as a formal event; yet you are more likely to choose a slightly alternative approach—a penthouse loft space, or a rooftop garden, instead of a hotel. Perhaps friends will do the music, or a collage pal will do the flowers. Maybe you will have just a few close friends in the bridal party; you might select a color but let them find dresses they love. You are on a budget, but you know your wedding will likely fall into the national average of $22,000 to $25,000, so you will be looking to cut down on elegant and expensive extras and replace them with comfy and cool details. The dark side is that you may be too worried about pleasing others, including everyone, and giving all the people you care about something to do. While this can save you some bucks, it can also land you in the position of trying to keep a lot of people happy, and busy, with your wedding.

Warning sign: If you find yourself having to micromanage friends and family members who are helping out, or if you end up on the receiving end of complaints or so many "helpful" ideas that it is making your blood pressure rise, you might need to pull back and evaluate whether you have too many cooks at the wedding kettle.

The Offbeat Bride

If your answers were mostly C's, then you are someone who dances to her own beat and wants her wedding to reflect that. You see your wedding as a special and personal creation, and you intend to put your signature touch on every part of it. Because you are so creative and have so many ideas, you probably are an independent operator and would not enjoy hearing the input of others about what you should do or how you should do it. In fact, you probably want to surprise them all with the result. Since you will probably be paying for the wedding yourselves, you have some assurance of being able to create what you want on your own. You are most likely to choose a destination wedding with limited guests, or something larger and local that is different or kitschy. Whatever it is, it will be your own special design, and it will celebrate your love in a truly unique way. You will take from tradition the things that are meaningful to you and leave the rest behind. You might find yourself drawing from many different cultures and traditions to add just the right touches to your ceremony and party. You are likely to dress the part as well—a sari for an Indian theme or goddess gown for a handfasting. The dark side is that you may be so independent and offbeat that you leave people out of the celebration and press them into the role of observer rather than participant. This could hurt people's feelings or make them feel like observers at just another weird wedding.

WARNING SIGN: If you find yourself getting so lost in concocting your unique wedding that you stop caring about arranging it in a way that others feel included, you may have crossed the line. Be unique, but not exclusionary in your approach.

THE UN-BRIDE

If your answers were mostly D's, you are someone who would prefer to take a very low-key approach to your wedding. The idea of a wedding with all the trimmings does not appeal to you. You clearly prefer no frills, no fuss, no financial drain, and no relatives telling you what to do. This is good in that you have tremendous flexibility about where and when you wed, and whom you include. You can always include or adapt certain wedding traditions that suit you. For example, perhaps you would prefer to marry in a restaurant with just your parents and siblings present, or in a park with just one witness, yet you might still want to wear a bridal gown or get your hair and makeup done. Or maybe you would rather get married in a judge's office, or by a clergyperson in a house of worship, but would rather not dress in white. If you feel that as long as you are together, that's all that matters, it can be ultra-romantic. The dark side is that your desire to keep the wedding low-key could be related to a fear of getting married, family issues that you don't want to face (which could resurface again in your marriage), or even a negative attitude toward marriage.

WARNING SIGN: If you find yourself becoming obsessed with having it be an "un-wedding" and insist on treating your wedding day as just another day in your life, you could be missing the special joy and bliss that is meant to be yours on that day. If you keep all of your loved ones out of the equation, you may later regret that no one witnessed your marriage.

Who Is the Wedding Goddess Bride?

The Wedding Goddess bride embodies aspects of all of the above. She combines the best of all bridal personalities, and she knows she is entitled to create the wedding of her dreams. She aims to be creative, inclusive, and self-protective, and she never loses sight of the reason she is on the wedding path—she is in love and is getting ready to marry the man she adores! She is a bride who seeks an alternative to a traditional wedding, yet wants the option of including any traditions that call to her. She is a down-to-earth person who can get crazed from time to time, but she makes sure that she takes responsibility for herself and her reactions. She very much wants to stay centered in the face of wedding dramas. She sees her wedding as the stepping stone to married life—not a means to an end—and seeks to go through the experience with an open heart and mind, yet with boundaries and a good game plan. While she knows that weddings can bring out the worst in people, she also hopes that her wedding will bring out her best, and the best in her beloved and their loved ones. She sees her wedding as a form of self-expression and as a very personal declaration of her love.

WHAT YOU CAN LEARN FROM HER: A Wedding Goddess is the creator of her own reality and takes charge of all that goes on between engagement and the biggest ritual of her life. She embodies the most personally meaningful aspects of the bridal personalities, and she is a female in touch with the divine spark within.

Wedding Goddess: Joëlle Brassard
Arlene Sandler/Lensgirl.com

INTRODUCTION

Choose to Be a Wedding Goddess

You are a bright light . . . a gift from the heavens.

The hand of life pulses through you, imbuing you with sacred wisdom.

You are magical because you love . . . and you are loved.

Nothing enchants more than a woman who knows the key to the heart.

You are a bride, standing on love's pedestal, a Goddess.

—Isis, Egyptian Mother Goddess of all things,
and wife, consort, coruler, healer, and soul lover of Osiris

When I began thinking about this book, I had in mind that a Wedding Goddess was something of a wedding Superwoman. Like a power bride, with a big WG on her chest, she'd leap from task to task, planning her wedding with bridal organizer in her hand while comforting cranky relatives, friends, and vendors. She'd have a cool demeanor that nothing could ruffle. She'd keep an open heart and an open mind, let other people's opinions bounce off her opinion-proof chest, and have the perfect wedding with the perfect man in her own perfect way.

Then I got engaged. And the wedding drama began.

As a wedding officiant, I have for years helped hundreds of other brides through the oy's and joys of planning their wedding. I pride myself in my calm and loving manner, and the way I am able to put couples at ease as I help them find solutions for tricky challenges—anything from dealing with overinvolved moms to handling religious disputes. I kinda thought I'd be the same way as a Bride. But when I found myself at a time in my life when it was my time to be a Wedding Goddess, I realized that I would not be spared all the stresses of wedding planning. I really got to see how hard it is sometimes to stay true to yourself when planning a major life event. I also got to see how important it is to be flexible and open-minded, and to wisely pick the things to battle about and worry about. It made writing this book so much more meaningful, knowing that I was taking the journey down the aisle with all of you!

Fortunately, my beloved *husband*—I so love saying that word!—and I shared many of the same visions for our wedding. We both love ceremony and ritual, and we agreed there was more than one way, and one day, to bless our union. We decided we'd have a few different blessings over the course of a year. When anything we thought of planning became too stressful or just didn't feel right, we nipped it in the bud (including calling off our engagement party and instead having a "family unity ceremony"). By the same token, on the occasions when challenges arose that could have interfered with the things we truly did want, we stood our ground—yet sometimes chose to tweak our plans to adapt to new developments. I'd heard so many stories from my brides, yet it was interesting to experience just how many times in a day "situations" can arise when you are planning to marry. I got the chance many times over to test, firsthand, my philosophies on how to turn wedding stress into wedding bliss.

In this book, I blend my personal experience with years of working with brides, and with the many stories and situations encountered by so many of the brides and grooms who I have married over the years. I am glad to report that no matter how bumpy the road may get, it is a road you will travel for only a short amount of time, in the grand spectrum of things. You may as well enjoy it with all your heart!

Today's weddings have become so commercially driven and so stressful to plan that many brides feel as though they are dealing with a crisis rather than a joyous rite of passage. They sometimes forget about the sacred nature of the wedding ceremony. Many brides also forget—or never realize in the first place—the sacred nature of being a bride. To recapture the sacred nature of the experience—from engagement to wedding day—it is important to be aware of the emotional and spiritual pitfalls of wedding planning, and to *plan* for them so that they do not turn your joyous wedding journey into a wedding disaster.

In the process of wedding planning, many brides experience a period of intensity that challenges them on every level. When you are *in it*, you feel as though you are being pulled into a wedding-mania vortex. It can bring out a side of your personality that even you have never seen. What's more mortifying is that planning a wedding can turn even the sweetest-tempered people into maniacs; you might find yourself or your loved ones being pushed over the edge. That is why it is essential that you tread the hollowed ground of wedding preparation with the grace of a Goddess and, as much as possible, surround yourself with love, spirit, and divinely inspired support.

Many of us—no matter how cool, composed, and professional we are when we start the journey—find ourselves stressed, disempowered, and wishing we'd just eloped. But it doesn't have to be that way. What can set you apart from all who take a traditional Stress Express to the altar is to make a decision up front that you will go about the business of being a bride with the conscious intention to stay present, enjoy the journey, and feel the blessings of this very short yet intense period of your life. This means that you are not just the luckiest woman in the world with the most fabulous guy, the princess whose prince has arrived, the queen for a day, etc. You will be a Goddess—radiant, relaxed, ready, and excited as you step into your new life, onto your new path. A Wedding Goddess.

While attending an Orthodox Jewish wedding ceremony of family friends in 2004, I watched with awe while the twenty-year-old bride fulfilled the tradition of blessing her female guests. In Orthodox Judaism, it is held that the bride has special access to divine wisdom on her wedding day, and typically the women line up to kneel before her to hear whatever she has to share. I watched this young woman speak like one far beyond her years, encouraging friends and loved ones to go for their highest in life and, in some cases, to find true love, as she had.

From the moment you embark on your wedding journey, it is important that you realize that *you* are magical and blessed. And it is just as important that you treat yourself not just royally but divinely—like a Goddess. Adopt a mind-set and create a lifestyle that is nurturing, healing, and relaxing—and generous. From the moment you decide to marry, you will want to get on the Wedding Goddess track and forge ahead with wedding planning with a sense of joy, fun, inspiration, and grace.

I see the Wedding Goddess as someone who can have an awareness of the realities, stresses, disappointments, and disasters of wedding planning but also hold on to and nurture her vision of how she wants it all to be. She is someone who takes a special path to the altar, because she is committed to making that dream come to life—without losing her sanity, or her life's savings.

The best way to conquer wedding problems before they begin is plan for them like a Goddess would: Take charge of your wedding planning experience as if you are seizing the opportunity to create your own destiny; and own every moment of it, from start to grand, delightful, delicious finale.

Make every stage of planning your wedding as sacred as the ceremony itself. This book treats every step of the experience—from engagement and bridal shower to wedding day and post–wedding day—as its own rite of passage. It looks at the planning of the wedding as a sacred growing experience and incorporates exercises, prayers, rituals, meditation, music, healing techniques, creativity, spirituality, and playfulness into the experience.

In these pages you will find insight, advice, information, and many practical and spiritual hints on how to tap into the Wedding Goddess within you to bring your perfect wedding experience to life. It helps you deal with the most confrontational personal issues related to planning a wedding—your friends, your mother, your guest list, your groom's disinterest, wedding politics, fear, panic, the search for the perfect dress, etc.—as it shows you ways to:

- Visualize, imagine, dream, and pray your dream wedding to life.
- Enact rituals that put you at ease and help you relax and stay centered in the face of the inevitable wedding dramas and family issues that will come up, so you can reduce stress and bring out the best in yourself.
- Design proper boundaries with those around you, and energetically protect yourself from well-meaning but meddling relatives, negative friends, and insincere well-wishers.
- Give your marriage the best start with special prayers, blessings, and ceremonies in the months before the wedding.
- Incorporate loving experiences and feel-good moments with your groom that will empower you both to remember *why* you are getting married.
- Experience each step on the path *toward* the altar as a sacred rite of passage unto itself.
- Bring out and enhance feelings of confidence, self esteem, and self-assuredness so that you feel fabulous, calm, and confident on the days leading up to the wedding, as well as on your wedding day.
- Find inspiration, creativity, and self-expression on your personal path to the altar, and give yourself permission to do your wedding your way.
- Look and feel divine on your big day.
- Calm wedding-day jitters and walk down the aisle like a Goddess.

- Gather great ideas for a fabulous, memorable, personal wedding.
- Create a wedding that embraces your personality and values, and is a unique celebration of your love.
- Take charge of the experience so that your big day goes your way.

Many brides seek an empowering alternative to traditional weddings and traditional wedding-planning stress. This book is designed to give you the tools, ideas, exercises, and spiritual support that will help you travel the road to matrimony with serenity and peace, self-esteem and personal power, always remembering the love that will bring you to your wedding day—not the arguments you are having with your mother about the guest list.

So when the next little problem arises—such as when your parents try to control you, your bridesmaids can't agree on a dress, your sister-in-law is bent out of shape because she's not in the wedding party, your grandparents are freaking out because you are not getting married in a church, your in-laws are not getting along with your parents, etc.—you can rise to the occasion like a Goddess.

This book offers a nondenominational, interfaith, creative, contemporary, spiritual way to be the Goddess Bride that you are meant to be—not just in dress, hair, and makeup, and not just for photos, but in your heart and soul.

Rev. Laurie Sue Brockway
New York City

Arlene Sandler/Lensgirl.com

PART ONE

The Engagement

A BLESSED BEGINNING

Outwardly you walk down the aisle with family and friends looking on,

a passage of only a few minutes.

But inwardly you are undertaking a much longer journey,

enacting a transition from one way of life to another.

—Gertrud Mueller Nelson and Christopher Witt, from *Sacred Threshold*

This is the dawning of the journey that will forever change your life.
The ring you now possess heralds the start of the precious time
Between the decision to marry . . . and marriage itself.
Use this time to prepare yourself fully for the new life that will soon be yours.
Treat it as sacred, for it will open the door to all your tomorrows.

—Aurora, Roman Goddess of the Dawn, who presides over all new beginnings

Congratulations. Someday is here, and your prince has come. Now you are a bride-to-be, and in the-not-too-distant future, you will be a married woman. *Sigh.* It's all so exciting and romantic. Even the most nontraditional brides agree that the idea of getting married—of actually getting to that place in your life, stepping up to the altar, and taking that big step—is thrilling.

If you are at the very start of your journey, it might all feel surreal. That's not surprising. After all, you're about to embark on a new life, a new possibility, a new partnership. This is one of the most important and significant moments of your whole life. Of course, you want it all to be perfect and smooth, and you want your marriage to be blessed in all possible ways.

A wedding proposal is a precious thing to most women—whether he proposed, you proposed, or it was a little of both. For many, this first stop on the path to the altar is accompanied by the piece of jewelry that changes a woman's life forever—an engagement ring. Although in Sri Lanka they use string, and the Hopi used corn husks, most modern brides prefer something more sparkly.

THE ULTIMATE WEDDING GODDESS RULE

A Wedding Goddess is committed to taking a personal path to the altar.

From the moment you get engaged to the moment you say "I do," you pursue a path to the altar that enriches your spirit, empowers your relationship, and ensures that the planning of your wedding will be a soulful and magical experience.

Whether it's a huge diamond or a modest one, Chinese jade or pearl, a semiprecious stone or a Celtic Claddagh ring, it marks the formal end to your life as a single woman and heralds the dawning of a new era. And it represents the time in your life when you find yourself poised at the threshold of married life, anxiously waiting to walk through that new door, and planning the wedding ceremony and celebration that will take you over that threshold.

It's Official!

Your engagement ring is your first announcement to the world that you have chosen a partner—and that you have been chosen. It is a piece of jewelry that in many ways boosts your self-esteem with every sparkle, because, in this culture, it is considered a confirmation that you are loved and adored. Once the ring has been given or chosen, there is a feeling of "official-ness" that helps kick off the wedding adventure. You can't wait to call friends and family members to share the good news. From then on, the engagement will be the hottest topic of conversation in your life, and the *presentation* of the engagement ring is a time honored tradition for every bride who has ever been blessed with one. We flash them on fluttering fingers and love to show them—and show them off—to the world.

Wedding Goddess Exercises

HOW TO BLESS YOUR ENGAGEMENT RING

The image of a newly engaged woman flashing her ring has in many ways become a tradition. But it is a tradition that you, as a Wedding Goddess, can transform to strengthen yourself and ready yourself for the journey to the altar, as well as to the married life on the other end of "I do." Even before the guest list for an engagement party is put together, you can bring many blessings to your marriage by blessing your engagement ring.

1. **Instead of just flashing it at people, transform the experience into a brief ritual that you do over and over again.** This will enforce positive feelings and a sense of joy.

   • **Go within and be grateful.** During some Buddhist meditation retreats, a bell clangs every hour to remind people to stop to meditate on the blessings of the moment. Apply that approach to your engagement ring in this way: Every time you extend your hand to show someone your lovely ring, pause for a moment to count your blessings and reflect quietly on the happiness and excitement you feel—and on the love you share. This helps empower you to a state of grace by maintaining an attitude of gratitude.

• **Ask people to bless your marriage.** Since so many friends and loved ones will joyfully take hold of your hand as they seek a closer look at your ring, ask them for their blessings, their good wishes, or to share a bit of wisdom and love that will empower your married life. It can be spontaneous and relaxed, something that will make you glow with pride as it makes those who offer their blessings feel that they are contributing to your happiness.

• **Soak in the sunny rays of a smile.** Consider it a blessing every time someone smiles as they look at your ring or hear of your engagement. If you are game, you can count the number of people who have blessed your ring in this way and begin to feel the power of other people's positive energy. Sound labor-intensive? Not if you are using a spiritual abacus of smiles, and if every time you add one, your ring takes on a spirit of love that energizes you and empowers you as you move forward in establishing your wedding plans.

• **Share the Wealth.** Other women love to celebrate with us as we excitedly show our new jewelry acquisition—those we know, and those we do not know as well. It gets everyone excited about the promise and inherent possibilities of marriage; it makes some female friends and acquaintances wish they had a ring—and a chance at true love—too. It's quite natural for the women around you to yearn for success at love when they see you celebrating yours; your good fortune can inspire them! Be sensitive to those who are just getting over a heartbreak, and to those who are a bit jaded. However, as a Wedding Goddess, take on the mantle of a woman who is pro-marriage, positive about relationships, and who believes that love can be just around the corner for anyone, at any time. This will empower every single woman who sees your happy smile and your beautiful ring!

2. **Have a ring-blessing ceremony.** Invite some of your favorite women to dinner or tea—women you trust and adore—and ask them to help you start your marriage right by blessing your engagement ring.

• **Gather in a sacred circle.** Ask everyone to bring themselves into the circle by saying, "My name is _____ , friend of [your name]. I am here to offer my blessings, my good wishes, and my love."

• **Say a prayer.** Create a sacred environment for the blessing with a prayer. Ask for what you want and need from Divine Grace and from your girlfriends: "May my marriage be blessed in all ways. . . . May I be relaxed and feel supported through my wedding-planning journey. . . . May I honor my relationship with my beloved. . . . May this ring shine a light on my new path. . . ."

• **Pass the ring around the circle.** The ring itself represents the circle of life, of love, of eternity. Passing it around a circle to be blessed reenforces its meaning. Place the ring in a small, pretty box or pass it hand to hand and ask everyone to hold the ring and "charge it" with their love and good wishes for your marriage, and with a blessing that your wedding-planning experience be smooth and joyous.

• **Empower your single friends.** The Wedding Goddess has a special presence, power, and allure. Invite friends to cast an eye on the shiny, sparkly diamond (or whatever the stone or style) as you bear witness to their wish for true love. It is a generous way to share that "I'm getting married" feeling in a way that will bring joy to others, too.

A diamond is a powerful stone, the strongest, most brilliant of all precious jewels. But any stone or metal that your ring is made of has a power unto itself. I called on the power of the materials in the ring itself to enhance the blessings on my marriage, and blessings for my friends. I saw the ring as both a jewel and a symbol of the strength of our union, and I felt more powerful wearing it. Whether metal or jewel, the ring shines with possibility. I often said to people, "If this ring could find me and weave my life together with a man I love and adore . . . *anything* is possible." My engagement was very upbeat because my ring helped me meet new friends, make conversation with just about anybody, and generate a lot of love.

—*Janine, who married John on January 23, 2004*

The Engagement Begins—
Special Wedding Goddess Exercise:
Design Your First Wedding Altar

Whether you want a large, traditional wedding in a castle or a small, barefoot ceremony and shindig on the beach, you want your wedding to be well organized and perfect, personal and memorable, romantic and loving, and uniquely your own. Now that you've got the ring, here's your chance to define and create the wedding of your dreams.

Your dream wedding can begin to come alive in a corner of your home when you start your journey down the aisle with a special wedding altar. This is not *the* wedding altar, it's a small shrine to your special day that creates a spiritual statement, which will help you turn imagination into reality. This section outlines how to set up the altar, what to place on it, how it will change over time, and how to use it as a creativity center for making wedding choices come alive!

Designing your mini wedding altar will help build the foundation for your wedding-planning journey. It is designed to help you define what would start you and your marriage off on the right foot! It will help establish the path of a Wedding Goddess—and help you walk it—by encouraging you to visually articulate your dreams, aspirations, and goals. To get started:

1. **Meditate for *your* Perfect Wedding.** Play a piece of music that inspires you and puts you in a wedding mind-set, be it your first-dance song or processional music. Begin to imagine, dream, and fantasize about what your wedding might be like. See as many details as you can in your mind's eye, but also open your heart to feel the energy or vibe of your big day. Make a mental note, for instance, about whether you see yourself in a church, temple, chapel, or on a beach; under a bright summer sun or beneath a harvest moon; dancing in a formal bridal dress or something more low-key. As you dream, get a sense of the general ambience you want, and the time of year and time of day you'd like to be married, as well as the kind of place you are drawn to.

2. **Ponder these questions, and more:**
   * What would be the most auspicious time, location, and venue?
   * What kind of ceremony would start your marriage off right?

- What kind of officiant do you see marrying you?
- Will it be a big wedding, a small intimate one, or medium?
- What role will your groom have, and how can you empower him?
- How will your family be involved?
- Who will support you most on this journey?

3. **Begin to build a wedding altar in your home.** Place it somewhere that you can easily enjoy looking at it—in the bedroom, on a night table or dresser, or in the living room. Placing it in the southwest corner of the room is particularly auspicious; according to feng shui, that is your "marriage and partnership" corner. You can construct it on any flat surface, or even on its own little table. Although it might look something like an arts-and-crafts project as you get started, treat it like a mini-temple to your dreams. If you like, you can place a corkboard behind it to pin up and display some of the images that you will collect, and add to the altar over time. Some of the things you can use include:

- Bridal magazines to cut pictures from.
- A picture of you and your beloved.
- Images of the kinds of things you will include in your wedding— such as a postcard from a favorite venue, a business card from a photographer you like, and a CD of some songs you will dance to.
- A cake topper or small statue of a bride and groom that you relate to and think is adorable—a cat in wedding clothes, pigs on a Harley, an interracial couple, a bride and groom dancing or sharing a special glance, whatever.
- If you like, include religious imagery or symbols from the tradition of your birth and your beloved's (a statue of Mary, a cross, a Jewish star, Hindu *ohm*), or icons of any favorite soul-mate deities such as Egyptian Isis and Osiris or Hindu Krishna and Radha.

4. **Work on your altar over time, and change it as you go along.** The idea is to create a mini version of what you hope your wedding experience to be. It is like a visual prayer, and will help you avoid wedding pitfalls and problems by creating an image and making a statement of how you want things to be. It gives you something to focus on and is like your own little wedding world—a world you *can* control. Here are some ideas for content:

• When you have some time, flip through some wedding books and find pictures of happy brides and grooms getting married, dancing, looking out to the horizon, honeymooning, and loving each other. Place those images on the "floor" of the wedding altar, and place images, icons, and ideas around them.

• Perhaps you can buy a chalice that represents your two lives becoming one, which you can later use in the ceremony; or you can keep your unity candles there to represent you as two individuals merging into partnership.

• You can also add pictures of floral arrangements and bouquets that you really like, an image of parents, friends or even a celebrity marriage that made an impression on you; or a photo of an officiant who looks kind and loving.

• Find a great *peaceful* picture of you and your mom, dad, siblings, and/or any other key relatives you might have tension with, and write little affirmation prayers on the back of the photos, stating your wishes for how your want your relationships and interactions with them to be during wedding planning, such as: *My mother and I are getting along great and enjoying the experience; my sister is helpful and loving; my dad is cooperative and generous.*

• In the center of it all should be a photo of you and your beloved, looking happy—a gesture of bliss to come as you head toward the altar. If you are feeling creative, you can cut out your faces and paste them onto an image of a bride and groom from a magazine and turn it into a centerpiece by affixing it to a cardboard backing.

Over time, you will begin to see many new ways to turn your little wedding altar into a haven of images and knickknacks that begin to spell out the wedding you want to experience.

A PLACE TO REST YOUR RING

As a special boost, you can place your engagement ring on your altar each night so that it can take in the blessings of your ideal wedding and also cast its lovely glow on your dreams.

Wedding Goddess Wisdom

DOCUMENT EVERY STEP OF THE
JOURNEY — CAPTURE THE MEMORIES

Don't wait until the wedding day to take pictures. A camera is the Wedding Goddess must-have accessory. Whether you get a good camera or a bunch of disposables doesn't matter. Just find a way to capture the images of your Wedding Goddess journey. Take pictures of:

- Your parents' expressions when you tell them you are engaged
- Friends blessing your ring
- Shopping for dresses
- Trying on dresses (if the salon allows photos—some do not)
- Meetings with vendors
- Checking out venues
- Doing wedding errands
- Your engagement party
- Your wedding shower
- Picking out invitations
- Asking your attendants to be on your wedding team
- Meeting with your officiant
- Your wedding rehearsal

Having a record of your joy—and all your efforts and emotions—will be a fun thing to look back on when it is all said and done, and it will help you realize how much love and energy you have put into your wedding. While you are planning the big day, it is a great pick-me-up that you can go through in times of doubt or stress.

Collect memories through photos and memorabilia (such as receipts, menus, match covers, etc.). Have the photos developed as you go along, and create a truly meaningful wedding journey memory book.

Alternatives and additions: Keep a wedding journal of feelings and experiences, including the ups and downs; have fun documenting the wedding-planning journey on videotape.

WEDDING GODDESS BLESSING

With this ring . . .

I tell the world I am in love and I am loved.

I show my friends and family I'm changing and growing.

I set myself on a new path, and journey toward marriage.

I choose to navigate these days, weeks, and months before my marriage as a Goddess would . . . gracefully, joyously, lovingly.

May I embody the generosity of spirit on my journey.

I am a Wedding Goddess. And so it is.

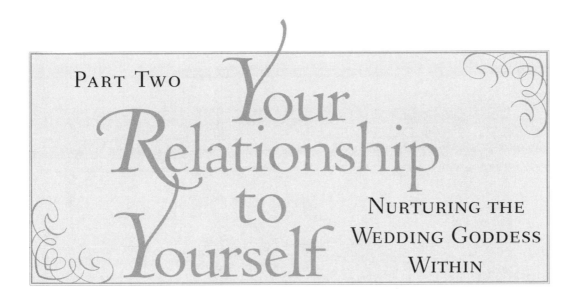

PART TWO

Your
Relationship
to
Yourself

NURTURING THE
WEDDING GODDESS
WITHIN

Take some time for yourself. Relax as you would normally.
Write a journal, pray, meditate, just sit quietly
and take deep breaths for even a minute. . . . It works.

—**Meenal Atul Pandya**, from *Vivah: Design a Perfect Hindu Wedding*

Arlene Sandler/Lensgirl.com

CHAPTER ONE

Spring Cleaning for Your Heart and Soul

Call now to the three directions—past, present and future.

This is the time to look back, to let go, to walk freely into your future.

Become ready, now, for the new life that awaits.

—Hecate, the Greek triple Goddess of the Crossroads,

who represents past, present, and future

Agreeing to marry the man of your dreams doesn't necessarily mean you are automatically good to go for marriage. If you have been living with your beloved for a while, chances are you've already tossed out your little black book and the big furry bear that your first boyfriend won you at the county fair. Yet many of us cling to remnants of relationships past and need a bit of closure with certain people, certain aspects of our romantic history, or past behaviors and ways of thinking. Some are subtle, some are more obvious.

The mere decision to marry begins to transform us, because it kicks off the process of journeying to the threshold of a new door and a new life. In order to open that door fully—and be open to it fully—we have to find peace and closure with our past.

This doesn't mean giving up your happy memories, the feeling of love you have for those who have touched your life, or the growth and lessons—even tough ones—that came with the relationship before the marriage you are preparing for now. But it could mean donating to charity the overstuffed chair that Mr. Wrong gave you because it doesn't belong in your new living room, or passing along a few trinkets from former relationships to friends. For some, it might also mean taking a good, hard look to make sure there are no attachments—to an ex-love, a former lifestyle, or things associated with single life—that you are holding on to that will get in the way of your happiness down the road or prevent you from being fully present in your new marriage.

Spring cleaning for the heart and soul requires taking time to reflect, release, and rampage through your closets, your drawers, your finances, your thoughts, and your life—not to mention your memorabilia, photos, diaries, and old letters. The idea is to take into your marriage those things that warm and empower you and release that which will not serve you and your beloved in your new life together. Once you have taken some personal time to go through the sentimental girl stuff that your husband-to-be is not meant to share with you, and once you have done the releasing and healing on your own, you can partake in purification rituals with your beloved.

A Wedding Goddess knows that if you take time on your own, first, to release, reflect, and heal, you can truly enter your marriage like a "spiritual virgin"—a woman renewed by the grace of love and the willingness to change, grow, and do what it takes to ready her heart and her life for a soulful union.

WEDDING GODDESS RULE #1

A Wedding Goddess has courage.

You allow yourself to see clearly the truth about anything that may be standing in the way of your happiness with the man you are about to marry. You set about consciously working through the issues and releasing old baggage— physical, emotional, and spiritual. You let go of the old to welcome in the new.

How to Create a Fresh Start

*M*any traditions believe that the power of the commitment you make on the day that you marry gives you a fresh start, a new beginning. You can take fullest advantage of this if you take responsibility for your feelings, fears, and unresolved romantic issues up front. A powerful way to do this is physically and symbolically ditching the unneeded baggage you've been schlepping around from relationship to relationship. As a wise fortune cookie once revealed, "Cleaning up the past will always clear up the future."

Saying a proper good-bye to past loves. For some women, it means seeing an ex-love, just to confirm that you never want to see him again. There is a scene in the movie *Monsoon Wedding* where the bride-to-be leaves her parents' home in the middle of the night, on the eve of her wedding, to take a ride, park, and make out with her bad-boy ex-boyfriend. Police come snooping around the car, win-dows now steamed, and the ex-boyfriend acts in only his own defense and interest, leaving the woman to fend for herself. Awakened to the fact that her ex is still a creep, the woman drives away in his car, leaving him to deal with the police. She now knows she is marrying the *right* man, a man worthy of her love.

You may not need to go to the same ex-treme as this movie bride, but it may be important for you to do your own version of saying good-bye. We've all had past loves that represent the "best sex" or "most fun" in our lives, and as we are heading to the altar, there may be a little part of us that just wants to make sure those sparks won't reignite. "I had to see him one more time, just to make sure," said one bride, who stopped by the office of her former lover just to "do a reality check that it was so over." Another bride, who was about to marry her true love, set about healing a re-lationship from the past before she said "I Do." "I went to see my ex," she said. "We had ended very badly, and I wanted to just have closure. I really didn't know exactly why I had to see him, but I did. Maybe it was to make sure I had no attraction to

> One night, I poured myself a glass of wine, turned off the phone, took off my clothes, and surrounded myself with boxes of memorabilia and memories that I began to sift through. It was tough, because I would find letters and photos and get sucked into the memories, and then I'd tell myself, "I am not of this anymore. . . . Let it go, it's just a memory." When José got home, he asked what I was doing and I just replied: "Let-ting go of stuff that I don't need anymore; mak-ing more room for you and me." He looked at me, naked, with my glass of wine and two wastebas-kets, and he got the picture and gave me space for a while to finish. That was great for me.
>
> —*AnaMaria, who married José on January 24, 2004*

> I did a visualization (adopted from something I had once read in a Native American book) where I went deep into my womb and saw luminous cords of light belonging to previous lovers. These cords kept me connected to them on a psychic level. So I blessed them, cut all the cords, and re-leased them.
>
> —*Arielle, who married Brian on June 22, 1998*

him or that it was truly over in my heart, or to release my anger for him. I needed to make a physical statement, so I gave him back a ring he once gave me. When I walked away from him, and that ring, I knew it was over for good."

Identify the challenges. I hope that by the time you wed, you will no longer be in love with or attracted to your ex—or anyone else, for that matter. And you might find that you have no need to pay any visits to former loves. But you may find that you are not quite healed from the broken hearts and romantic disappointments of the past, or you might assess that there are some painful issues or unpleasant memories that you would rather not cart (physically or otherwise) into your marriage. Sometimes we sabotage what is good because of heartache, fears, and unpleasant associations of the past, so think about nipping it in the bud before it nips you in the butt. You can start this process in a very simple way. Take a piece of paper and make a few lists.

1. **I am so happy about** . . . List the joys and pleasures of planning your wedding and married life with the man you love. For example: "I love Jason. He is my true partner. I have never felt so loved and adored in my life."

2. **I feel I still might need closure on** . . . List any baggage you suspect is lingering in your life, such as feelings about a relationship that ended badly, guilt, or a sense that you are hanging on to a fantasy about an old relationship in an unhealthy way. For example, feelings like: "Jim was the best lover I ever had. Jason is so wonderful and tender, but Jim was so hot. I still think of him sometimes. I think I need to close the door on Jim so I can open the door to deeper passion with Jason. And maybe I need to also own up to the possibility that my husband may not be the best lover I've ever had, and that's okay."

3. **Things that are definitely in my way** . . . List any and all things that you *know* need to be resolved, healed, or released before your wedding day. For example: I am holding on to Mark's phone number, thinking I might call him someday, but that would be so stupid. I still have the punch bowl set my ex-husband's mother gave me, and it brings back bad memories every time I look at it. That shoebox filled with old love letters and break-up letters is a memento that holds me back in time.

Now you have a checklist that can help guide you in the process of letting go and moving on.

Choose to move forward. Sometimes it is important to walk toward the future by ritually leaving your past behind. Marriage represents a new beginning, yet also an end; it is part of a very natural cycle of life. As you prepare to marry, there is a part of you, or portion of who you have been, that comes to an end—the single woman, the solo wild woman, the lonely woman, the woman who perhaps thought she'd never marry, the woman who was hurt by men and was once too scared to love, etc. It is meant to be a healthy ending to an era, and the start of a new one. But it certainly can come with the feelings of loss that are associated with any transformation.

Mourn those things that must end. Some brides can't wait to be married, change their names, and start anew. Then there are those of us who actually feel sad, and who mourn the ending of our old selves as if there has been a death in the family. Those kinds of strong emotions stir up a lot of confusion, because as a woman about to be wed, you are led to believe that happiness is the only emotion you are supposed to have. However, alongside happiness can come grief and sadness—not to mention stress and fear. You are letting go of being single, of certain levels of privacy and independence, and of your option to *ever* date other people; perhaps you are forsaking the monthly practice of locking yourself away for two days when you have PMS, or your habit of running off to be alone when you are in a bad mood. If you are moving to a new home or town, or changing your name, you might feel sad—even though you are happy to be doing so. Let yourself mourn what you must leave behind—the old you and your old life, your past loves, and relationships that didn't work out. That is an important part of the process.

> This was a second marriage for us both. My husband had died six years before. I had put my wedding ring away, but had his wedding ring sized to fit me, and I wore it for six years. I could not imagine finding the love I had with him . . . until Tim. On my wedding day, I took the ring off, kissed it, and told my beloved first husband that he would always be in my heart. I did this alone, but it was important to starting my new life with Tim.
>
> —*Patti, who married Tim on April 25, 2003*

Be proactive in making change. Marriage will not magically make your problems disappear. Rather than just being changed by marriage, take a proactive approach to changing your life. Being loved by a wonderful person will not guarantee that you will never feel pain again. And it won't guarantee that there will never be a little, tiny part of you that longs—from time to time—for someone other than the one you have married, or for a life other than your married life. However, you can take full responsibility for entering your marriage with the cleanest slate possible if you identify some of your painful or unresolved issues up front.

Clean up your life. Once you've grieved appropriately or have had a few good cries if needed, and once you know it is time to move on, go on a rampage to clean up your house of love, and clean up in general! Get rid of memorabilia from formerly broken hearts and times you would rather not remember. Clean up your bedroom, your life, your spiritual attic, and your emotional basement so you can move on to marriage with a fresh—or at least fresher—slate. In some feng shui traditions, this is known as "energy clearing." It follows a natural law which tells us that when we release the old, the new has room to come in.

Wedding Goddess Exercises

1. WEDDING GODDESS RAMPAGE

*I*n order to be truly ready to engage in a serious kind of love, you have to be committed to bringing order into your life on *all levels*—physical, psychic, emotional, financial, and spiritual. It is often a process of gently identifying, releasing, letting go, and giving up that which stands in the way.

There is a very specific spiritual law that states: "Nature abhors a vacuum." Get rid of something, and something new can come in. If your life is too cluttered or filled up with "stuff," if your house is messy or your mind is disorganized, if you are not honoring your body or your spirit, it is very hard to feel connected to your own divine nature. Therefore, it is difficult to create a life of your choosing, and impossible to connect to the divine nature of the one you plan to marry.

It may seem wacky to think that a pile of old magazines or relics from relationships past that are collecting dust can interfere with your marriage, but clutter can impact your love life. A good, soulful spring cleaning will bring you closer to that fresh start you seek. The best bet for a fresh start is to make symbolic gestures in the physical realm.

An episode of the TV show *Friends* illustrates this well. It was Valentine's Day, and Phoebe, Monica, and Rachel did not have boyfriends, so they decided to do a "boyfriend burning" ritual to exorcise the bad memories of relationships past. They tossed old theater tickets, trinkets, and other mementos into a garbage pail that contained the fire, and enjoyed it . . . until Rachel threw in some alcohol-based cologne from a heartbreaker ex. It started a bigger fire, and the fire department had to come, which made it possible for the women to meet three cute firefighters. Mission accomplished.

You don't have to start a fire to be free. Clearing the decks of disarray will help you create a healthy foundation for your life and your marriage. These things take time. Be gentle with yourself, but start somewhere!

Try some of these "life cleaning" tips:

• **Start with one drawer.** Then a closet. Next, a whole room. Rampage through your physical space one step at a time, as a symbolic gesture of cleaning up your life and making room for a wonderful relationship with the love of your life. Take a big, black garbage bag—or ten!—and dump things. Give anything you don't need anymore to the Garbage Goddess, or to charity.

When my husband and I first started dating, I had quite a bit of memorabilia from past relationships that felt to him like the needles of a cactus surrounding me. With time, I was able to start letting go of things, but I was afraid at first, thinking of them as parts of me that I needed. Each time I let go of something, it became easier, because my past was not erased, simply put behind me, making more room for my future to fill my life. By the week before our wedding, as I came across items from the past, I couldn't get rid of them soon enough. I had discovered that the space created for future items and mental clarity was much more valuable to me than myriad relics sending me stumbling around my past.

—Sharon, who married Michael on March 20, 2004

• **Let go of memorabilia from past or failed relationships**. This includes anything that ties you inappropriately to the past, or to a love affair that is long over. Save or sell anything that is valuable or sacred, but pack it up and place it in storage—at least for now. You should not be looking at pictures of your old loves on the mantle, or stuff that reminds you of them, while trying to get ready for the new. Keeping a photo of your ex on display energetically keeps him or her around your house. Unless he is now one of your best friends, or if he is the father of your children and you keep his picture there for them, his picture should be tucked in a photo album, in a box, out of sight! If you find yourself thinking of someone who you probably shouldn't be thinking of, see if there is something of his around the house that keeps zapping you with reminders of him. Find it and ditch it.

• **Sell off the good stuff.** Thank God for eBay. If you are confronted with the fact that you have some big-ticket items, collectables, or jewelry related to a part of your life you want to be over and done with, but they are too valuable to give away, sell them. Use the money to buy wedding favors or a new pair of shoes for your wedding day. That way, you can know that the stuff is going to good use, you can make a few bucks, and you can use the money to walk down the aisle on a strong foundation of what came before, yet it will be all new and fresh.

• **Make cleaning up your life a fun and rejuvenating ritual.** Play music, such as "Open Your Eyes, You Can Fly," sung by Vanessa Williams on *Ain't Nuthin' But a She Thing*; or "I Am Changing," sung by Jennifer Holliday on *Dream Girls*. Of course, for getting past the tough reminders of romances gone awry, there's Gloria Gaynor's classic "I Will Survive." Or watch wedding movies that make you laugh and cry as you clean up your old life (such as *Father of the Bride, My Best Friend's Wedding, Four Weddings and a Funeral, My Big, Fat Greek Wedding, American Wedding, The Wedding Singer, The Wedding Planner, Runaway Bride, Monsoon Wedding*, etc). Relish the fact that you, too, will be a bride very soon!

2. WEDDING GODDESS EMOTIONAL RELEASE

As you prepare for marriage, certain feelings and fears may be floating around in your head: *I'm not ready . . . not sure . . . not over my former love . . . not confident I can be a good partner in marriage . . . afraid it will turn out like my parents' marriage . . . scared to death of commitment*, etc. Since we are all trained to believe that marriage will make all things better, and that love will make us complete, you may be shocked by some of the darker, fear-based thoughts that cross your mind. Some of these may be due to the normal anxiety that bubbles to the surface as you plan your wedding. Some may be related to deeper, more challenging issues. The first step is allowing yourself to admit how you are feeling. Many things can help you begin that healing journey.

• **Speak now or forever hold your peace.** Go to the source of the challenge or pain. Is there anyone you need to talk to, see one more time, call, or even scream at in order to release the holds of the past? Now's the time. This is not a job for the meek-hearted, yet there is a certain power that many women find around the time they choose to marry; they feel more empowered to deal with some of the men and issues of their past. You may have more confidence to find closure with an ex, because you know there is someone who loves you and who is waiting for you. You may also feel more internal motivation to be free of any loose romantic ends.

- **Consider counseling.** Not every issue can be cured by a good chat with the offending party. Sharing your story with a trained professional is often very helpful, especially when you are going through a high-anxiety time when many deep emotional issues are surfacing. A psychotherapist or clergy person could be very helpful.

- **Write it out.** If talking is not for you, try journaling or writing long, detailed letters to the ones who hurt you. There's no need to mail them. This is to help get the pain out of you.

- **Forgive.** As Jerry Jampolsky, M.D., author of *Love Is Letting Go of Fear* and *Forgiveness*, always says, the person who does not forgive is the one who is in a self-imposed prison. As you stand at the cusp of your new life, wherever possible, forgive the indiscretions and stupidity of others. Holding on to anger is toxic to your hearts, and your heart, especially now, wants to be filled with love, joy, and hope.

WEDDING GODDESS VOW

*I vow to let go of the past gracefully
as I embrace my future, now.*

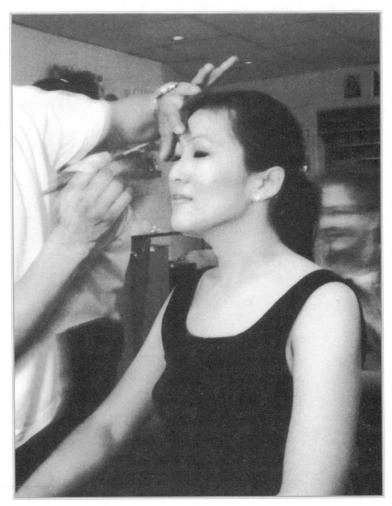

Arlene Sandler/Lensgirl.com

CHAPTER TWO

Bridal Beauty and Grace

Self-Care to Bring Out the Goddess in You

You are a goddess in human form. You are beautiful and worthy of the best of all things. Self-care and pampering are your birthrights. Look at your reflection and never fail to see the beauty before you.

—**Venus, the Roman Goddess of Love, Beauty, and Sexuality, who loves being a girl**

*E*very bride wants to look her best on her wedding day. A Wedding Goddess also wants to *feel* her best and *be* her best. She wants to feel beauty, grace, and confidence radiating through her. She wants to experience a deep sense of comfort in her own skin. She wants to embody a sense of health, balance, serenity, security, joy, and excitement, and be her most natural, gorgeous self.

Evoking this kind of bridal balance and loveliness is not something you want to have to figure out a week before your wedding! From the moment you embark on your wedding journey, it is important to focus on lifestyle changes and enhancements that are nurturing, healing, and relaxing. These can include basic beauty treatments and dietary changes, but don't stop with the basics. Pursue activities and practices that enhance you and put a song in your

> ## WEDDING GODDESS RULE #2
>
> **A Wedding Goddess Takes Care of Herself.**
>
> You gently ready yourself for your big day by taking time to relax, reflect, and rejuvenate—*every day.* You create experiences that enhance your beauty and peacefulness as they make you feel like a Goddess. You evoke beauty, confidence and grace from within. As you tend to your body, mind, and spirit, you pamper your soul.

heart. Anything you do to soothe and nurture yourself through this time of transformation will have the added advantage of showing up in your wedding photos!

One of the great delights associated with being a bride is that you are treated like a Goddess Queen on your wedding day. Get into the habit of treating yourself royally *now*, and it will boost your overall well-being—and you will radiate the beauty that lies deep within. As part of her premarital preparations, it is important that the Wedding Goddess put into place a self-care program for the body, mind, and spirit.

How to Treat Yourself Like a Goddess

Self-care is as essential as breathing for a Wedding Goddess. It is the time spent nurturing yourself, taking care of your unique needs, and consciously preparing yourself for marriage that will make your journey to the altar so much more enjoyable and graceful. While planning your wedding—and managing the myriad responsibilities, relationships, and emotions that come along with the package—it is truly important that you try not to cut corners when nurturing yourself!

There is so much pressure on a bride to please others while planning her wedding that sometimes she forgets to take care of her own needs. Dr. Patti Britton, relationship coach and ivillage.com advice columnist, suggests that for a happier trip down the aisle, it pays to be a little selfish. She calls it "extreme self-care."

Some brides get so caught up in the preparation—*things to do*—along with the pressures from others that they are afraid to slow down for a little "me time." Britton suggests that if you feel guilty about being selfish with your time and energy, give the word a new meaning. Take each letter of the word and imbue it with a more expansive and positive definition. Here's an example:

S: Nurture your **spirit.**

E: **Enjoy** moments alone.

L: **Love** yourself.

F: Keep **fit** and **feel** good.

I: Make your unique needs **important.**

S: **Shower** yourself with gifts.

H: Be **happy** and open-**hearted** as you plan your wedding.

Fortunately, brides today are blessed with many options for self-care. Massages, facials, manicures, pedicures, and other beauty treatments are a standard part of many brides' ritual preparation for their wedding days. Many brides include improved diet, fitness, and exercise in the months before the wedding. The Wedding Goddess goes beyond the typical and into the realm of the fabulous by making traditional pampering more meaningful, and by seeking self-expression, physical exercise, emotional support, and spiritual pursuits that massage her spirit and exercise her soul.

There are myriad ways to tap into the Goddess within. For some brides, a spa day is the key; for others, it's a swim at the health club. Some find a day at the beach rejuvenating, and others find peace in the country or in spending quality time with a girlfriend. Some need a periodic getaway, or just get away to a warm bath. If you can figure out early in the game what will most support you in your journey to the altar, you can make sure that you schedule relaxing and healing pleasures along with wedding responsibilities. The energy of these experiences will bring out your natural beauty, grace, and confidence, and will ultimately support you in that walk down the aisle.

> I decided I wanted my skin to look its best, so a month before my wedding, I went and purchased a new beauty-skin regime for my face, including toner, moisturizer, eye cream, lip conditioner, and night cream. (I would normally just buy moisturizer and cleanser.) When I went to purchase these products, I signed up for a free makeover. It felt nice to treat myself to the makeover, and it helped me see how beautiful I could look on my wedding day. I also drank a lot of water and ate right. A week before my wedding, I booked a day of beauty, including a pedicure, manicure, facial, and massage. If felt great to take care of myself, and the fun part was that my fiancé came with me.
>
> —*Jessica, who married Michael on September 13, 2003*

Wedding Goddess Exercises

Your wedding day will be the most photographed day in your life, and your wedding photos will be your treasures forever, capturing the essence of your special day, so of course you want to look great. Yet this day is also the most important rite of passage in your life to date, so you want to make this transition consciously, soulfully, and in the healthiest way possible. An upcoming wedding, in many ways, is an opportunity (or excuse) to get your life more together. Consider one or all of the steps in this Wedding Goddess thirteen-step program. Here are some ideas to bring out the Goddess in you!

1. **Take care of your health and medical well-being.** See all your doctors, your dentist, and your health-care specialists, and aim to clear any nagging health or dental issues, or at the very least get a clean bill of health.
- Have an overall checkup.
- See your gynecologist to make sure everything is in order and to update your birth control.
- Have your teeth cleaned, as well as examined, and deal with cavities or other issues, and look into whitening if you desire.
- See an eye doctor if you need to, and update your glasses and contacts.
- Make appointments to see any specialists that you might need to consult with—a dermatologist, for example, for skin issues, or orthopedist for that old knee injury—as well as holistic health-care practitioners or healers.

2. **Eat well.** Many brides fret about their bodies. Often, one of their biggest issues is losing weight before the wedding—whether it's five pounds or fifty pounds. You have to consider that if you have a weight issue before your wedding, it may be unrealistic and cruel to force yourself to try to "resolve" it by your wedding day. Assess your current reality with compassion—be kind to yourself—and don't expect to change your body issues overnight. Instead, work toward greater acceptance of who you are right now (the woman your beloved fell in love with!), and initiate healthy

lifestyle changes that include a better relationship with food. Balanced, healthy eating might require a little more time in planning, yet it is so much *less* stressful than eating foods that are bad for you. Whether you want to drop some pounds, gain some, or just get healthier, if you start now and work toward eating right, you will have much more energy, as well as a clearer head to deal with the tasks at hand. Also, be sure to select lifestyle changes that you can maintain after the wedding! Here are some tips:

• First, always check in with your physicians, and consider consulting a nutritionist who can get you started on an eating plan that is right for you.

• Notice the kind of foods that make you feel good and nurture you. Notice which foods deplete you by making you sleepy, cranky, sad, or depressed. Many people have hidden sensitivities to flour, wheat, sugar, yeast, and other ingredients. Keep a food journal of what you eat and how you feel afterward, and it will help you track your reactions to food; it will also help you do a reality check on how much you are eating.

• Modify your eating habits. Steer clear of fad diets. Instead, eat smart. Have smaller portions, put your plate in the sink before going for seconds, push the dessert dish away from you at the dinner table, or get up and do something else. Consider cutting down on foods that tend to cause weight gain and water retention—i.e., sweets, sugar, caffeine, bread, potatoes, sauces, and salty and spicy foods.

• Eat consciously, mindfully, and with a prayer. If you are used to grabbing quick bites on the run or eating without reading the labels or knowing the ingredients, slow down and take time to taste the food you are eating. Bless it before you put it into your body.

> I quit drinking caffeine and ended up losing ten pounds!
>
> —*Brooke, who married Joshua on October 10, 2003*
>
> Like a typical city girl, I walked. Sounds simple, but that's what I did. Instead of taking cabs or the subway, I walked everywhere. It cleared my head and kept me in shape. I also did not starve myself, like many brides do. I am a vegetarian, so I eat pretty healthy to begin with. I just continued to eat healthy so I could have the energy to do the important yet exhausting things I needed to do (like registering, following a budget, buying my dress, etc.).
>
> —*Randi, who married Christopher on August 9, 2003*

• Anchor your dream. Every time you get a food craving, switch to a mental image of you in your wedding dress at your ideal weight, looking and feeling fabulous!

3. **Move your body.** Being fit is a very real life goal, and a super-important wedding goal. Programs such as "bridal boot camp" are popular (the theme is "You'll look gorgeous on your wedding day . . . and that's an order!"). It is important to assess your true exercise temperament—including your level of fitness and your favorite kind of exercise—so you can choose something that is right for you. If you are someone who is up for a little adventure you might want to try something different; or perhaps for you the adventure is doing *any* exercise at all! Here are some ideas:

• A health club or gym membership could be your best friend if you enjoy taking classes and working out with equipment. Find an exercise regimen that works for you; work with the gym's personal trainer to get you started.

• Swim. It tones everything and is so relaxing.

• Walk. Try to leave the car and hoof it whenever possible. Use stairs instead of elevators. Keep your body in motion.

• Yoga will gently stretch your body as it expands your mind. It can clear your sinuses, your head, and any creaks in your body.

• Take dance lessons—not just to make an impression during that first dance with your new husband, but to keep you moving and to get your wedding groove on.

• Belly dancing is the ancient movement that gets you into the primal rhythm of the Goddess and can bring out your sensual self as it tones you all over. (You might find side perks in your love life, and perhaps you'll be able to shake it like Shakira on your big day!)

• Buy home exercise videotapes. You can learn anything, from aerobics to hula dancing and how to strip for your man in the privacy of your own home. You can also choose more than one exercise to suit your needs—including all of the above.

4. **Love your face.** This is a great time to begin to appreciate how the glow inside you shows on your face, and even transforms the way you look, naturally! Love does amazing things to soften your features, and also to help

you see yourself through more self-appreciating eyes. Don't be surprised if you hear people say that you "have that glow." To enhance the natural beauty that is emanating from you, you might want to indulge in some of the traditional bridal beauty treatments to further enhance your skin and your look.

- **Get that facial you have been wanting for so long.** Estheticians say the ideal solution is to begin having monthly facials about six months before the wedding. The wonderful thing about facials is, in addition to the ways in which they can improve your skin and restore its glow, they are also a way to cleanse your past. Say good-bye to impurities from past life experiences as they are exfoliated away. If you haven't had one for a while, a facial might sting and pinch a bit—consider it a release of the old to make way for fresh, clear skin. If a facial series is not in your budget, invest in some new skin-care products such as an at-home facial and skin-care kit.

- **Try a new look.** While you are focusing on your face, check to see if it's time to reshape your eyebrows or find new make up. Sometimes just a new lipstick will bring even more brightness to your face, symbolizing the brightness in your life. Perhaps there is a color that is more befitting to a soon-to-be married you! (Check out the Tony & Tina's Goddess-inspired makeup line, with its Herbal Aromatherapy Lip Gloss, with names like "Goddess," "Enchantress," and "Prophetess.") Of course, it is always recommended that you do an advance test run of the makeup that you plan to use for your wedding day, so enjoy a bridal makeover.

- **Appreciate the beautiful face in the mirror.** Throughout your wedding planning stages, make sure your use a mirror—not to just asses your flaws, but to see your true beauty. There is nothing like the natural glow of a woman in love.

5. **Get pampered.** Massage is always a great way to relieve stress and release toxins from your body. There are also many other kinds of bodywork that might work for you. For the best stress relief, try reflexology. You lie back in a dimly lit room and let the reflexologist's fingers do the walking—all over your feet! It is like a heavenly foot rub, but, more important, says Laura Norman, top reflexologist and author of *Feet First*, "It targets spe-

cific areas of the feet that represent organs and areas of the body. It helps bring healing and rejuvenation, gives you energy, and relaxes you." Norman explains that because the feet have about fifteen thousand nerve endings, targeting these reflex points can speed relief to the nervous system. Having your feet worked on has a way of grounding you and bringing you back into your body. This gentle and delicious healing technique—said to be about five thousand years old—can help you connect to your own heart and soul, and can enhance the way you relate to others. Not only is it an amazing stress reliever that clears your mind—it also clears your face. The aftereffect is a "reflexolgy facelift"—a very healthy glow.

6. **Meditate.** There are so many ways to meditate that it's easy to include it in your prewedding self-care plans. You might choose to learn a formal meditative practice, such as transcendental meditation, use a meditation tape, CD, video, or DVD, or just take ten minutes a day to be quiet and still. The act of taking time to slow down, reflect, release tension, and center yourself will do wonders to help you cope with the trickier parts of wedding planning. "Meditation helps us to take a break from chaos," says meditation and ritual expert Barbara Biziou, creator of the DVD *Momentary Meditations*. "If a bride makes some form of meditation a regular part of her well-being routine, she will find that she wastes less and less energy on worry and reactive behavior, and that her capacity for coping with wedding ups and downs increases."

> I had a lot of emotional stuff come up as I was in the planning phase. I went back to therapy for a session to work this out. I also appointed a friend, who had just been married, to be my "getting married sponsor" (like a twelve-step sponsor). I asked her to keep me grounded and keep me going forward. That was important for me, to have someone to share with when I was freaking out!
>
> —*Susan, who married Robert on July 3, 1999*

7. **Find someone to talk to.** Whether you have a designated listener, a support group, or a therapist, make sure you have a way to blow off steam, work off stress, communicate about cold feet and fears, and complain about wedding annoyances in a safe place (without driving your friends nutty), and also to make sure you do not get stuck in a perpetual state of complaining or whining. Consider connecting with other brides. No one understands you better than some-

one in the same "sorority." Perhaps you can find a support group, such as The Bridal Survival Club,™ available through The New York Wedding Group and Boston Wedding Group. There are so many chat sites and message boards on the internet (www.theknot.com and www.wedding channel.com, for example), where brides can share their experiences, swap ideas, refer vendors to other brides, and moan about the downsides of wedding planning. To unload your wedding woes and worries, visit "Bridezilla Confession Booth" at www.goingbridal.com.

8. **Connect with the womenfolk.** Many cultures insist on rituals designed to pamper the bride. The women in some African cultures adorn the bride with native jewelry before her wedding. In the Hindu tradition, the wedding can go on for weeks, and sometime months; the women from both sides of the family gather for Mehndi (decorative staining of the hands and feet with henna); they decorate the bride and each other and they make sure the bride is rested for her wedding day. In China there is an ancient custom of combing the bride's hair, where a friend or relative runs the comb through for good fortune. In Turkey, "the bride often takes a five-day break from premarital stress," according to *Timeless Traditions* by Lisl Spangenberg. "They pamper themselves and take time relaxing with friends." Look into your culture of origin to see if there is a way you would like to connect to womenfolk and friends and honor a particular family tradition. It's also nice to spend nonwedding time with friends just to relax, unwind, and recall where you came from. Whether it's tea together every couple weeks or an occasional pajama party, make time for your good friends.

9. **Soak and shower.** There is nothing more healing than a hot bath, and nothing more cleansing than a shower after a long day of doing "wedding stuff." Water is one of the five sacred elements, and baths and showers cleanse and purify the body. To restore electrolytes to the body, put a cup each of sea salt and Epsom salts in your bath, and dunk yourself completely a few times. In the shower, enjoy a standing meditation and allow the water to wash away your worries and carry them down the drain. There are also so many options in aromatherapy bath oils and scented candles, which can fill the bathroom with an uplifting or relax-

ing energy. You will always find some solace and spiritual cleansing in water.

10.   **Breathe.** Taking time to literally catch your breath is something you can do anywhere, anytime. "One gateway back into the body is conscious breathing," says Dr. Patti Britton. "Consciously follow your breath in and out, for maybe four or five minutes. It helps anchor you back inside your skin." If you need a boost of energy, or a moment of stress reduction, breathing can bring immediate relief.

I did many things to help remain calm. For the spirit, I took time out for early-morning walks to watch the sun come up, or evening walks to watch it set. I also spent time with my girlfriends, who seemed to be able to bear endless questions and worries from me, like *What if I cannot find the perfect favor gift?* By finding the right audience to talk with on certain matters, it helped alleviate my stresses without adding stress to my fiancé. I am such a girly-girl, so I really treated myself to the full Goddess package. I began using "whitening strips" on my teeth six weeks before the wedding so my teeth would be their whitest. Two weeks before the wedding, I got a nice haircut. A week before, I got my overall color and highlights done with a shiny gloss, so my hair would be it's healthiest. A full two weeks before the ceremony, I had a spa day—I got a facial and got my brows cleaned up and dyed to match my new hair color. The day before the wedding, I had a massage, had my toes and fingernails done, and got a bikini wax.

—*Summer, who married Tony on September 20, 2003*

11.   **Journal.** Writing down your deepest thoughts and documenting your feelings during this time of transition is a great way to make it go more smoothly. It's a chance to communicate what disturbs you and release it onto the paper, and it is also a way to capture your goals and create new ones. Just taking fifteen minutes a day to journal can do wonders for adjusting your attitude, when needed, and enhancing feelings of confidence and hopefulness. Make it your sacred diary by using a notebook and decorating the cover, or by getting a specific wedding journal that you'd love to write in. "Journaling is a great way to help a bride reduce stress before her wedding," says Dr. Linda Olson, clinical psychologist and Imago relationship therapist. "The physical act of writing and the visual act of seeing the written word are therapeutic." To help make the process easier, she's created beautiful, leather-bound or white satin books called "The True-Love Bridal

Journal." Part of her "True Love Collection," the leather version feels like butter and is lovely to write in.

12. **Use Aromatherapy.** Filling your home, office, and even car with specific scents can help in many ways. Aromatherapy draws on the healing essences from a variety of plants. It might use plant oils that are mixed together to create a certain effect, or essential oils, which are the purest essence of a plant. Research by Young Living Essential Oils shows that essential oils, when inhaled, provide both psychological and physical benefits. An essential oil such as lavender, or a combination oil such as "Peace and Calming" from Young Living, can do wonders for calming the nerves. You can dab the oil on a tissue and hold it to your nose for a quick lift, or use a diffuser. Young Living has a state-of-the-art plug-in system for delivering the aromatic molecules into the air. Or buy a candle diffuser or clay pot diffuser (which releases the scent when you light a small candle beneath the diffusing pot), or even an aromatherapy fan. (See more on aromatherapy in Chapter 17.)

13. **Pray, daydream, and make some wishes.** To stay connected to Divine Source—and your dreams—it is so important to take time every day to make a wish, get lost in a daydream, or say a prayer when you need some support. Don't be shy about taking time to lovingly fantasize about your big day. It will make you feel good to focus on your vision for your wedding, and it will bring a smile to your face. Remember, when you smile it is impossible to frown or feel stressed.

Set Aside Goddess Time

*I*n general, being kind to yourself is a healthy habit for a Wedding Goddess to practice. Get into the groove by setting aside Goddess time each week for you and you alone! Despite the fact that you have a million wedding-related tasks to complete, agree to do things that pamper, heal, and revitalize you. Treat yourself royally—if only for at least a few undisturbed hours each week. Pick something that will bring you great pleasure—an activity, an experience, or even a material gift—and agree to give it to yourself. Use this time to pursue some of the aforementioned steps, or try some simple delights, such as the following.

- Light a scented candle, or try an aromatherapy diffuser with a calming scent (lavender, for example) and relax in a favorite chair.
- Sit in your garden or take a walk in the park.
- Take yourself to a movie, out to dinner, or to a museum exhibit that you've been meaning to see.
- Get your hair cut or have (or give yourself) a pedicure and manicure.
- Dig in and read a great book.
- Go to sleep early or sleep in late.
- Engage in an activity that makes you laugh . . . and laugh.
- Buy yourself a small love gift.

The best way to keep your soul nourished is to create an ongoing environment for this nourishment. Although you of course want to focus on activities that you can share with your beloved, now is also a good time to spend some special moments on your own.

WEDDING GODDESS VOW

*I vow to take good care of myself
and treat myself like a Goddess.*

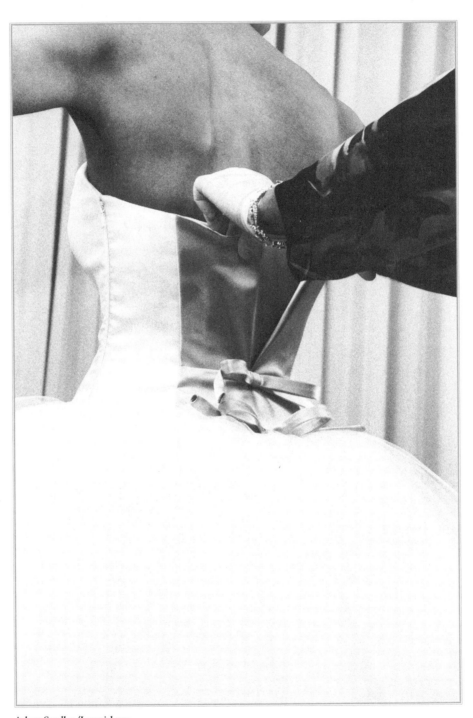

Arlene Sandler/Lensgirl.com

CHAPTER THREE

Finding *the* Dress

Worry not . . . the perfect dress already exists for you.
Free yourself from convention and look toward what suits you best.
It will be as easy as Cinderella's ballgown if only you believe in
a little bridal Bippity . . . Boppity . . . Boo.

—The Fairy Godmother, the wonderful, magical, mystical being of fairy tales

Nothing quite sets a girl's heart afire like the idea of looking fabulous in an amazing gown on her wedding day. Even the most nontraditional Wedding Goddess can find herself taken with the idea of "the dress."

The wedding dress is more than just an outfit. It is a symbol of all your romantic dreams of true love and partnership. And it's a cultural icon that evokes hope, optimism, promise, and a sense of fairy-tale magic. The concept of happily ever after has long been associated with the image of a bride in white dress and veil, with her tuxedo-clad groom beside her. They are the magical couple whose marriage gives us all reason to hope, and whose love seems to conquer all things. To us, they are divinity . . . in human form. As Arielle Ford, author of *Hot Chocolate for the Mystical Lover*, puts it, "Weddings are where fantasy meets reality."

When you go from being someone *who dreams of getting married someday* to a woman who *is shopping for her wedding dress*, you have arrived at a milestone that is a rite of passage unto itself. For some, the task is daunting and exhausting, because they are searching for a dress that will help them *look like the fantasy* rather than one that will help them *live the fantasy*. Your wedding dress is your real-life opportunity to dress up and go to a ball where all eyes are on you and your prince. On that special day, in that special dress, you get to feel like a movie star, princess, queen . . . a Goddess.

As a Wedding Goddess, you can make the entire dress experience—from shopping and going through umpteen fittings to accessorizing and finally wearing the dress—meaningful and fun!

How to Find Your Perfect Wedding Dress

When you think about shopping for *the* dress, your first thought will undoubtedly be white. White may not even be a color you like, but it is the color you know. Women are lured, like moths to a flame, to that sacred white dress. "For as long as I can remember, I have always stopped to watch when a bride and groom leave a church or to catch a glimpse of a bridal party taking photos in a park. . . . it encouraged me to fantasize about the day I would wear a wedding dress," says one bride. "I don't even like the color white, but I can't seem to imagine getting married in anything else."

Now that it's your turn to go for the big white dress, you might be worried about whether you can pull it off. Remember Parker Posey as the sobbing bride in *The Sweetest Thing*, complaining, "I look like a magazine bride." And Nia Vardalos in *My Big Fat Greek Wedding*, shrieking, "I look like a snow beast."

> ### WEDDING GODDESS RULE #3
>
> **A Wedding Goddess dresses her way for her wedding day.**
>
> You feel free to embrace the elements of tradition that feels right for you, and feel free to dress outside the bridal box. You use a combination of research, creative visualization, daydreaming, and feminine magic to find your dress and draw it nearer. And when you find it, you trust your decision and make the dress your own. When you wear it, you are a Goddess, a Divine Bride to behold.

You may be amazed by how amazing you look when you first put on that big white dress. And it may be surreal.

Get familiar with the wedding-salon scene. The shopping experience itself is somewhat surreal. Most salons advise you to make an appointment in advance so they can give you the most personal service. You typically *must* register during your first appointment and give all your pertinent information (wedding date, etc.) before you try on dresses. While some salons have sales racks that you can browse, many have sample racks. And you are not always welcome to go poking through them on your own. In many cases, you can "look" and point to some of the dresses you like, and the sales associate will bring those to you. Or you can show pictures (this is the best idea) or explain the kind of dress you are looking for. The sales associate will usually round up some prospects, one at a time, and bring them to the fitting room. These folks generally have well-honed skills and can help size up your body type immediately, and the truly helpful ones will steer you to the best styles for you. But, depending on the salon, they might also steer you toward whatever they think you will buy.

In some salons, the salespeople gather around and fuss and tell you you look great the moment you step out of the dressing room to look in the mirror. It is very seductive—and overwhelming. It can also be confusing, because the dress samples are not always exactly your size, and they don't always have all sizes in the store, so you kind of have to guesstimate how it will look once it's fitted properly. You might end up making a purchase without knowing exactly what the final dress will look like. It is truly a unique shopping experience. One that may require a little bridal salon combat training before your hit the front lines.

> I first looked for my dress in the mother-of-the-bride section because I just could not imagine wearing one of *those* huge, white dresses. The salesperson kept bringing real gowns to me in my size, and finally I tried one on. I was stunned. I couldn't believe how magical I looked. The saleswoman asked, "Are you feeling it?" And I was. It was this thing that came over me that said, "I am a bride ... wow ... and I can wear one of these dresses."
>
> —*Charlotte, who married Avi on March 6, 2004*

> I couldn't find a dress from a shop that fit me correctly or that suited the style of wedding that I wanted. So I found some beautiful material and had a wedding dress made to the pattern of an evening gown that I already owned and that fit me perfectly. The dressmaker modified the style of the dress slightly to make the most of the fabric, and the occasion, and it was beautiful. I intend to wear my dress whenever I can.
>
> —*Monica, who married Simon on December 8, 2003*

Be prepared. Any bridal magazine can familiarize you with the different dress styles for different body types, and prices of dresses, as well as give you pointers on how to work with a salon and utilize the salespeople to help select the perfect dress. They are also super-thick and full of ad pages to give you inspiration. It is a time-honored custom to get the lay of the land from magazines and it is so much fun to flip through the pages of *Bride's, Modern Bride, Bridal*

Guide, Martha Stewart Weddings, Wedding Bells, The Knot, and regional publications. Yet one industry insider says that it is also super-important for brides to be savvy, emotionally prepared consumers.

Ilene M. Shack, vice president and managing director at WeddingChannel .com and founder of Independent Visions Couture Expositions, is an expert in this area who runs couture trade shows for wedding designers. She says a Wedding Goddess must "find her center point, her vision of herself as a bride" before she heads to the bridal salon. Otherwise, your calm can very easily be undone by the overwhelming nature of it all. "They call it 'snow blindness' and 'white-out,'" she says. "The bride gets overwhelmed from being around and trying on so many white dresses. The seller wants to make a sale, and because of the emotion of the moment, the bride is vulnerable. She's never tried on wedding gowns before."

> I must be the luckiest woman on earth—I did have an idea of what I wanted, but I went shopping with an open mind about styles and colors. I took my best girlfriend with me, tooling around New York. I was on a pretty tight budget. We found a gorgeous, simple, off-white, formfitting gown that marked down to—get this—$28.00. No joke. I knew the second I tried it on it would be mine. I borrowed a pair of diamond earrings and bought a shoulder wrap, and that was it. I was happy to have my girlfriend with me—an honest opinion, and more adventurous than my mom would have been.
>
> —*Courtney, who married Ray on October 26, 2002*

Consider the challenges, and meet them head-on. Anchor yourself before you even walk into a bridal salon, and bring the right support team with you. Shack says you can help avoid bridal-shopping stress by having an awareness of some of the emotional, spiritual, and physical undercurrents at work when buying a dress, including the following.

1. You are shopping for something to wear on the most important day of your life.
2. You are shopping for something in a color that most people never wear and that is not flattering on most people.
3. You are shopping for a kind of dress that you've never worn before.
4. You know you will be the center of attention when you walk in the showroom, and you'll feel a little uncomfortable.
5. You may be shopping with your mother, who may have very different

opinions about the perfect dress, or with friends, who also might have varying opinions.

6. You are basically hanging around naked in the fitting room while the salespeople get you the clothing to try, and they don't like you flipping through the aisles yourself.

Warm up to white. Even with preparation, white can be a tricky color for some women. As wedding lore has it, white was not the norm until Anne of Brittany wore it to marry King Louis VII of France. Queen Victoria of England later solidified the trend in the 1800s by shirking the traditional silver gown for white. Hence the white wedding dress tradition was born. Prior to that, some brides wore pink, and Christian brides sometimes wore blue because of its affiliation with the Virgin Mary. Many brides would just wear their best dress, in whatever color, on their wedding day.

The traditional interpretation of white is purity, innocence, and virginity. But let's face it: How many brides—other than pop singer Jessica Simpson—are actually virgins when they wed? A new marriage, itself, offers bride and groom a "clean slate," so the notion that white represents something new and fresh still stands. But it is also important for the Wedding Goddess to be able to redefine "white" for herself. Here's one way to give it a new meaning:

> I shopped alone for a long time with no success. Then I asked a friend to come along, and success! We returned to a shop I had been to alone. I found a sample dress that was still double my budget, but with my friend's support, I went for it. I felt this dress was meant for me. The designer was very amazed that it fit so perfectly. He usually had to do major alterations or remake a dress to fit the brides. But his dress fit me all over. I told him that I believed he made the dress for me, many months ago, and now I had shown up for it!
>
> —*Susan, who married Robert on July 3, 1999*

W: Womanly
H: Heavenly
I: Inspirational
T: Time-honored
E: Enchanting

Kathryn Weber, a feng shui master practitioner and consultant based in California, points out that bridal white and the groom's traditional black actually represent the famous yin/yang symbol. In that sacred symbol, the white represents male energy and the black represents the feminine, yet each always has within it a tiny dot of the opposite color. "This is to help balance each color, and because you cannot have one without the other," says Weber, who is also editor of *The Red Lotus Letter*, a feng shui e-zine. In the context of a wedding, it is a powerful balance and a metaphor for the sharing of energies that a marriage requires.

"In Western ceremonies, the traditional black and white is wonderful because the male wears the female color of black and the female wears the male color of white," she says. "This makes the bride and groom both balanced and harmonious. It is a perfect pairing, in my opinion."

Consider the best color and style for you. The Wedding Goddess might decide to shirk the traditional wedding dress and even the idea of white. I've worked with many brides who from the very start decided to wear something they looked and felt great in, rather than something they were expected to wear:

Margaret married Jerry in a fabulous black dress. Amy married John in a sequined gown with spaghetti straps that was fit for the Academy Awards. Monica married Simon in a beautiful blue velvet evening dress that she had had made especially for her. Another bride wore a green tweed suit and red shirt because she said it made her feel most "like myself."

Give yourself permission to select a non-wedding wedding gown, or try something in a different color, if that suits you best. You are not obligated to wear white. Many other cultures have wedding gowns in other colors, also considered auspicious. Indian brides generally choose a sari in a shade of red, and Chinese brides also often marry in red with gold trim (for good fortune, good romance, and celebration of a social occasion, says Weber). In other parts of Asia, bridal costumes can be a wide range of hues—

My husband is Chinese, so my dress was very Chinese-inspired—but still in the traditional white lace. I had it custom-made, and it came out just right. I felt like a princess in it.

—*Katerina, who married Xingmin on January 6, 2001*

I knew exactly what I wanted, but I almost couldn't believe my eyes when I made my first trip to look for a wedding dress. There it was, sitting in the window, in the first place I decided to look. It was old in style, similar to what princesses wore in fairy tales or what Maid Marian wore in *Robin Hood*. The salesperson told me that the dress was a new arrival and that there was only one for trying on. To my disbelief, the one dress was actually my size. I tried it on, came out, looked in the mirror, and thought: *Oh my gosh, I can't believe it. I'm wearing a wedding dress and I feel like a princess. This is the dress I am going to wear on my wedding day!*

—*Ana, who married Bill on August 25, 2002*

green, blue, gold, silver, etc. In America, many brides these days select soft pink hues or light blues and off-whites—as well as red and colorful trims—for their wedding day. Dare to be different!

The Wedding Goddess is not immune to the allure of finding the perfect dress, but it is so important to seek a dress that highlights *who you are inside* as opposed to a dress that will turn you into someone you are not. Your dress should feel comfortable and as natural as possible. Before you begin to shop for your wedding dress, have a clear vision of what you want and a way to stay grounded in reality as you make your way through the fantasyland of bridal salons. Keep in mind that you may not always know exactly what you want, but in your heart you know the essence of it. While on the journey to "destination wedding dress," also allow for the possibility that the dress you've had in mind since high school may not be the right style for you after all. No worries. There is something even better just waiting for you to find it.

Wedding Goddess Exercise

CREATE A WEDDING GOWN TREASURE MAP

Visualizing exactly how you want to look on your wedding day is a way you can use the magic of your mind to draw the perfect dress into your life. This gives you a clear visual image to use as a road map to help you find what you are looking for—and to help it find you! It is also important to get a sense of how you want to feel, and be, on that day. What it feels like to be in that dress, walking in it, dancing it in, sitting in it, and, yes, even peeing with that dress on! This is where visualization meets the feelings you have inside, and where you can use your feelings to conjure images of how you want to look.

1. **Buy wedding magazines and cut out pictures.** They all have a kazillion photos of brides in different dresses and different poses, with different attitudes. Flipping through the pages and selecting images will heighten your visualization skills—and it's fun! Tear out every image you like, and put them in several categories, such as the following, that explain why you cut the picture out.

• How you want to look, and the kind of dress you want to wear.

• How you want to feel—model brides with facial expressions that show a certain attitude you want to embody (sexy, sultry, happy, elated, in love, gorgeous, fabulous, relaxed, etc.).

• Things you want to experience (that first dance, lots of attention, alone time, fun, enjoying friends and family, etc.).

2. **Wedding arts and crafts**. All you will need is a big piece of oaktag or poster board, glue, scissors, and the magazine images to begin to "design" your perfect dress and "create" the experience that you want to have in that dress.

3. **Make a collage of your perfect wedding day.** Cut, paste, and create your wedding dress treasure map with your own hands, heart, and spirit. Images can be pasted any way you like, including overlapping one another and at angles. Have fun and be creative! Include anything that relates to your wedding-dress goals: images that reflect the way you want to look, feel, be, behave, and be treated. Include headlines, quotes, and neat sayings that give language to your thoughts. For example, you might use an image of a bride boogying on the dance floor and a headline that says: "Make sure you enjoy your own wedding." Or find what you believe is your perfect dress and cut out headlines that have words or say things such as: "Easy to find," "Affordable," "Perfect Fit." Maybe you will find some images of movie stars and famous brides who you would like to model yourself after. It's fine to utilize their images as symbols of the kind of look, experience, or even financial ease you hope for your wedding.

4. **Display it proudly.** Your treasure map is a very personal and sacred blueprint for your wedding dress and wedding day. Make sure the images you choose truly represent what you want, because they will act like visual prayers, offered on paper to help capture your dreams! Place the map somewhere where you can see it daily—perhaps in your bedroom, where it is the first thing you will see when you wake up and the last thing you'll see before falling asleep. The treasure map will help to manifest your dreams by placing images that represent those dreams and hopes right in front of your face! It will stimulate conscious awareness and conscious

creation of goals, and will act as a visual message board for the brain. In a gentle and quiet way, it will feed images of the perfect dress to your subconscious mind in a way that draws you closer to your dress and draws your dress closer to you.

5. **Use your energy and attention to give life to your treasure map.** Get up every morning and meditate in front of your poster, further visualizing the way you want to look and feel on your wedding day. You will be amazed at how this will accelerate the process of finding your perfect dress.

WEDDING GODDESS VOW

I will look and feel like a Goddess in my wedding dress.

Arlene Sandler/Lensgirl.com

CHAPTER FOUR

Play Dress Up and Have Fun!

Lighten up and be more playful. This is the dress you will wear to your date with destiny. Rejoice. This is a happy dress, for a happy time. In it, you will feel like a goddess and look like a queen. Enjoy the vision reflected in the mirror ... you are becoming more beautiful as your special day approaches.

—Amateruseau, Japanese Shinto Goddess of Beauty, and Uzume, Japanese Shaman Goddess, who together reflect sunshine and laughter, beauty and healing

S ooner or later, every bride is likely to have a mini-meltdown somewhere along the way to her wedding day—a moment in time when fear can get the best of you. Juggling the details of the big day can make even the most level-headed bride go a little bonkers, yet what often puts pure panic in the hearts of the about-to-be-married are worries about the ceremony.

Many brides wonder, *How will I get through it?*

Although it is a time-honored tradition, a rite of passage that many brides have fretted over yet survived, the concept of professing your love before an audience in such an "official" setting can be a little nerve-wracking. Some brides fret about it so much that they begin to associate the ceremony with fear and disharmony, and get locked into a mind-set of apprehension and dread. Instead of looking forward to the ceremony, they look forward to it being over. This is not a fun way to say "I do" or a pleasant way to start a marriage!

The Wedding Goddess understands that anxiety comes with the territory and that it is totally natural to be nervous and concerned about everything going smoothly. Not only are you making a mega-promise to love, honor, and cherish

> The dress stayed in the garment bag, but the headband and veil were a critical part of my highly personalized prewedding celebration. In the months, then weeks, preceding our ceremony, I would wait until I was alone in the apartment I shared at the time with my then-husband-to-be, and I'd take the veil down from the shelf, put it on, and admire myself shamelessly. Then I would put on the music from a sample tape given to us by a dulcimer player who we ultimately hired for the wedding ceremony, and I danced. I pranced around my house for weeks before my wedding, wearing my veil and playing bride.
>
> —*Amy, who married Steve on October 21, 1991*

one man for the rest of your life, it is a public appearance and may involve public speaking. It is a time when all eyes will be on you. Just thinking about it now might send a little shiver of excitement (mixed with stage fright) through you. That's perfectly normal. It is important, though, to not allow performance anxiety to drain the joy out of the experience.

Your wedding is a hugely important and sacred experience. It is, in fact, your statement to friends, family, and the world that you are ready to embrace a very serious love. Ironically, though, one of the biggest challenges of planning a wedding is not taking it too seriously or getting so uptight that you lose your sense of perspective, humor, and joy. When the going gets rough on the road to wedding planning, you can bring a playful energy to the wedding experience by inviting some of your girlhood lightness and pleasure to your bridal experience.

If you are worried about your performance on your wedding day, it may help to act out the way you want to be on your wedding day, and fake it until you make it. Play-acting being a bride is not a goofy thing—it can actually be a fun way to empower yourself to the feeling of grace and confidence that you hope for on your special day. When you practice being the bride you want to be, it can help you create an image and an energetic signature that will elevate you on your wedding day.

WEDDING GODDESS RULE #4

A Wedding Goddess uses playfulness to help her on her special day.

You have been waiting for this day for so long, and you want to make sure that you prepare yourself so you can enjoy it thoroughly! Of course, you will take your commitment seriously, but you don't have to take yourself so seriously! You bring a sense of playful, hands-on practice to your wedding experience that will make it lighter and easier—and more fun.

How to Practice Being a Bride . . . and Enjoy it!

A Wedding Goddess has to learn to recognize when she is starting to take herself, and her wedding planning, *too seriously*. You may get a feeling that you are out of balance, or you may feel way too stressed for this to be a "normal" state of being. Or perhaps those around you will mirror it back to you in their discomfort, annoyance, and resentment of your behavior. A telltale sign is that you feel pulled in a million directions, and you've become obsessed with the details of how things will look and what others will think. And you feel yourself being whisked into a world where planning a wedding amounts to a series of business arrangements, and where relatives and friends get on your last nerve and you get on theirs. What's worse is that planning the wedding gets in the way of *your relationship to yourself, your relationship to your beloved, and your sense of joy*. In that scenario, many brides say they find themselves completely distracted and feeling like a nervous wreck as their big day gets nearer. Before that even happens, bring some fresh, playful energy to the situation.

Nip stress in the bud. One bride realized that she was starting to lose it when every time she thought of her wedding ceremony, her stomach began to hurt. Instead of feeling the tinglies of excitement, she saw herself more like a lamb being led to slaughter. "I tensed every time I thought of us standing in front of the minister, before friends and family," she says. "I had never been married, and I was afraid it would all be too overwhelming."

Another bride said all the wedding-planning stress had begun to wear down her confidence. When she began to see her ceremony as a *task* that she had to accomplish, she tried to lighten up by thinking back to the days when being a bride seemed like a natural thing. "I remembered that I have been practicing being a bride since I was five, when I'd bor-

> What girl doesn't prance around in her dress in anticipation of the big day? I admit I put mine on a couple of times because I really wanted to get that feeling of being a bride, a sense of what it would be like to wear that dress on the big day. But I will never admit to the fact that I used my dog as a stand-in for my husband.
>
> —*Deborah, who married Chris on July 15, 2000*

> I would actually stand in front of the mirror, look at myself, and give myself pep talks. I felt it was the only way to calm my nerves, because it connected me to myself. As weird as it may sound, I think it really centered me and helped me stay present. It's so easy to fly away into unconsciousness when planning a wedding. When you stay connected to yourself, you feel you have more control over the whole experience.
>
> —*Charlotte, who married Avi on March 6, 2004*

row mom's hairpins and my friends', and I would make bridal veils out of white toilet paper, streaming down our backs," she recalled. "We'd always have to convince someone's brother, or one of the girls, to play groom. It was such a joy!"

Practice makes perfect. Just as kids practice grown-up things to help themselves grow, a Wedding Goddess can benefit from practicing kid things to help herself relax into her new adult starring role as *the Bride*. It is great to slip on your wedding dress, practice in the mirror, and get the feel and sound of what it will be like that day. It will help you acclimate yourself to being bridal. If you practice by marrying yourself first, you just may step up to the altar with more confidence on your wedding day and feel freer to exchange the deepest kind of love and communion with your beloved.

Wedding Goddess Exercises

Wedding Goddess Reflections. When you feel yourself stressing about details related to your wedding ceremony, take some time out. Allow yourself to remember a time when you were a little girl, and when being a bride was just about equal to being the Queen of the World. You'd sometimes dream about being wed, and perhaps even orchestrate pretend weddings, enlisting little brothers, dolls, dogs, or even a chair to be the groom. As you got older—even after your first broken heart and your latest Mr. Wrong—you still seemed to carry that dream in your heart, hoping and longing for the day it would happen to you. Sometimes, when you met someone terrific, you'd fantasize that perhaps he was the one, and you may have mentally written out your wedding guest list as you dreamed of that first kiss at the altar. There was a time when that daydream seemed to lift your heart and make your spirit soar, a time when it was so much fun to let your imagination run wild. Recall the feelings it stirred within you, and how you wanted so much to be a real bride.

Even if you are not someone who has always dreamed of taking that walk down the aisle, or if you are someone who has a hard time seeing herself being "bridal," it is important to be able to think back to *any* time when being a bride seemed like fun. Find a way to tap into that energy through memory. Even if it was the day you got engaged, remember back to the point in time when that fantasy was fresh and new, and when you looked joyfully toward the day that you would walk down the aisle like a Goddess and get married.

When it feels like wedding worries are getting the best of you, remember: Through the ages, many little girls have enjoyed "playing bride," and many grown-up brides have walked down the aisle before you. You are simply taking your place in the circle of life.

A PRACTICE WEDDING CEREMONY

Prepare for an at-home practice wedding ceremony just for you! For this ceremony, you will need ample time alone, your wedding dress (or something wonderful to wear if your dress is not ready yet), a candle, flowers, a mirror, music and a "first dance" song, celebratory food and libation (a glass of wine or grape juice is fine), and anything else you would like to include.

A. Clean house and make sure things are neat and comfortable beforehand.

B. Prepare a reception for afterward, including a libation and favorite meal or whatever would be pleasing (alcohol not required). You can prepare it prior to the ceremony.

C. Have everything you need ready and handy. It is recommended that you stay home and bask in the energy of your experience rather that going out afterward.

D. Shower or bathe, and when you do, imagine that it is an exercise of purification that will wash away your worries and concerns.

E. Play some music that inspires you and opens your heart as you prepare the wedding altar—in your living room or on a small table in your bedroom.

F. Include a candle and flowers on the altar if possible.

G. Have a makeshift bouquet of flowers ready.

H. Have a full-sized mirror handy.

I. Have your wedding dress and accessories, such as shoes and veil, ready for wear.

J. Make sure you have undisturbed time alone, and begin.

YOUR WEDDING CEREMONY FOR ONE

1. Light a candle to bring light into the room.

2. Say a brief prayer if it feels comfortable, such as:

> *Divine Spirit of all there is, please fill this place with your sacred presence.*
>
> *Support me in my efforts to playfully experience and express myself as a bride.*
>
> *Help me see my own divine light and joy.*
>
> *Help me have fun as I prepare myself for the big day. Amen.*

3. Take a look at yourself in the mirror without judgment, and gently place your hands on your belly, which is literally the center of your body. Let your feet sink into the floor. Feel supported by the ground beneath you. Let the power of the earth uphold you.

4. When you feel centered, grounded, and ready, step into your wedding dress (do the best you can to get it on by yourself). Don't put the shoes on yet. Even without full makeup and all the trimmings, slip into the dress and begin to feel it on you—not just the material but the energy of the dress and how it feels to be in it. Look at yourself in the mirror and become familiar with this image of you as *the Bride*.

5. Now close your eyes for a moment and remember back to a time when you played dress-up as a child, or when you dreamed of being a bride as an adult. Remember the tingly excitement, the fun, the sheer joy, the hopefulness, the ease of fantasizing about the big day. Let that feeling sweep over you, and at the same time, continue to feel your feet firmly planted on the floor, grounded and centered.

6. Open your eyes and look at yourself, the bride, as you continue to recall the times when playing or imagining being a bride was so much fun. See if you can hold both the image of now and the memory of then together, in the same moment in time—while still feeling your feet firmly planted on the ground.

7. When you feel ready, connect with your own eyes in the mirror. Look deeply, beyond the pupils, and stay focused with open eyes. Begin to imagine yourself as the bride you truly want to be. Feel it inside. You are confident, happy, and joyous, and feeling beautiful and connected to your beloved. Get a sense of how you will stand, how you will feel, how poised you will be. See yourself in all your glory, as if it is happening in this moment, right now. Continue to feel all these sensations while looking deeply into your own eyes—until you get the sense that it is time to stop. This will help you integrate the many feelings—those of the moment, the memory, and the hopes for the future—and create a positive energetic signature for your wedding day.

8. Know that on your wedding day, when you look into the eyes of your beloved, it will be like looking into your own eyes, and that these feelings will flow back to you and you will feel centered, joyous, like the bride you are meant to be.

9. To celebrate your practice ceremony, head over to the boom box and start your "first dance" music. Slip on your shoes and dance yourself across the floor. After that, play something you can boogie to. Enjoy dancing in your dress, and feel the fun you will be having in that dress!

10. Bring the experience to a close with a sip of wine or juice, and a feast.

Although your wedding will be more elaborate, the practice wedding is a fun way to get the party started in your heart! Soon enough, the fantasy will become a reality. When the big day comes, you'll be lighter and you'll look forward to playing bride for real!

QUICK PICK-ME-UP:

Get in the mood and groove. If you find yourself stressed and don't have time for a full practice wedding, nothing helps shake out stress like a little uninhibited dancing. If you can play some tunes that remind you of childhood, it will help stir up the cellular memory of playfulness and abandon. Then play some songs on your wedding playlist and dance away the stress.

WEDDING GODDESS VOW

The excitement of being a bride courses through me.

I vow to enjoy each moment leading up to the big day!

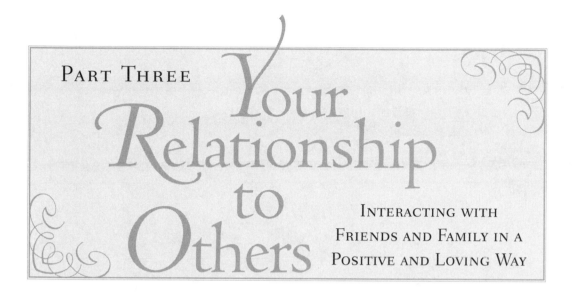

PART THREE

Your Relationship to Others

INTERACTING WITH
FRIENDS AND FAMILY IN A
POSITIVE AND LOVING WAY

Knowing how deeply our lives intertwine, we vow to not harm self or others . . .

—Stephanie Kaza, from "Buddhist Vow," in *Woman Prayers:*
Prayers by Women from Throughout History and Around the World

Arlene Sandler/Lensgirl.com

CHAPTER FIVE

Building Your Bridal Dream Team

Your journey to the altar is a precious life experience. Follow your heart in choosing the beloveds who will walk with you to your wedding day. Seek to surround yourself with those who will uplift you and honor you. Select sisters and brothers who know your soul and want only the best for you.

—Calliope, Greek Goddess and Muse of Epic Poetry, eldest of the nine Muses,
known as the fair-voiced one and as a mediator.

*I*n the old days, all the members of the bridal party would dress exactly the same as the bride in an effort to fool ill-wishers and throw off evil spirits who might try to attack the woman who was about to wed. This custom of protecting the bride—who was considered pure and blessed—was similar to the custom of protecting and serving royalty. Queen Elizabeth II of England had six maids of honor carrying her long train at her coronation, all trailing behind in the same dress, ready to deflect any negative vibes.

The days of feeling honor and obligation to serve the bride as if she is the queen have dwindled somewhat in modern times. Many potential bridal attendants get stressed when they think about the time, money, and emotional commitment that they may be asked to invest in your wedding. And the process of selecting wedding attendants can create a lot of anxiety for brides. The bridal party becomes a political hot potato for some, and an experience with the darker side of feminine nature for others, because there can be a lot of confusion and resentment related to formulating or being part of a bridal party.

Brides fret about who to select as maid or matron of honor, and they worry

> We included a vow renewal for my brother and sister-in-law at our ceremony. So once we decided to ask my brother and sister-in-law to participate in the ceremony, it was only natural to make them the maid of honor and best man. The only regret I have is not being able to make my other bridesmaid, my best friend from college, feel more included in the wedding. As a med student living on the opposite coast, her time was limited.
>
> —*Sophia, who married Zvonko on October 11, 2003*

about showing favoritism, creating jealousy among friends, upsetting siblings if they are not chosen to head up the team, and ruffling feathers in general. They sometimes try to include people they aren't even close to, to honor family ties or obligations. Worse, they drag in team members who they *know* are inappropriate—too envious, angry, cranky, nervous, demanding, difficult, financially strapped, or recently heartbroken—just because they are old friends of the bride, and she feels obligated to include them.

When you think about it, you really want a team of people who can grow with you and stand by you during your wedding experience. This is your big moment to shine, and you want to avoid scene-stealers. And it is your moment to offer special blessings, so you want to be with people who will appreciate them. This is your moment to enjoy the process of planning your wedding, and you want a team that can enjoy it, too.

WEDDING GODDESS RULE #5

A Wedding Goddess picks the right wedding team.

You select the people who will be there for you on this wedding journey, the ones who can truly appreciate the experience and graciously celebrate it with you. You are gracious, loving, and generous of spirit with your bridal dream team.

Take a fresh approach to your bridal party, and look toward tweaking tradition and making it more balanced. Even the old titles are a little goofy and discriminating—"maid" and "matron" of honor. Forget about titles and family politics. Instead, round up the women (and/or your guy friends) you love most and who will truly support your journey to the altar and bestow upon them the title Goddess of Honor or Hero of Honor.

A Wedding Goddess removes herself from the possibility of bridal party blues and invites the right people for the right reasons to partake in her wedding.

How to Select the Right Attendants for the Right Reasons

*T*here is a story about Eris, the Greek Goddess of Discord, which is reminiscent of some of the horror stories that brides share about their attendants. Eris, insulted that she was not invited to the wedding of Peleus and Thetis, tossed a golden apple (the Apple of Discord) into the wedding feast. This act ultimately led to the Trojan War—and you better believe it ruined the wedding!

This is not the kind of Goddess that you want on your wedding team. Yet you may have an Eris lurking in your circle of friends, who for whatever reason will be disruptive and unpleasant with you and other members of your bridal party. Try to figure out in advance who is truly right for your wedding dream team, and who you would invite because your feel obligated. For a peaceful journey to the altar, it is so important to make sure you select Goddesses of Honor (as well as Heroes of Honor, if your good friends and family members happen to be male) who will truly celebrate your wedding experience with open hearts. It is equally urgent that you weed out the drama queens—even the ones you love—if they are disruptive in any way. Remember, it takes only one bad apple to spoil the whole barrel. From time to time, a bride has to fire her maid of honor or a bridesmaid because they contribute so much stress to an already stress-filled time.

I chose a friend of mine from work to be my maid of honor. After getting together with her a time or two, I started freaking out. She was nervous about being a first-time bridesmaid and wanted to do everything right. I was put off by her overzealousness to help, and felt my emotions colliding with her personality. After meeting with her one night, I let my feelings out to my fiancé and our wedding planner. They allowed me to rant and release all my fears and frustrations about having chosen her to be my maid of honor. I didn't see her for several days, and by the time the wedding rolled around, all of my frenzy was gone, and she turned out to be a splendid maid of honor. I am now very happy and thankful that she was at my side. The day of my wedding, she was very helpful, and having spent that time together, we are much closer now. I no longer regret my decision, and I am very happy that my ranting was enough for me to release my frustrations before they got in the way of the big day.

—*Callie, who married Arnie on April 17, 2003*

Many brides feel let down. Arlene Cronk, MSW, founder of The Bridal Survival Club™, sponsored through The New York Wedding Group and The Boston Wedding Group, estimates that one in four brides complains about a problem with at least one of the women in her bridal party. Often it's the maid of honor. One of the problems is that some brides have high expectations about what a maid of honor and other attendants are supposed to be responsible for, and another is that some friends just are not up to the task of being in a bridal party, and they don't know how to, or are not willing to, share their true feelings. It is so important to be aware of the dynamics of those you intend to have in your wedding party, before the fact. In addition, you should also do a reality check on your own demands and behavior to make sure *you* are not the one causing the problems. Cronk says that many brides report:

- Disappointment because the maid of honor is not as involved in the process as the bride hoped or expected her to be.
- Feeling shocked when her maid of honor *disappears* from the process. She begins missing dress fittings, falls out of touch, refuses to get involved, or gets involved minimally with shower and wedding preparations.
- Discomfort with a friend's feelings (or expressions of feelings), such as acting cranky about performing bridal-party duties or acting out by complaining about every bridesmaid dress she tries on.
- Feeling let down because a maid of honor lacks enthusiasm for the whole process. It is difficult for a lot of brides to understand why their friends are not as happy as they are.

"Sometimes the friend you select just can't do it," says Cronk. "She can't say to herself, 'this is my best friend, I will be there for her. I know my turn will come. I will get over my feelings of sadness because I feel I am being displaced by the groom, or I will get over my jealousy or my disappointment that I am never going to have this for myself. I'll just rise to the occasion.' Not everyone has that level of self-awareness that they can rise up and be there for their friend."

Try to resolve the issues. If you can't, then you might consider taking a break from each other. When a friend does not come through for you, it is very disappointing. It gives you yet another set of issues to deal with, on top of everything else. Cronk suggests that the best way to resolve problems with an attendant is to communicate with her. After all, she's a good friend; see if you can talk it through. "Go out to lunch, and in a diplomatic way, try to talk it through," she says. "Create an environment where the friend may be able to express her feelings. Don't say 'You are really disappointing me' or 'You are just not there for me.' Use the word 'I' instead of 'you' and say how *you* feel. If it's impossible for your friend to give you what you need, try to accept that, and hopefully it won't damage the relationship. Maybe by talking about it and getting it out in the open, it will help."

Sometimes a maid of honor or bridesmaid will opt out of the bridal party. Yet, as Cronk points out, this may just be one of the ins and outs of a lifelong friendship that continues.

Ask only the people who want you to win. Before you ask anyone to be on your team, give some thought to what they bring to the bridal party. While they may be willing to throw parties, do physical work, and spend money, they may be emotional time bombs just waiting to erupt. It's essential that you ask only the people who believe in your marriage and truly want to support you; otherwise, you will end up with your own version of "As the Bridesmaid Turns," like Jeannie, who opted to ask an old friend to be on her bridal team. The only catch: This woman did not agree with Jeannie's decision to marry; she didn't even like Jeannie's hubby-to-be. "Everyone always says you find out who your real friends are when you are planning your wedding," said Jeannie. "Ain't it the truth!" Jeannie's first choice for maid of honor turned her down because she had such a hectic work schedule and traveled so much. So she selected an old friend who lived on another coast. She felt this person would do a great job, plus her hubby got along with Jeannie's hubby-to-be. But her old friend Kim, one of the bridesmaids, took issue. "Kim, although an old friend, turned out to be a disappointment. She caused stress and hurt feelings, and alienated other members of the bridal party, especially my maid of honor, Renée." Kim complained that Renée wasn't doing her share, while Kim, who saw herself as "just a bridesmaid," was doing more work. As Jeannie realized, "It turned out that she really had issues with my husband and our short engagement but didn't have the nerve to say anything. So she took it out on the maid of honor."

Pick your battles wisely. Sometimes you just have to go with the flow and not get yourself crazy with the drama within the bridal-party circle, especially dress drama. When it comes down to it, is their attire really as important as yours? After much frustration with that issue, Delia decided it wasn't. Choosing her wedding team wasn't hard for Delia. She'd been bridesmaid for her sister

Jane, so she asked Jane to be matron of honor for her. Her other two sisters were bridesmaids. But they had great difficulty finding dresses. "One sister complained about every dress we tried—something she did for the other two sisters' weddings as well," says Delia. "One sister was pregnant but was going to have the baby before the wedding; another was pregnant and was going to be even more so for the wedding. I finally gave up and told them to find a dress. They did—and nice ones at that." With special circumstances like these, sometimes it is best to just give them your color choice and let them find their own attire.

How does tradition fit in—or does it? The Wedding Goddess has to truly assess the traditional obligations of the maid of honor and figure out if those obligations are right for her bridal party. Technically, according to a dictionary definition, the maid of honor is "the chief unmarried woman attendant of a bride, and an unmarried *noblewoman* attendant upon a queen or princess." And a matron of honor is "a married woman serving as chief attendant of a bride at a wedding." Yet, if you look at the long list of what tradition dictates a maid or matron of honor must do, you might find it is like a full-time job. According to WeddingGazette.com, these are some traditional functions.

- Go shopping with the bride and for her own gown.
- Lending a hand with tasks, such as addressing envelopes and preparing favors.
- Offering objective opinions on anything from the cake to the flowers.
- Throwing a bachelorette party and a shower with the help of other bridesmaids.
- Taking notes and recording all the gifts received at the various wedding parties.
- Attending the rehearsal and dinner.
- Rounding up the bridesmaids to make sure they get to the wedding on time.
- Holding the groom's ring at the altar.
- Prepping the bride before she takes that walk down the aisle.
- Holding the bride's bouquet during the ceremony.
- Signing the license.
- Dancing with the best man at the wedding.
- Offering a toast at the reception.
- Helping to keep the bride calm.

• Making sure the bride eats so she doesn't get swept away on the adrenaline rush.

• Listening to the bride's concerns and fears.

And those are just the main functions! Figure out if you really want to ask one person to do all those things or if you want two people to share the responsibility. It really is a lot to ask someone to take on in their busy life, and you can see how it could exhaust even your best friend just thinking about it. Rather than expecting to put this all on the shoulders of one committed friend, think of spreading these responsibilities among several attendants and friends.

> I had seven bridesmaids, much to the dismay of my mother (who said nothing, but I could see it in her eyes when I told her). I was totally nontraditional, even though I had a formal wedding. Instead of bouquets, I had my gals carry little lanterns with tea lights and coordinated satin ribbons. The lanterns were engraved with my husband's and my name and the date. They kept them as mementos.
>
> —*Summer, who married Tony on September 20, 2003*

Bringing balance to the bridal party. If you do away with the hierarchy, you can create a true and intimate circle of friends and family members who can cooperate with you and with one another to help make your wedding wonderful. Rather than calling them maids and matrons, address them all as Goddesses. Goddess of Honor is a term passed along by Arizona nondenominational minister Rev. Paul Michael, who officiated for a bride who wanted to make all of her team feel special and equal. When you honor them with a title like Goddess, they become more like the noblewomen who serve the queen rather than the maids who are schlepping and working so hard for the bride. You can also welcome men into the bridal party (as your groom's attendants or yours) as Heroes of Honor. Like the days of yore, when men stood at the altar, swords by their sides, ready for action, the Heroes of Honor can be special energetic protectors of the bride and groom.

How to avoid hurt feelings. Rather than designating one person to be chief among attendants, you can organize and send them down the aisle in order of height so no one feels offended. Or, if you have a best friend or sibling who

> The best decision I made was not to have a bridal party. It was simple, and no feelings were hurt. My best friend did a reading, and my sisters walked with us to the altar, each holding our rings on a silver swan, because swans mate for life. It was a very cool touch!
>
> —*Randi, who married Chris on August 9, 2003*

truly wants to be in the chief role, you can bestow the title Goddess of Honor of the Highest Order. Just think of the fun the women in your life will have feeling that they can at least share a little bit of the Goddess spotlight with you!

Wedding Goddess Exercises

1. **Know your bridal-party priorities.** It is so important that you have your priorities straight when selecting your bridal party, and that you approach it with compassion and wisdom, taking into consideration the point each person is at in their life and being clear about what you need and what you expect from them, and also finding out what they can realistically take on. Each member of the team might have something very special to contribute—if only you are open to it. By the same token, you might have something very special to contribute to them. Make four lists before you ask anyone to be on the team. These will help you clarify your goals:

> A. What you *need* help with—number-one priorities.
> B. What you hope they can be part of but can do without.
> C. The ways you believe each can contribute.
> D. The ways you can contribute to them.

Give some thought to each person you are considering. What's going on in her life? Is she free to partake if she chooses? Does she have so much on her plate that it might be overwhelming? Is she in a relationship herself? How might this affect her feelings about your wedding? Just think through all these little issues. Once you are done, and clear about whether your choices are truly right, call them to discuss it.

2. **Goddess of Honor night.** Once you've figured out the best people for your bridal party, invite them over as a group for a Goddesses night. Serve dinner and use a fun ritual to initiate your best female friends as Goddesses of Honor. (This evening for the ladies of your court can be expanded to include your Heroes of Honor). In a sacred circle, or with a

raised glass, you can tell them how much you appreciate them and why they are an important part of your wedding journey, and thank them for

their participation. Rather than delegating chores and assuming that they are there just to serve you, ask each of them how they see themselves being part of your wedding journey. What would they like to do, and what would they like to get from the experience? This sets up a gracious dynamic from the start. If your Goddesses (and Heroes) of Honor get their needs met and do not feel put-upon, they will rejoice in your happiness and lovingly serve your needs.

3. **Offer your blessings.** Since you are becoming spiritually ready for

> I chose only one person, my sister, as my maid of honor. I have too many good friends to have to put them through tacky dresses, financial strain, and stress. Instead, they became my bridal management team and were assigned jobs to help me with during the wedding planning. For example: Sara did my invite design; Gabriella was wardrobe and flowers; Maritza did hair and makeup; Anna Tulia did crisis and best-friend management; and Larisa, my maid of honor, designed my shower and oversaw the whole production.
>
> —*AnaMaria, who married José on January 24, 2003*

marriage with every step of your wedding-planning journey, you already embody the special powers attributed to a bride on her wedding day. Share these special powers with friends in special ways. At author Arielle Ford's wedding to Brian Hilliard, she threw small bouquets to all her single friends, to make them feel special and to bless them with the love that she was experiencing that day. If your Goddesses (or Heroes) of Honor are single, offer your blessings to them to help them find true happiness in a relationship, as you have. If they already are in a relationship, offer blessings for love in all forms, and for prosperity and success. You can do this simply, by following these steps:

A. Take your friend's hand.
B. Look her (or him) in the eyes.
C. Connect your heart to hers (or his).
D. Offer a blessing, such as: *"May you find your true love. I know that special soul is out there. May you experience love all around you."*
E. Close with a smile.

WEDDING GODDESS VOW

*I will select attendants who support my marriage
and who will joyfully share in the experience.*

Arlene Sandler/Lensgirl.com

CHAPTER SIX

A Bridal Shower Fit for a Goddess

It is your time to be showered with riches, material and spiritual. Open, now, to good luck, good fortune and the abundance of the universe. Allow your womenfolk to fuss over you as they offer love, friendship and wisdom. Let them help you step onto the path of new possibility and celebrate your path from unmarried to married woman.

—Fortuna, the Roman Goddess of Prosperity and Plenty,
whose domain includes luck and lotteries

What's the first thing that comes to mind when you think of a bridal shower? *Oh, gee, can't wait to go,* or *There goes another fifty bucks and a Sunday afternoon, here comes spiked punch, a goofy hat made of ribbon and bows, a series of annoying ooohs and ahhhs over toaster ovens and towels, and a boring time with boring relatives and bored friends of the bride?*

Although it is always fun to include or adapt familiar elements in your shower, most brides want more than a typical hen party these days. The Wedding Goddess wants a shower fit for a Divine Bride! You may need that toaster oven, and of course you want to share the experience with the women you love, yet you want a shower that is personal, unique, meaningful, and truly fun.

WEDDING GODDESS RULE #6

A Wedding Goddess goes for the extraordinary.

You want a bridal shower that truly blesses your rite of passage from single gal to married woman, from past relationships to present. The main focus is on spirit, on growth, on being supported—in the style of a Goddess—from one stage of life to another. And on fun and lightness! The gifts you receive will be both material and spiritual.

Consider a gathering that truly honors your rite of passage, acknowledges the wonderful hosts of the shower, and celebrates the people who have taken the time to be there. Invite the women you love to a truly meaningful Goddess-style bridal shower. Celebrate, have fun, get lots of presents, and do it in your own special way.

How to Have a Bridal Shower That Will Truly Transform You

*T*he concept of the bridal shower originated about three hundred years ago. According to wedding lore, a Dutch woman's father refused to give her a dowry because he did not care for her choice in mates, so all the womenfolk in the village got together and *showered* her with gifts so she could marry the man she loved.

Obviously, three hundred years ago, and even thirty years ago, a bride needed lots of household items to get her marriage off to a good start. These days, so many couples are living together before they wed that they probably already have plenty of dishes and pots and pans. Wedding showers can be far more creative and personalized, and your shower can bring you gifts that appease both your material and spiritual needs.

1. **Give some thought to the shower you want.** There are so many options and variables. Think about what would best suit you, including your ideal level of participation and whether or not you want it to be a surprise. If you could have your druthers:
   - Where would you like it to be?
   - Who would you want to be there?
   - What kind of theme would you like?
   - What would you like to experience?
   - Would you rather a nighttime or weekend shower?
   - What kind of gifts would you most appreciate?

• What kind of gifts (material or spiritual) would you like to offer?

• Would you want to include a ritual experience?

• Would you want boys there, or would you want to make it an exclusively Goddess thing?

• Do you feel you can have all the elements that you want most in one shower, or might it be best to have two—one for family and one for friends?

2. **Ask for what you want.** Even if someone else is throwing a shower for you, you can make requests about how you would like it to be—unless it is a total surprise. Be clear up front that you want something that really addresses who you are and where you are going. You can even pick a theme. "Showers are more themed than they used to be, because brides and grooms are older and established and have the typical gifts," says Sharon Naylor, bridal expert and author of many wedding books, including *The Ultimate Bridal Shower Idea Book*. "There is more focus on their hobbies or home decor. They are not themed around starting your first home."

3. **Bridal showers have gotten more exotic.** Themes range from a lingerie party (where the bride gets only sexy sleepwear, underthings, and naughty toys), to a romantic beauty shower (where she is gifted with beauty products, Victorian-style romantic items, and anything that inspires romance), to a backyard barbeque and luau shower for both the bride and groom (where you can roast a pig, play lots of goofy games, and give the bride and groom Hawaiian leis—and all the jokes that you can think of. Here are some fun themes for the Wedding Goddess to consider.

> Just being the center of all that girl attention was a treat. And having someone else plan the whole thing made me feel taken care of. I made the guest list and helped pick the date and suggested the place (my mom's house). I had a lingerie shower. So I gave gifts to my maid of honor and the four others who helped make the shower: I tucked a $25 Victoria's Secret gift card into each thank-you note.
>
> —*Jessica, who married Terry on November 15, 2003*

• **A Goddess gathering.** Women gather with sacred intent to spiritually support you through this right of passage, and maybe bring gifts of the Goddesses from the world's traditions or gifts fit for a

Goddess—such as elegant perfume bottles, gift certificates for massages, or inspiring artwork.

• **A Feng shui shower.** Guests bring feng shui items for the home, such as wind chimes, crystals, golden icons, water fountains, bamboo flutes, plants, Chinese good luck symbols and coins, or cash in red envelopes.

• **Showering you with wisdom.** At this shower, you receive gifts of wisdom and advice. The shower gifts can be anything you need, and a wishing well can include books, prayers, and plaques with pithy sayings and quotes. The women go around the circle and offer you advice for married life, or they write down their advice and place it in a special wisdom book.

• **A wedding memory and keepsake shower.** This shower is devoted to honoring your past and documenting your wedding experience and marriage. Guests bring keepsake gifts, such as beautiful photo albums, picture frames, memory boxes, disposable cameras (or they can chip in for a new camera), scrapbooking supplies, a frame for your wedding license and your vows, and even a wedding time capsule, into which you can put a copy of your wedding invitation, a photo of you and your groom, a favor, dried flowers, etc. Someone can also bring a retrospect of the bride in photos—usually Mom—and one or more people share a story of how you went from shy child to awkward teen, to the beautiful swan that you have become.

• **Special cultural customs shower.** Many cultures have their own version of women gathering to honor, celebrate, and assist the bride

> I had three showers, and they were all fabulous. The best was the tea party that my bridesmaids threw for me. At the shower, there were two special albums waiting for me. One had recipes, and the other was a pressed flower–covered album that contained a page for every woman at the shower—twenty in total. Each had received the page in the invitation, and they were instructed to fill the page with memories and advice. I got twenty very different pages covering all the years of my life! There were photos of me building sand castles at age five with one of the gals, and then pictures of us at the prom, and then at her wedding. Some of the gals did quotes and photo collages; some just wrote me a poem and drew pictures. It was the loveliest book I have ever seen. I get teary-eyed every time I look through it.
>
> —*Summer, who married Tony on September 20, 2003*

through her rite of passage, which can be adapted or included in some way in a wedding shower. Indian and Middle Eastern cultures paint the bride's hands and feet with henna and then paint one another in preparation for the wedding. In Bali, the womenfolk take the bride to a river, help her remove her clothes, and let the clothes float down the river, says ritual expert Barbara Biziou. This is to symbolize releasing the old. Then they dress her in fresh, new clothes.

4. Picking your bridal shower team. Essentially, you should pick a bridal shower support team that truly wants to take this part of the journey with you, a team that you can easily communicate with. Typically, it is the maid of honor who plans the shower, but it might be your family or other friends who pitch in to help. "Whoever it is," says Naylor, "go to them. Don't be shy. Tell them you don't want a typical shower. You can't tell someone to give you a shower, but if you are already aware that one is being planned, that assertiveness will be welcome. The maid or matron of honor will be relieved to have direction. They want to give you a shower that you really want."

5. Decide on your guest list—or guest lists. Take some time to jot down your guest list. That way, you can get a sense of the full group dynamic of these women—and whether you can do what you truly want with the entire group. And then you will also have a list (or lists) to give your bridal shower team.
- Take a look at who you *truly* want to invite.
- Who do you feel you *have* to invite?
- Make note of who you feel can truly support your desire for a more meaningful rite of passage.
- Acknowledge who will "sort of" be there for the punch.

You may find that each person you truly want to invite is someone who will totally support your chosen theme—terrific! Then again, it could be that your family, or his, is on the conservative side. Since you may need some practical items, and you won't want to exclude your mother, mother-in-law-to-be, and assorted relatives (who always bring *the big gifts*), you can ask that parts of your shower be more traditional. Or perhaps *two* showers are in order.

6. **Two showers may be better than one.** There can be one for family members and another for your closest circle of friends. These are the friends who truly understand the magnitude of the commitment you are making—and all you have had to *get over* and *grow into* to get there. These are the friends who want to make sure you move toward your new life in your best emotional and spiritual shape ever!

Some brides allow their moms to throw more traditional showers for the relatives and friends of the family, then the maid of honor or a good friend will throw a more personalized shower. Some brides just take it upon themselves to have the personalized shower that they truly want.

• Comedienne Caroline Rhea took eight of her closest friends—including her sister—to a very hip jewelry store that offers jewelry making parties. They sat and joked as they strung beads and baubles and ate Brie.

• Another bride had a "hearts and crafts" shower, where she took her closest girlfriends to a paint-your-own-pottery store. They were each given dried clay hearts to paint, with the prayer that all the single women in the group would soon find true love and that all the married women would have renewed passion and love. The bride asked all her friends to bless her own multicolored heart. She took the heart to the shower thrown by her mother a few weeks later and kept it on display on the gift table. It helped her get through the more traditional shower.

• One bride had an astrologer come to the shower and do a reading for her in front of friends, highlighting the chemistry and challenges she and her husband-to-be shared and offering pointers on how to have the best marriage. Then the astrologer gave mini–astrological readings to everyone in the group.

> I think the most divine part of my shower was having my husband there to share in the festivities and the embarrassing moments. It made me really feel like part of a couple. I loved having him there. My mom made a presentation board with photos from my youth. My husband's friends from college did the same for him, although the pictures were funnier and more incriminating.
>
> —*Dawn, who married Dominick on July 6, 2002*

> A great friend hosted my shower at her house along with my mom and my maid of honor. Everything about it was great, and it culminated with an entire cake made out of rainbow cookies—my favorite cookies in the whole world.
>
> —*Jackie, who married Brian on July 27, 2002*

• Another bride asked Urban Shaman Donna Henes to do a drumming circle for her close friends. They worked up a sweat and worked their energy into a high pitch to assist her rite of passage.

7. **Women and men can shower together.** Many brides and grooms are sharing the shower experience. Sometimes there is a small shower for the bride, thrown by girlfriends, and then a bigger joint shower, where the girls and the boys get together and both the bride and groom open the presents. "Coed showers are the big thing, because eighty percent of grooms are planning the weddings with their brides," says Naylor. "So it's no longer just a female thing." Joint showers make a strong statement about partnership, and have a nice "we're in this together" feeling.

8. **Tweaking traditions.** There are many ways to adapt some of the familiar parts of a shower to make it more personal for you.

   • **A blessing mobile.** The long-honored tradition of making a goofy paper-plate hat for the bride with the bows and ribbons from the presents—and writing down random comments that she says when opening gifts and reading them back—can be adapted for the Wedding Goddess. Instead, have the supplies on hand—such as small scissors, red string, tape, a stapler, and a hanger—and create a mobile with all the bows.

   A. Cover the hanger in pretty wrapping paper, and then tie on a series of bows and decorations.

   B. Instead of randomly writing down things the bride says, ask her what her wishes, hopes, and dreams are.

   C. Attach a comment to each bow.

   • **A true wishing well.** Instead of a traditional wishing well, which people bring sponges and spatulas to place in, ask that the wishing well be a true collection of well-wishes and spiritual items. Guests can write a blessing and place it in the well, adding a small gift, such as a spiritual book, a crystal, a sixpence for your shoe, or a good-luck charm.

   • **Capture the memories.** Instead of asking relatives and friends to give out advice or recipes, create a "blessing book." Give out small pieces of paper or index cards, and ask everyone to write down a blessing or good wish for the bride. Take a photo of each woman who writes a blessing (a Polaroid, if possible). Read them all to the bride at intervals during the shower. Then press the blessings into the memory book, along with the photo of the person who wrote it.

• **Tie the knot at the shower.** For a joint shower, use some of the massive ribbons from the gifts to give the bride and groom a taste of the bonds of matrimony. During the opening of the presents, tie various pieces of ribbon together. After the gifts are open, have the bride and groom stand facing each other, and wrap that long piece of ribbon around their whole bodies. Tie it in a knot as they hug. Give them a moment to make some fun promises to each other, such as: "I promise to love, honor, and listen to you—even when you ramble on!"

Wedding Goddess Exercises

1. A SHOWER OF BLESSINGS

*B*lessing circle. Create a circle of love, friendship, and good energy. Hold a moment of silence, and let everyone in the circle speak a heartfelt blessing to the bride, one by one. As Sharon Naylor says, "For the most touching and memorable showers, sometimes it's not the games you play or the gifts you display, but the words you say that can make even the most modest bridal shower priceless."

2. A GODDESS SHOWER—AND BATH

The Aphrodite ritual. High Priestess and author of *The Love Spell*, Phyllis Curott believes a woman who is about to wed should be treated like a Goddess—a love Goddess! She often helps brides through this rite of passage by evoking Aphrodite, Greek Goddess of Love and Beauty, because she is a divine female known for bringing joy and laugher, says Curott. "She is also very special, because each year she returns to her temple on the island of Cyprus to bathe in the sea, purifying herself from the remnants of past loves and relationships. She becomes, once again, a virgin—a woman unto herself, and thus she is renewed and liberated, free to enter into the great love that comes to her."

Currott's *Aphrodite Ritual* takes into consideration that most brides have had a number of relationships before they find the person they will marry, and that all relationships were the stepping stones to both the experience and the recognition of true love. "When we fall in love and marry, there is an aspect of love that we have never known before," says Curott. "Like Aphrodite, we are again virginal."

This ritual is very similar to a bridal shower, in that friends and family can be invited to participate (of course, you can also choose to do this with just close girlfriends). While Curott has led this ritual with womenfolk *right there in the bathroom*, the more modest bride can have her privacy and the support of her womenfolk as well. Currott says these are the components:

- Each guest is asked to bring a gift that symbolizes the powers and blessings of a Goddess of love, of the hearth, the home, family, sexuality, or creativity, such as: rose essential oil for love, candles for fire and warmth in the hearth, or an icon of a Mother Goddess or Mary to represent family.
- A purification potion is prepared with rosemary, lavender, peppermint, chamomile, oatmeal, sage, and sea salt in a handkerchief sachet. These are all items easily obtained at the supermarket. (Use approximately one teaspoon each of rosemary, lavender, peppermint, chamomile, and sage. Use a tablespoon each of oatmeal and sea salt.) If you don't have those ingredients, you can replace them with chamomile tea, which is light, sweet, and purifying.
- Aphrodite oil is made of almond, lavender, rose, and patchouli essential oils. (Mix three parts almond to one part of the other oils, and about twelve drops of almond oil to four drops of each of the others.)
- The bride-to-be is escorted to the bathroom, where a tub has been filled with warm water and some of the potion has been bundled into a handkerchief that floats in the water. Into the tub she goes. (You can wear a bathing suit, or go in the buff if you are comfortable.)
- All the while, there is a lovely chant that everyone sings: "I am the Goddess, I am the Mother, all acts of love and pleasure are my rituals."
- The bathroom is also filled with pink and red candles. The bride's name is carved on the pink ones, for the Goddess, and both husband and wife's names are carved on the red ones, for love and passion.

The women can leave the bride in the bathroom, where she can disrobe and step into the bath. There she can give herself a good soak and scrub, using more of the potion, which is a good exfoliant as well. Then she washes her hair, usually with an herbal shampoo. The Goddess of the hour is left alone for a while to meditate on love and her future. Meanwhile, the guests gather in a different room and help prepare for a feast.

"When the Bride first arises from the tub, she does so as the Goddess Aphrodite, cleansed, purified, renewed, and ready for new love," says Curott. Once she's dried off and slips into a robe or underclothing, the women can rejoin her and help her dress, as friends would on her wedding day.

"We help dry her hair, style it, make up her face, help her dress in something beautiful and sexy. And then she's escorted back to the living room, where she stands in the center of the circle of women, who dance around her chanting her name and calling out blessings that she will need in her marriage such as 'Passion!' 'Honesty!' 'Gentleness!' 'Strength!' The energies of love and joy rise with the chanting and are finally directed to the bride-to-be by simply extending one's hands and visualizing the love you feel flowing from your heart to hers. It is a very simple, very powerful experience for all."

There's generally a lot of humor, as well as wine and all sorts of yummy things for a feast, when the ritual portion is over. Then the bride-to-be opens her gifts as guests explain their meaning and significance to her future.

"This is one of my favorite rituals to do whenever a friend is about to get married," says Curott, who also describes this ritual in her book *The Love Spell*. "It takes the idea of a bridal shower to a whole new experience of joyful Goddess empowerment and pleasure."

WEDDING GODDESS VOW

*I will enjoy my Goddess gathering, and I will take to heart
the many gifts of love showered on me that day.*

Arlene Sandler/Lensgirl.com

CHAPTER SEVEN

Dealing with Wedding Dynamics

Getting the Support You Need from Your Family

Open your eyes . . . you will see many sides of the people you love . . . and you will see sides of yourself once hidden. Aim to cut through darkness by shinning a light on these emotions and behaviors. Seek creative solutions, stand your ground and transcend petty arguments. Remember, forgiveness is, ultimately, the only way to neutralize anger.

> —Kali, Hindu Goddess known as the Black Mother,
> who reins over life, death, regeneration, and the ego

Weddings are notorious for stirring up the emotions of the clan. Even the most centered, focused, loving, and graceful Wedding Goddesses might come across some of the stereotypical behaviors that have long plagued brides—the ornery mother who thinks things should be done *her way*, the sister who is so envious of your joy that she gets reactivated in a very passive-aggressive way, or the conservative father who just can't see beyond tradition. It's not easy to deal with the many dynamics that can arise when planning for your big day, but understanding them will help you keep your footing.

The reality of wedding planning is that it pushes people's buttons all around. And it can bring out the soap-opera stars and drama queens in every family. Your best defense is to understand and accept up front the fact that part of the journey involves allowing for people's dark sides to rise to the surface—including yours and your beloved's—and counteracting negativity with spirit, love, insight, communication . . . and really, really clear boundaries.

How to Deal with Wedding Dynamics and Get the Support You Need

*U*ltimately, a wedding is like a production," says one bride. "Whoever funds it has a say in what happens, unless your generous benefactor has granted you complete creative control. It also brings out a lot of human drama. However, it is still your day! Stand strong. Speak clearly. Try to maintain your grace, and a smile."

Nothing is more aggravating than having your buttons pushed by the people you love—except perhaps experiencing this while you are planning your wedding! This is a major milestone in your life and can be filled with an alternating array of emotions—anxiety, fear, and confusion, along with joy, elation, and anticipation. Of course, you want to have family and friends involved, yet sometimes it feels as though they are adding aggravation and unwanted emotional work to your already *huge* to-do list.

> ## WEDDING GODDESS RULE #7
>
> **A Wedding Goddess is gracious . . . and establishes appropriate boundaries.**
>
> You take charge of your wedding from the start. Although you love, appreciate, and want to honor and/or include your family, in-laws, and friends, you set forth a game plan that works for *you.* You identify the kind of wedding experience you choose to have, and assess how the people you love can best partake. You want your wedding to be a true celebration, and so your organize the troops and do all you can to stay in command!

1. **Strike a balance.** It would be unrealistic to think that your wedding journey would not include a few bumps when it comes to family. In order to have the wedding experience you truly want, you will have to find ways to invite your loved ones to participate, as well as find ways to create healthy boundaries. Sometimes you have to weigh the benefits of having a lot of support with the amount of interference and dramatics that could come along with it. On one level, wedding drama can ultimately be good for the soul because it gives you a chance to become emotionally stronger and more congruent about the

choices you are making as you individuate from Mom and Dad. It is also an opportunity for you to take responsibility for your own meltdowns and upsets. At the same time, you do not want your wedding-planning experience to be one ongoing confrontation—even if you triumph, it will exhaust you.

2. **Bride and groom as the projection screen.** People will have, and will want, their own view of *your* wedding. There is no getting around it. Susan Cheever sums up one of the maladies of getting married in her book *Looking for Work*. "A Wedding isn't for the bride and groom, it's for the family and friends," she writes. "The B and G are just props. Silly stick figures with no more significance than the pink-and-white candy figures on the top of the cake." Depressing as it may sound, certain family members have their own ideas about what your wedding day should be all about. People will project their fantasies, and it is par for the course that someone, or a few someones, will be a pain in the neck. You can't ditch your entire family and all your friends, but you can try to manage and organize them. When you know where they are coming from, and what their needs are in this whole wedding scenario, you can orchestrate their roles in your wedding more appropriately.

> I think when you have a big, traditional wedding, you have to bend a little to keep the peace. It is important to show respect to others. However, this should apply only to certain things. My grandmother brought a couple of friends to my wedding, and that was fine, because it made her feel good. Other than that, I wouldn't allow anyone to dictate to me who should or shouldn't be at our wedding, especially since my husband and I paid for it ourselves. Do what is comfortable for you. It may be your day, but you are asking others to join in the festivities. Just try to keep your cool and remind those pushy people that this is your moment to shine.
>
> —*Debbie, who married Chris on July 15, 2000*

3. **Weddings can bring out the shrinks within.** Loved ones tend to act out some primal, archetypical roles when it comes to weddings. Some get snagged in some very stereotypical behaviors. Your marriage may tend to trigger a lot of different feelings in the people who love you, just as it is triggering many feelings for you. Another way to help head off the problems at the pass is to clearly understand the psychological dynamics that

can go on with people involved in your wedding. And to realize, even people who love you can get crazed.

"Getting married is a crisis . . . but a normal crisis," says Virginia Rachmani, CSW, M.A., formerly a psychotherapist with the famed Karen Horney Clinic and now in private practice in Manhattan. She says it's a crisis for you and your beloved in that you are making a huge commitment, a decision to truly grow up and be responsible, and in that these are your final, formal steps away from your parents. It's a crisis for your loved ones because they are along for the ride, trying to help you deal with your stress and tasks, and yet still dealing with their own issues.

"Very often, if someone is stressed-out—whether they have emotional problems or not—they regress to being preschoolers," she says. In effect, everyone involved in your wedding—including you and your groom—can act out as if they are a bunch of kids in a sandbox. Rachmani suggests that giving language to some of the "freak-out" behaviors that might arise will help you cope with and manage the emotions in the sandbox more effectively. She sites these as some of the most common problematic behaviors that can surface in families:

• Your mother may talk incessantly about the wedding planning, relationships with the groom or his family, or decorating your home. Conversely, she may become aloof or even depressed. She may be experiencing a revival of her own fantasies of the perfect wedding—or the perfect marriage. She may also be dealing with midlife issues associated with aging, work, or her lifestyle.

• Your dad may become increasingly possessive, and perhaps will relate to you as he did when you were a small child. Or he may constantly complain about the wedding expenses, when you know the money is available; he might alternatively distance himself from you or any wedding planning whatsoever. Frequently, these behaviors emerge because a father can feel out of control or unable to protect you. Perhaps he never disclosed his discomfort with your living with your fiancé before marriage, or the fact that your fiancé's family seems to live in a different world. Like your mother, he is also dealing with aging and post-child-rearing changes in his marital relationship.

• Your unmarried sister may act out in an assortment of ways, such as missing fittings for her dress. Married sisters and brothers sometimes behave in a proprietary way, hovering—or conversely dismissing—the importance of your wedding or "putting you in your place." Siblings may resent the attention that you are being given or the fact that you are happier than they are themselves.

• If your parents are divorced, any difficult family dynamics may intensify, since the wedding or your relationship with your fiancé and his family may trigger lingering feelings of loss that can appear as anger, frustration, and sadness.

As one bride says, "Pick battles wisely, and ignore some of the things that can't be changed." Sometimes the best defense is a smile, a hug, and a thank-you. Your family will not transform overnight, but you can use the experience to transform your behavior around them.

4. Resolve the issues wherever possible. The problem individuals may or may not admit or even be aware of their behaviors, so as a Wedding Goddess, you really have to stay aware of how loved ones are responding to the whole wedding situation. With some, you will be able to call negative behaviors to their attention and clear the air. With others, you won't. But whenever possible, talk to your loved one and see if she or he is willing to discuss the situation. Find out her or his point of view as well. Share what you are feeling. Telling the truth, and opening the door to the other individual telling the truth, is the first step toward liberating you both from a negative pattern that you may be stuck in. See if you can open the dialogue for some compassionate and honest exploration. It's always a more pleasant experience if you can deal with things in a conscious, loving way.

5. Graciously learn the lessons. Keep your eyes—and heart—open to the lessons being offered. Your family and your groom's family will likely bring up some of your unresolved issues and force you to revisit and reflect on things within you that need some attention and healing. As Alan Cohen, author of *The Dragon Doesn't Live Here Anymore* says, "Everyone who lives outside of you lives inside of you." Wedding planning brings up all our childhood "stuff," big-time, because being around all these folks zaps you back in time. Having these things come to light is not necessarily a bad thing. Intimate relationships of any kind beg us to explore our shadow selves. In many cases, these parts would never be discovered, were it not for the people who push your buttons! The gift is that this is a chance to look more deeply into yourself. You might gain insight that will be helpful to your growth. This is a chance to get out of the sandbox of youth and grow up, especially with the people who make you feel like a kid.

6. **Stand up for your choices.** When people start butting in and telling you how to plan your wedding, it can be downright annoying. When they start projecting their own needs and desires onto your big day, it can be infuriating. And if they do anything to sabotage your happiness and peace—even unconsciously—it is devastating. Some hefty emotions and old patterns might rear their heads while you are planning your wedding. The questions are: How will you deal with it? And how can you use the experience to grow? When you stand up for yourself and your choices, like the Wedding Goddess you are, the dynamics begin to shift. Whether dealing with your mom or dad, a sister, or in-laws, your general stance must be: "I love you. I want you to be part of this big day. But it's my wedding, my day, my way. Please respect my preferences and boundaries. And thanks for being here!"

> Stay true to yourself and what you want. You shouldn't be pressured by "tradition" or what "everyone" does. Do what you want, even if the whole family screams to the heavens. It's your day. Have grace, patience. Listen to annoying information with open ears. Respond honestly and clearly, and be grounded in your decision.
>
> —*AnaMaria, who married Jose on January 24, 2004*

7. **Organize the clan.** You can save yourself a lot of headaches by sitting down with your spouse-to-be to decide who you want to involve and how you want to involve them—*before* you bring it to the family for open discussion. If you figure out what you would like everyone to do, you can then invite people to partake in a very specific way. This will save you the chaotic feeling—à la *My Big Fat Greek Wedding*—of people randomly trying to pitch in however they want to. You can also create a project chart. That way, you can better manage everyone's participation. One bride I married came up with a great plan. Jane has a large family

with several stepparents, and she found a brilliant way to have them all support (and enjoy partaking in) her wedding, along with her groom's family. Here's how Jane and her beloved, Adam, assigned everyone specific tasks:

Adam's parents: arrived in New York four days before the wedding; went with Adam to his tux fitting; planned/ran the rehearsal dinner.

Adam's sister: signed the wedding certificate as a witness; did a reading in the wedding ceremony with Jane's brother & sister; helped Adam's parents with the rehearsal dinner.

Jane's dad: helped select the wedding venue; hosted an "immediate family" dinner on the Friday night before the wedding, including parents, aunts, uncles, and grandparents; walked Jane down the aisle.

Jane's mom: shopped for the dress and shoes; made the bride's garter; arrived in New York one week before the wedding to help with final preparations (filling out place cards, picking up the cake topper, cleaning the apartment, making sure everyone arrived safely, helping with Jane's trial run of getting ready).

Jane's stepdad: took the bride and groom out for cocktails on the Thursday night before their Sunday wedding; gave the champagne toast at the wedding.

Jane's stepmom: shopped for makeup with Jane; helped with Jane's trial run of getting ready (and did a trial run of the makeup); did Jane's makeup for the wedding. Her brother (Jane's step-uncle) was the one who styled the bride's hair, and she helped with that as well.

Jane's second stepdad: helped Jane's mom with her tasks. (Also, see below for a list of activities that included immediate family only.)

Jane's sister: Went with Jane to her dress fitting; helped with Jane's trial run of getting ready; helped Jane get dressed the day of the wedding (she laced the dress, etc.); did a reading in the wedding ceremony with her brother and Adam's sister.

Jane's brother: signed the wedding certificate as a witness; did a reading in the wedding ceremony with Jane's brother and sister.

8. **Use creative strategies for the trouble spots.** Some wedding issues will have an emotional charge no matter what, and some family members will truly challenge your patience. Worse, these are folks you just can't communicate with honestly, because they can't—or just won't—hear it. When dealing with individuals who are in their own little worlds, it may be time to construct some creative boundaries.

• **Political boundaries.** Anne's mother wanted to invite everyone in her address book to her daughter's wedding. Since she was paying for part of it, she felt entitled. She wanted to be in on the entire invitation list process. That idea was completely unappealing to Anne and her fiancé; they knew her mother would criticize all their guests and try to replace them with hers. So they sidestepped the problem by giving Anne's mother twenty-five blank invitations to invite anyone she wanted. That way, they alleviated the need to pick and choose—not to mention argue—with the bride's mother.

• **Special needs boundaries and being prepared.** Sheila was very nervous about including her mom in her wedding plans because of her mom's mental illness, and she was afraid her mom was going to be a handful on her wedding day. So she gave her mother a specific sewing task as part of the preparations, something she could easily do and that made her feel involved, and she put her brother on "mom watch" on the big day to make sure that her mom did not become disruptive at the ceremony. Her mother was surprisingly calm at the wedding, but at least Sheila had a contingency plan.

• **Energetic and emotional barriers.** Pat's sister-in-law was the ultimate wedding know-it-all. Having married the year before, she acted as if she was the ultimate source for wedding do's and don'ts. She was so pushy with her advice that Pat found conversations with her to be very vexing. Since Pat's brother was in the wedding party, it was tough to avoid his wife. When Pat was around her sister-in-law, she felt edgy. At first she would argue and resist the advice, but this only got her engaged in even more annoying conversations. So she would imagine herself under a dome of protective glass, and it would help her tune out the yapping, and she would just say "great idea" to everything her sister-in-law suggested instead of resisting. Eventually, with no resistance to push up against, Pat's sister-in-law stopped putting her two cents in.

• **Physical boundaries.** Jan had problems with her grandmother's interfering nature. She loved the woman, but her grandmother was on her about something every moment, and it drove her crazy. On her wedding day, Jan set a policy that it was *bridal party only* in the bride's suite—no relatives allowed! She felt hearing her grandmother's nagging before the ceremony would wear her out. She asked the venue to keep the bridal suite locked and to keep all guests away from the area, and they complied. This gave Jan the space to chill out before the ceremony. When grandma complained that she didn't get to see her beforehand, Jan said, "Sorry, I guess these folks kept us in lockdown."

9. **Acceptance of what is.** Sometimes things happen that you simply have no control over, and you have to find a way to cope with the disappointment in the moment and rise above it. Weddings are a bit like the entertainment world—the show must go on, even if the cast and crew are not all present.

• One bride discovered, at the last minute, that her maid of honor wouldn't make it. "The most challenging part of my wedding was that I got a phone call at the salon a couple of hours before the ceremony," recalls Kelly. "My maid of honor had been in a bad car accident and wouldn't be able to make it. It could have put a roadblock in our day, but I figured we could easily find a volunteer to be our witness. I was just happy that Kelley was okay!"

• Another bride had a father who was missing. "My wedding had one disaster that could have been avoided if I would have planned getting to Central Park a little better," says Barbara. "We didn't make arrangements until the day before, and we didn't all ride together. So when my dad got lost, it was a little stressful. My stepmother ended up giving me away—but it all worked out."

Wedding Goddess Exercises

1. **Come up with wedding-planning policies—with your fiancé.** True, it is not romantic, but it will help take the stress and strain off your relationship if you figure out your wedding ground rules from the get-go. You've got to clearly draw the line at your boundaries, and then you both have to stand your ground and support each other. Dissention among the in-laws or bickering within your own family will drive you insane. But when your spouse-to be does not support you, or if he constantly caves in to his mother's pressure, it will drive a wedge between the two of you. So try to get it straight between you, and before you even begin to get family and friends involved, clarify who you want involved and how. Ponder questions such as:

- If your parents are involved, how much input do you want parents and in-laws to have? If they are paying, how can you maintain your position in the driver's seat?
- What family members do you want to include and why? Do you feel obligated, or would you be happy to have them involved? Make a note of all obligatory inclusions and think them through carefully. Do you really want a relative who rubs you the wrong way to have an intimate role in planning your wedding?
- Which friends can you depend on to support your big day—even the ones who are not in the wedding party?
- Who will be truly thrilled to help if you just ask? Are there people you trust who will help without needing the glory or the formalwear?
- Who can you put in charge of helping you manage relatives?
- What tasks can you assign to those you choose to involve?

The two of you should bat some of these ideas around and also think of other wedding policy questions: Will we marry close to where we live now or at a venue close to our parents' hometown? Will we invite kids? Is there an age cutoff, such as twelve and up? Do all the fathers and brothers have to wear the same tuxes? These are all things to mull through together. Get as clear as you can on as many points as you can before you start gathering with the family to discuss details. Even though you will likely learn a lot about compromise during this experience, you will also have a chance to hone your negotiation skills and your confidence.

2. **Make peace with your parents whenever possible.** Some of us are best friends with our folks and grew up in a household with two loving parents who are still together for their children's weddings. If your parents were the perfect models for love and respect, you can joyfully build your marriage on the wonderful foundation and example they set for you. If there were issues between them or between you and your mom or dad, now's the time to reckon with them and liberate yourself from carrying the worst part of their relationship into yours. If you feel you can talk to your father, mother, or any significant person who you feel you have unfinished business with, do so during the wedding-planning time, before emotions flare—and do so as gently as possible. Ask for their support in creating a fabulous wedding and a loving, lasting marriage. For example, one bride who was fretting over her dad's drinking finally got the courage to tell her alcoholic father, "Daddy, I love you, but it hurts me when you drink. If you want to see me, do not drink when I visit, and if you want to come to my wedding, it has to be without drinking." He came and stayed sober, and he never drank in front of her again. Sometimes the wedding is the very thing that helps us individuate from Mom and Dad.

3. **Protect yourself from negativity.** If you must deal with very negative people when planning your wedding, protect your precious energy. Judith Orloff, M.D., a California-based psychiatrist and author of the bestseller *Positive Energy*, says that brides must beware the "energy vampires" who can drain them. "Brides who are naturally empathic and sensitive might struggle with relatives and friends who are negative, pushy, or needy," says Orloff. "They might want to try to include these people and make sure they are happy, but sometimes a bride is putting herself at risk. Even family members and good friends who love you can be energy vampires. That is the last thing a bride needs when planning her wedding." Orloff says that if after interacting with someone you feel drained or nauseated, have a pounding headache, or feel dizzy, oddly uncomfortable, or overwhelmed,

> Be grateful and thoughtful when dealing with all those who love you and want you to be happy, but remember, at the end of the day, they will be *your* memories. Be honest with what you want and need, and know that ultimately that's what everyone wants for you anyway.
>
> —*Courtney, who married Ray on October 26, 2002*

it's a sign that you've been zapped by an energy vampire. Maybe this individual is very stressed, tense, freaked-out, or angry, and when you are around them, you start taking on their symptoms. Whether it's their constant complaining or their bulldozing their way into your bridal experience, you have to protect yourself from their intrusive energies. And you might have to consider removing those kinds of people from your plans, or lessening their roles.

To deflect and recover from experiences with people who drain your energy, and to ground yourself, Orloff offers this life-saving Root Planting Meditation. "Sitting in meditation is a lifeline to your center, to the earth," she says. "By calming the mind, you can realign with your essence." Follow these steps:

- Close your eyes. Focus on your breath.
- Then gently extend your awareness downward to strata, bedrock, minerals, and soil.
- From the base of your spine, begin to feel continuity with the earth's core.
- Picture having a long tail that roots in that center.
- Allow the earth's energy to infuse your body and stabilize you.
- Meditate for five minutes, or an hour if you like. This is sacred time to ground yourself.
- Repeat as needed.

The more grounded you are, the better you will be able to handle drainers without getting whisked into a state of depletion. The more time you allow to meditate and reconnect to yourself, the stronger you will be, and the less you will be willing to let others siphon your energy.

4. **Use the colors of a spiritual warrior.** In feng shui, the colors red and gold are introduced whenever there is tension, as these are the colors that create happiness and harmony. You can wear these colors when you meet

with family members and friends to discuss the wedding, or even host a lunch with a tablecloth, paper plates, and napkins in those colors. "These are wonderful colors to select anytime, but especially if there are family difficulties or other kinds of disagreements," says feng shui master practitioner and consultant Kathryn Weber. "They will help unify difficult people or emotions and inspire a peaceful, harmonious gathering."

WEDDING GODDESS VOW

It's my wedding, and I am ready, willing, and able to take charge of it all!

PART FOUR

Your Relationship with Your Beloved

STAYING CONNECTED THROUGH THE CRAZINESS

There is within each of us, I believe, a deep and holy hunger for sacred union. Our souls yearn to unite, to live in concert and connection with other souls.... On earth this deepest, sweetest desire for sacred union is most often expressed in a committed, passionate and soul-filled partnership with another; we long to interlace our hands and hearts with a beloved as we make the pilgrimage toward our own spiritual evolution.

—Sue Patton Thoele, from *Heart-Centered Marriage*

Arlene Sandler/Lensgirl.com

CHAPTER EIGHT

Staying Close to the Man You Will Marry

Keep the Love Fires Burning Bright

Keep Close. Let there be no distance between your hearts . . . your flesh.
Reclaim your love, if you must, at any point in the journey. Freely express
your devotion and your charms. Offer many kisses to your beloved as you
plan your wedding.

—Innana, the ancient Mesopotamian Goddess of Love and Sensuality,
known as "Queen of Heaven," who rescued her lover from
the underworld when forces drove them apart

Remember back to the times when all you could think about was *him*? At
work, out with the girls, off on that vacation you booked long before you
met him—he was always at the forefront of your mind. In the beginning
stages of your relationship, you were both so enthralled with each other that being together was magical and sublime. There was nothing you wanted more than
to be closer—and even closer yet. The man you fell for was the one who made
your heart sing and who made you feel that in his arms you were home. The
woman he fell for was the one who made him feel safe enough to open his heart
and give his love.

The day he proposed, or the day that you mutually decided to marry, was
likely one of the most significant moments in your life. You can probably still re-
count the story with a crystal memory of the entire engagement experience.
However, all too often, brides go from kissy, loving partners to wedding-crazed
women on a mission, and they forget to nurture the very thing that brought them

> ### WEDDING GODDESS RULE #8
>
> **A Wedding Goddess stays present in her relationship.**
>
> You remember, every day and every step of the way, the love that brought you two together. And you honor that love by continuing to date the man you will marry as you plan your wedding. He is still your boyfriend—and you treat him like the fabulous man you fell in love with.

to this important milestone—the relationship. The last thing you want to be is one of those brides, yet you'd be surprised how the stress and pressure that comes along with wedding planning can take the fun out of a relationship.

That's why it is so important that the Wedding Goddess makes sure that love, romance, nooky, and *just being together* are still on the menu in those months before she gets married. If not, your guy will feel cheated of his beloved and left out of the wedding experience. And you will be missing a special time to connect with your true love before you officially become husband and wife.

How to Date and Stay Close to Your Fiancé

*I*ronically, even though you are both happy to be getting married and looking forward to sharing your lives in a richer, more committed way, one of the first things to fall to the wayside during wedding planning is romance. With so many to-do lists, people to deal with, vendors to manage, and life changes to ponder, couples sometimes lose touch with each other. A Wedding Goddess knows she has to side-step the negative side effects. Here's some advice from two top relationship therapists about how to prevent those problems.

Don't take each other for granted. The magic begins to dim when you get too comfortable with your engaged status. As Dr. Judy Kuriansky, world-renowned clinical psychologist, sex therapist, and radio host, points out, "Once you've made the decision to marry, don't fall into a trap like so many other engaged couples, where you think you are already committed to each other because you're getting married, so you stop being seductive with each other and you stop putting your best foot forward. The feeling of security is great, but there is a danger in starting to go your separate ways now that you feel secure with each other. It's healthy to have your independent life, and to take time for yourself, but a healthy relationship means you maintain a balance between your independence and interdependence."

Kuriansky's solution? Date! Each other, that is! "It's exceptionally important to keep dating," says Kurianksy, author of many books, including *The Complete Idiot's Guide to a Healthy Relationship*, a book that gives many exercises that couples can use to deepen their commitment, communication, and cooperation with each other for lasting love. "The best thing for wedding planning . . . the best thing for a healthy relationship . . . and the best thing for a long-lasting happy marriage is to keep on dating each other." That means to treat each other with the same excitement and attention as you did when you were first falling in love. She says to keep coming up with new ideas of places to go and things to do that interest the two of you, and that you can do together. Find activities that

> My partner and I really focused on the wedding as a gateway to the rest of our lives together. Viewing the wedding as part of the journey and not the end game relieved quite a bit of pressure. We spent time discussing where we had been in our relationship, as well as discussing our future vision. These sessions were often over some good food and wine, just relaxing in each other's company.
>
> —Monica, who married Simon on December 8, 2003

> Throughout our whole relationship, we have had a tradition of date nights—one night a week, we go out on the town, even if it's just to dinner. Somehow, the time we spend out together feels more special than time at home. Our dates help us keep the romance alive. Even when things got really busy on the wedding front, we would still have our date nights. There were many dates where we were reviewing to-do lists over pasta, wine, and candlelight. Somehow, talking about wedding details in a romantic atmosphere made it easier to swallow.
>
> —Laurie, who married Chris on September 27, 1997

overlap your interests, whether it's gardening, wine-tasting, or home repairs. And certainly be creative about ways to seduce each other, and to enjoy love-making.

Try not to veer off the sex trail. Some couples seem to *forget* about sex or lose interest in intimacy. Dr. Patti Britton, a sex coach, columnist for iVillage.com, and coauthor of *The Complete Idiot's Guide to Sensual Massage*, says to avoid veering off the love-and-sex trail; couples should include nooky and sexual connection in the wedding-planning equation. Couples can feel so overwhelmed by the planning process that they sometimes forget to take a moment to reconnect—to look into each other's eyes. Britton points out that many things plague a couple's life as they're escalating in time toward what she calls "W-Day." She says it's important for you both to be aware that you are under enormous, high-intensity pressure; that you are stressed because you are playing beat-the-clock; that your bodies, just in the waking hours of wedding planning, are in high-rev mode often, with lots of adrenaline pumping; and that there is lots of negative stress in your lives, which has damaging effects.

Dr. Patti's solution? Sex! With each other, of course! "Considering all these things, a couple in that stage is often not feeling well . . . they are stressed to the max . . . and are often under enormous pressure they can never escape," says Britton. "This is the perfect time for an orgasm! Even a single orgasm can help change the chemical soup of your body. It helps alleviate physiological stress you feel, and sometimes gives you the emotional pain relief you crave." Here are some other ways to keep your relationship healthy.

Bring a breath of fresh air to your love affair. There is a state of being in the early stages of romance known as *limerance*, the time when all is perfect in a relationship and two people see each other through the eyes of love, without noticing flaws and issues. It is also known as the grace period or the "honeymoon period." No relationship can maintain that new, fresh, lovey-dovey vibe continuously every moment, but it is important for the Wedding Goddess to find ways to keep the possibility of that energy alive. In a long-term relationship, many couples find that the feeling comes alive when they make up after a fight (i.e., makeup sex). Yet one of the key elements to limerance is an unconditional appreciation and love of the other person. Kindness is a way to keep it flowing. If you decide to look upon you beloved with kindness and appreciate what he is doing to make you happy, it will help return your relationship to a state of grace. Say thank-you for the little things.

Make your bedroom a wedding-free zone. Don't bring wedding-planning issues and dilemmas to bed. The bedroom is for peace and rest—and for loving. Planning your wedding can take up residence in almost every area of your life—don't let it take over the bedroom. The time you spend loving each other, and lying in each other's arms, is a time of tender connection. Your beloved will be happy to revel in those moments with you, but if you start bringing up issues related to your wedding during those vulnerable moments, he may shut down or feel put-upon.

Establish rituals that make you both feel loved. In your day-to-day life together, remember to stay connected in small but significant ways. In his book

Soul Mates, Thomas Moore talks of those little life rituals that make the soul feel content. It's these things that keep us connected—a call from the office every day, romantic dinners at home on Fridays, going to your favorite restaurant or inn. Even if it is just calling out "I love you" when he is in one room and you are in another, these are small acts that keep your hearts entwined. When you establish loving rituals to look forward to, they will never become boring, and you will always have a sacred space of connection with the man you love.

> The most challenging part of the whole process was making sure not to let "the process" get bigger than it needed to be. It's so easy to get consumed with it all. When we felt that happening, we took some time away from it and got some perspective. Our wedding day would come and go, but getting worked up about the small stuff—all of that stuff—wasn't worth it. We laughed a lot at moments of stress. It took a while to be able to laugh, but we did. Keep thinking in the "long term," and today's stresses won't seem so unbearable.
>
> —*Courtney, who married Ray on October 26, 2002*

Wedding Goddess Exercises

1. **Keep clearing the air.** If ever you find yourself stuck in a rut or being unloving with each other, or if you just need to take some sacred time to share what's on your mind, designate a special "us time."

- Make sure you have an appropriate setting and privacy, and take a few moments to sit together quietly, decompressing from everyday stress.
- Then share a few moments of meditation. Just hold hands, look deeply into each other's eyes, and breathe in unison.
- Once you feel calm and connected, take turns sharing what is on your minds. For example, you speak for fifteen to thirty minutes, then he speaks for fifteen to thirty minutes.
- If you are feeling unhappy about something, be careful not to blame or dump on your partner. Instead of saying, "I hate when you . . ." or "I am so upset because you did this . . ." use statements that allow you to take responsibility. For example, "It would really support me if you would . . ."
- Tell each other what your needs are, so that you do not have to argue or try to act out your anger. Make sure each of you gets a

chance to share, and that the other listens in silence so you can both clear whatever is weighing on you.

- Although each of you must bear witness when the other talks, don't hesitate to touch each other or look at each other tenderly.
- Once you've both had a chance to say all that's on your mind, seal it with a hug and a kiss—and a vow to keep the channels of communication open.
- If you find yourself coming up against an issue—over and over—that neither of you seems to be able to come to a truce about, consider counseling. Even a session or two with a trained therapist can be helpful.

2. **Stay connected through breathing.** Dr. Patti Britton recommends synchronized breathing whenever stress and tension are getting the best of your relationship, or even as a bit of foreplay. "It helps couples focus on themselves and their union," she says. "If they are feeling anxious or a disconnection has occurred, if they are stressed or even when they are feeling loving together, it's the perfect entree into sex. It is a form of spirituality that unites. . . . After all, isn't marriage essentially a spiritual ceremony that is created to unite two persons and their spirit into one?" Here's her recipe for synchronized breathing:

- Set aside ten minutes to sit together, or lie down on the bed together.
- Listen to your partner's breathing, and begin to synchronize your breath to his.
- Feel the peaceful feelings of your heart as you both share the breathing pattern. Breathe into it. Let the connection deepen. This helps align the two of you on a primary level.
- Stay with it as if it is a meditation. When you are both connected, you can relax into each other's arms, snuggle, or let the energy take you . . . wherever!

3. **Pep up your love life.** If you have been together for a while, you might find that your journey toward married life is a good time to enhance your sensual loving. David Deida, a teacher and author who speaks to the needs of modern men and women, says a woman's openness awakens a

man's heart and takes the relationship to even deeper levels. The challenge of wedding planning is that there is so much activity that demands an *outward* expression of energy, while deeper sexual exchange asks that you be receptive. "The art of deep sex includes your capacity to relax in your own body and receive your lover so deeply that he is drawn beyond himself into your love," says Deida in *Finding God Through Sex*. Looking for deeper, more spiritual ways to connect in the bedroom can help balance all parts of your life together. Britton says that even a hot night in a hotel room could be the ticket to rekindle the heat of those pre-engagement days!

> The thing that helped us the most was finding time to plan the wedding, and then finding time for other activities. It was so nice to be able to turn that off for a while and escape to a movie, share a hammock, read a book, or even take a walk. The wedding pieces will fall into place; just make sure you don't neglect yourselves during the planning.
>
> —*Summer, who married Tony on September 20, 2003*

4. Try a little Tantra. Tantric sexuality is a sacred expression of romantic love that comes out of the ancient Hindu tradition, which honors the divine feminine and divine male. It teaches that divine love can be attained through a loving partnership between a man and a woman. Because Tantra treats the exploration of sensual connection and sexual pleasures as a sacred act, it can unite partners and inspire intimacy on all levels. It honors the body, the mind, the soul, and the sensual nature of humans, and it's healthy for both partners. The word *Tantra* means "expansion" in Sanskrit. The basic premise of Tantric sexuality is that people who practice Tantra together share a deeper ability to communicate, a spiritual connection, and an extraordinary expression of erotic love. This kind of intimacy and devotion comes with practice and patience. Men love it, and you will, too, because Tantra is a spiritual practice in which the female is revered and treated like a Goddess—her pleasure is the first priority. What a fun thing to practice on the way to your wedding day. It offers a way to develop deeper intimacy and sharing between partners.

Modern teachers, such as Charles and Caroline Muir, have brought Tantra into the twentieth century. Their *Secrets of Female Sexual Ecstasy* is a home-study video course that is highly educational (and also graphic).

Dr. Judy Kuriansky, Ph.D., has created a comprehensive, easy-to-follow, hands-on Tantra guide that offers a spiritual view of sexual power in *The Complete Idiot's Guide to Tantric Sex*. Both give you the historical perspective on Tantra and guide you on how to have more magical, playful, and loving relations with your partner.

5. **See the love in each other's eyes.** During the planning of your wedding, you often forget to just sit and gaze at each other, like you did in the days before your engagement, when you were falling in love. One aspect of Tantra that you can use anytime, without necessarily being romantic or sexual, is eye contact. Anytime you need to remember why you have chosen to get married, stand before the man you love and look into his eyes. It is there that you will find the "soul connection" between you.

* Look into his eyes and let him peer into yours to see the love you each have inside, as well as the love you feel for each other.
* Look for that familiar twinkle and warmth. Even on the dark days, or the hard-to-communicate moments, the love is always there, visible in the eyes.
* Utilize eye contact to develop immediate rapport—even when he's miffed at you. When you look deeply into his eyes, you will connect with him intimately and completely.
* Look into his eyes so you can know him on an even deeper level; the deeper you search, the more you sink into his soul.
* Kiss him with your eyes. It is wonderful practice for your wedding day, when you will have a chance to stand before family and friends and look deeply into each other's eyes and say "I do."

WEDDING GODDESS AFFIRMATION

*We vow to nurture our relationship and
celebrate our love as we joyfully plan our wedding day.*

Arlene Sandler/Lensgirl.com

Including Your Groom in the Wedding Planning

A woman's essence is that of feminine potency. It is up to women to take the raw energy of the masculine and give it direction and form. Empower and inspire your beloved to become engaged with the wedding experience.

—Binah, a Hebrew Goddess who represents "Understanding" and the
Supreme Feminine Principle on the Kabbalistic Tree of Life

*I*t's no secret that the work of planning a wedding has typically fallen to the bride and the womenfolk. But times are changing, and as a Wedding Goddess, you'll have to make sure that your wedding-planning experience is not hoarded by you, your mother, and the other female members of your wedding-support team. From the very start, you've got to *invite* your guy to get involved in the process and help him feel welcome.

True, there are still many grooms who just want to say "I do" and be done (those are the ones that will need a bit of coaxing), but today's marrying man is far more likely to partake in the decisions and process of where, when, and how (and for how much) you will wed. Wedding expert Sharon Naylor, author of *The Grooms Guide*, says it is estimated that 80 percent of grooms are involved in wedding planning. Some grooms will choose to be full partners from the start. Sometimes, even the guys who are willing to share in the full wedding experience may still see weddings as a "she thing." The trick is to guide your beloved through any unfamiliar feminine territory, and to call on your feminine wisdom and compassion to bring you both through the experience.

Planning your wedding will probably be your first major opportunity to make major decisions together, so it is great practice for marriage; in fact, wedding

> ## WEDDING GODDESS RULE #9
>
> **A Wedding Goddess works in partnership with her beloved.**
>
> You know that sharing the wedding planning is a way not just to prepare for your wedding but to prepare for your marriage. You establish up front the role each of you will play in the planning, and you honor and encourage his participation. You use this opportunity to further develop trust and strength in your partnership.

planning is a microcosmic look at how you two might divvy up the duties of married life, and it is a chance to develop a rhythm for how you can best work together. It's a journey, taken together, that can strengthen your bonds, deepen your trust, and help you get to know each other better.

Gregory J. P. Godek, romance expert and author of *1001 Ways to Be Romantic*, concurs that it's essential to include the groom in the wedding planning: "So the two of you can stay connected . . . so he doesn't feel left out . . . so the two of you can remain a team, a unit, that can stand united in the face of the onslaught of *the wedding*." It's important, he says, that "the bride-mother team does not supercede the bride-groom team. Also, when the groom is more involved, he's less likely to get cold feet."

By the same token, since your beloved may not be as intrigued by all the nitty-gritty details of the wedding day as you are, or in the same way you are, find the aspects that will truly turn him on. As in marriage, fifty-fifty does not always mean splitting up a list of "things to do." It may mean dividing the chores based on expertise or passion. Be creative and have fun sharing the experience.

How to Share the Wedding-Planning Experience with Your Beloved

*P*art of your Wedding Goddess mission is to encourage and help create the right balance between you and your mate while planning your wedding. One of the ways to do this is by welcoming your groom's support, input, participation, and company on the journey. Your marriage will require a balancing of female and male dynamics, and so will planning for the big day. "There is a yin and yang to everything, including wedding activities," says clinical psychologist Dr. Judy Kuriansky. "Yin represents the feminine, and yang is the masculine. It is important to consider both and tap into your future husband's feelings and interests so that he doesn't think it's just a female thing to do." It will be a relief to have someone to bounce ideas off of and help make decisions with—and yet there are some things you will enjoy doing on your own or with girlfriends or your mom.

We divided up the responsibilities according to the things we were interested in. He was in charge of music, DJ, officiant, photographer, etc. I was in charge of finding the florist, cake maker, etc. We did a great job working together. I had to put all my trust in him that he was making the right decisions for what we wanted, and he did the same. It was a wonderful experience to plan the biggest day of our lives together.

—*Teresa, who married Stephen on July 5, 2003*

Goddess things, groom things, and shared activities. Finding your dress and accessories, dealing with bridesmaids, doing your beauty treatments—these are all things your groom may pass on. But when it comes to decisions and legwork, meetings and negotiating, and creating and choosing aspects of your ceremony and reception, you can each take on the roles that are right for you. Is he a whiz at research? Then let him find the leads and phone numbers for vendors and venues, officiants and bands. Are you more talented at closing a deal? Then you should be the one to confirm the details of the contract with the photographer and caterer. There are also certain things you will want to do together, such as figuring out *his* wedding wardrobe, meeting with officiants, working on your ceremony, and dealing with finances.

What's his wedding-planning IQ? Assess and recognize your groom's level of wedding-planning expertise and interest. If he is very detail-oriented, perhaps he'll be *better* at many of the wedding tasks than you. If he is more of a vision holder, or the one with the finances, then perhaps he is best at *assisting and supporting you* while you create exactly what you want. If he is extremely creative, per-

There were some activities I would do with my mother and girlfriends, like picking out the dress, but otherwise Jim and I did almost everything together. That was really a gift from him, because I am much more into decorating and party details than he is. I did a lot of the phone work, but Jim was there for every in-person meeting. It really was a team effort. Plus, to make up for the extra time I spent on the wedding-planning legwork, he planned the whole honeymoon—from soup to nuts—and it was out of this world!

—*Laurie, who married Jim on September 27, 1997*

haps he will excel at special touches for the reception and finding readings for the ceremony. The mind-set of splitting everything down the middle works for only some couples. If you are one of them, great; if not, divvy up the tasks in a way that makes the most sense for you both.

Don't just give him a to-do list. For the Wedding Goddess, the most fruitful experience will come from really getting to know who your guy is and working with him based on the way you know he can best contribute. In some cases, you may have to assign specific tasks as well as offer suggestions and instructions on how to accomplish them. Then there are those grooms for whom wedding planning is a grand adventure, so don't be afraid to surrender to your guy's wedding-planning prowess.

Here Comes the Groom

When Barrie wed Howie. Barrie Singer married hubby Howie Singer on a rolling green hill overlooking a valley in upstate New York. Since Howie, and now Barrie, are bikers, they wanted to have motorcycles as part of the theme, including bikes lined up and spread like angels' wings from their wedding altar. They also planned to ride off on their bike after being pronounced husband and wife. "Howie was extremely involved," says Barrie, explaining that her husband had a hand in every nuance of the wedding ceremony and reception. "Being that he is in sales for a living, he was quite a negotiator. He really took charge when it came to negotiating a contract. He is also extremely detail-oriented. Our wedding turned out to be spectacular and exactly the way we wanted it."

Summer's dream. On the other hand, don't be devastated if your husband-to-be is not as devoted to the details as you are. Actress Summer Moore married her director husband Tony Glazer on September 20, 2003. For her, love was in the details, and she paid close attention to *every* aspect of her wedding, from the candles carried into the processional by her seven bridesmaids to small personal touches throughout her reception (such as individual framed photos of her, Tony, her parents, and his parents on every table). She had only one regret.

"I wish I had not gotten so mad at my fiancé when he didn't really want to be included in all the little details—like picking the color of the ribbon for ceremony programs," she says. "Now, in my current state of mind, I realize that of course he wouldn't care—he can barely match his tie to his suits. But in the crazed planning stages, I took it as a personal insult—that he didn't care about the ribbon meant he didn't care about the ceremony or me. Cut the groom some slack," says Summer. "He is doing the best he can, and his only real desire is to make you happy and commit his life to you forever. Remember that, and pick out your own ribbon!"

> I did all the detail stuff, and my groom helped make the big choices: where to have the ceremony and reception, who to use as our officiant, where to go on our honeymoon, how much to spend on each item, etc. I did things like pick flowers and color schemes and invitations. He did help with registering. He liked to hold the scanner gun while I picked out stuff. So it worked out well for us.
>
> —*Summer, who married Tony on September 20, 2003*

Wedding Goddess Exercises

*I*t's often been said that women tend to initiate men. Even in equal partnerships, a Wedding Goddess will typically take the lead in managing the details of the relationship. This holds true in many cases of wedding planning. More often than not, the woman is the overall project manager for "Project Getting Married." Consider some of the following.

1. **Hold a vision.** A Wedding Goddess needs to start by using her powers of initiation in a subtle, spiritual, and sublime way, says Ray Bergen, Ph.D., creator of HeroGoddess couples workshops and the audio series *When Hero and Goddess Love*. "A bride needs a clear vision of how she wants her man to 'show up' for her on her wedding day," he says, explaining that this vision will become the guiding light for the planning stages of their wedding. Ask yourself: "Do you want to be standing next to a lion in all his radiance? Would you maybe like a knight of old kneeling to kiss your feet? Or maybe someone standing there with arms wide open to fully embrace you? Or do you see yourselves as two doves cooing and kissing at the altar? Whatever it is, let that be your guide for the directions you give your groom," he says.

When a woman sets forth a vision, and can actually *feel* the essence of how she wants her wedding experience with her mate to be, it creates a context for the entire journey. "It provides a context for the myriad of practical directions," says Bergen. "And it can create a context for every wedding conversation they have, allowing them to keep focused on what is important so they can find their way back when they get derailed."

2. **Try to see things from his point of view.** It is also important to tune in to where your man is with this wedding adventure. Women tend to be able to charge into the wedding process and get lost there for a while. Being a bride is something that spurs us to action. Being a groom could be a slower or different process. Many brides admit that they fantasize about their possible wedding in the early stages of a relationship, even before an engagement, while for men it often does not become the same kind of reality until the later stages of wedding planning. So don't be surprised if it takes a while for your groom's sense of reality about the wedding to catch up to yours. It doesn't mean he's less committed. Here are some tips for bringing you both through the wedding-planning process with compassion.

* **Know your man.** It helps to understand where a man is coming from. How flexible is he? How inflexible? Some men want to be full partners. Some guys are very laid back and just want to be helpful but not in charge. Some just want to be involved in the parts of the wedding that they can relate to. Some want to be a hero. Figure out the man you are marrying, and manage the wedding experience for you both.

* **Communicate effectively.** Timing is everything. Try not to ask him to chalk up another $2,000 for flowers after he's had a bad day at work, and don't describe the details of a wedding-related chat with your mother when he is about to head out to a huge, stressful meeting. Know that there is a time and place for wedding talk, and be sensitive to his needs and the best times for chatting.

* **Let him contribute in his own way.** Forcing a groom to trail along to every vendor meeting is not useful; giving your groom a task that will confound him is also no fun. "The most important thing is to find a way to include the guy in the plan that taps into his interests," says Kurianksy. "Otherwise, it can become a very stereotypical male-female experience, where the woman takes over and the guy follows along—which separates the couple."

- **Let him experience his own power.** Empower him and encourage him. This is the guy you're choosing for life, not just your "assistant" in wedding planning.

- **Try not to shame him.** Be gracious, allow space for a learning curve, and do not attack him when things do not always go the way you had hoped. Attacking him will set up such a negative relationship dynamic. During the planning process, uncover your diamond in the rough and embrace his imperfections. Once you give him a task to do, trust him and allow him to do it fully.

- **Recognize that some grooms are like little boys.** They often look toward their women for acknowledgment and guidance. And they take direction well when it is offered with love. If you are the wedding visionary, make sure you share the vision and offer instructions along the way.

- **Let him know what will make you happy.** Ultimately, there is nothing that a man wants more than to please his Goddess. If you empower your groom for all the times that he brings you happiness, there will be plenty more to come!

WEDDING GODDESS VOW

I vow to share the wedding-planning experience with my beloved and to honor the unique role we each play on this journey.

Arlene Sandler/Lensgirl.com

CHAPTER TEN

The Paperwork That Makes It Legal

And the Language of the Heart That Makes It Real

> This is the moment you have waited for. . . . Your relationship is more official! Yet this document cannot, and will not, bind the heart or secure love. This is up to you. Make an oath to be wise and creative in keeping the scales balanced in your marriage.
>
> **—Themis, the Greek Goddess of Law and Justice, considered the guardian of oaths**

Going to get your marriage license is a major historical event in your relationship. It represents the day that you two are no longer just dreaming and talking about getting married—you now have the legal ability to do so. It is a very "This is it!" moment in time. And it begins to subtly yet powerfully shift your relationship to a new level.

It is a rite of passage that every bride and groom must experience together—no one can marry legally without going together to obtain a valid wedding license from the state in which they will wed. It is an experience that many brides and grooms dread, especially in busy clerk's offices in some big cities, because it often requires waiting on a long line and means they must take time off from work.

> We took the day off from work to get our marriage license and spent the day together, nice and quiet. We celebrated by going to dinner and relaxing. We felt more in love and committed. We did not allow ourselves to get lost in all the planning and busyness.
>
> *—Elizabeth, who married Ross on September 6, 2003*

> ## WEDDING GODDESS
> ## RULE #10
>
> **A Wedding Goddess honors the milestone of the marriage license.**
>
> Rather than get lost in the busyness and the business of getting the license, you turn it into a sacred experience. You recognize this as an important step in your journey to the altar. You make the experience intimate and fun, and you utilize it as a moment in time in which to clarify all the contracts that you choose to make with each other.

Country clerk's offices and courthouses differ around the country, so the logistics of getting your license will differ from city to city, town to town. Essentially, though, it is a bureaucratic experience. On the surface, it doesn't look very romantic.

Although the license is exactly that, a license to wed, in most states the marriage is not official until the following conditions are met: you go through your ceremony; you, your witnesses, and officiant sign your license; and your officiant sends it back, filled out, to the city or county where you got the license. Usually within several weeks, a marriage certificate that legally recognizes your marriage will be sent to you.

That little piece of paper, the foundation of your future, will hold the key to the legal aspects of wedding bliss. It joins you in the eyes of the law and allows you the entitlements that this society offers to married couples. But it is only part of the contract you make with your groom when you decide to wed.

As a Wedding Goddess, you'll want to turn a bureaucratic experience into a blessing by making each aspect of the journey to get the license count. It will also be important that you two explore the other contracts that you intend to make with each other—contracts of the heart, of the soul, and for the spirit of your marriage.

How to Rise Above Bureaucracy and Enjoy Getting Your License

*M*any couples find that the day they get the wedding license is the day that their commitment gets wings. It is an experience that makes the wedding seem so much more real to your groom, and it carries a wonderful feeling of accomplishment for both of you. While the experience of dealing with the clerk's office may not be the most fun part of your journey to the altar, it is in fact the foundation for having a lawfully binding marriage. Look for ways to enjoy, savor, and enhance the experience.

Make the research fun. Each state has a different protocol for attaining a license, so your first step will be to research the legalities of your state and county. In the United States, essentially, both bride and groom must show up, usually at a city or county clerk's office, with proper identification and a small filing and processing fee, as well as proof of the dissolution of any former marriages or the deaths of former spouses. (Most states no longer require blood tests.) After answering the clerk's questions, you are given a license or affidavit for a license that your officiant will sign on your wedding day and send back to the clerk's office to make your marriage "official" in the eyes of the law.

Be prepared. Make sure you have all the paperwork and identification needed, and the correct processing fees in the correct form, so that you are not turned away or delayed for any reason. (For example, the clerk may not take cash, checks, or credit cards, so see if you need a money order; conversly, they may only accept cash.) Each city or state has its own protocol for the legality of a license—in New York, for example, you *can* have it in hand for sixty days before using it and *must* have it for at least twenty-four hours. If you are to be married in New York, you are permitted to get your license anywhere in the state. In Las Vegas, you can attain a licence from the Las Vegas Marriage Bureau practically 'round the clock and you can marry *immediately*.

Take care of yourselves. Make sure you take care of yourselves on the day you go to get your license. Get a good sleep the night before. Exercise or stretch

> We were getting married in New York, so we flew to New York on a Tuesday to get our license. My mother-in-law took pictures of us at the courthouse. To me, everything about getting our marriage license was special. I felt a very big commitment that day to Josh.
>
> —*Brooke, who married Joshua on October 10, 2003*

> I had to replace a lost out-of-state driver's license before we could get our marriage license. Luckily, everything worked out in time and we were so excited to have our marriage license in our hands, we hung it up on our bedroom door so we could look at it every day!
>
> —*Sharon, who married Michael on March 20, 2004*

that morning; eat before going, or bring a snack, so you don't get worn-out and cranky if the line is long. Treat it like a sacred moment, in which you want to be at your best.

Keep your spirits high. Couples sometimes complain about waiting in long lines or dealing with bureaucrats. They say they feel anonymous and treated like cattle in some cities. Try to embrace the realities of the marriage bureau office and seek to be pleasant to the workers. Getting cranky with the person who will be issuing your marriage license or complaining and suffering through the experience is not a great energy to bring into your marriage. It's one day in your life—such an important day at that—so make it fun.

Document the experience. Take pictures so you can remember where the legal part of your journey began. Pictures of you with a smiling county clerk would be a fun thing to show the kids someday!

Celebrate. Plan to spend time afterward, to celebrate this important step toward your life together. You might want to pack a picnic lunch and go to a park afterward, or go out to a favorite restaurant. Perhaps you'd like to buy a frame and temporarily hang your license on your wall, where you can proudly gaze at it while sharing a glass of wine at home. Maybe you'll keep it on the bedside table as you make love that night for your first time as an almost-married couple!

Don't rush through it. Getting your license is a moment in time to cherish. Don't wait until the last minute to get your license. Leave time to enjoy it and to savor it. Once that license is signed on the day you wed, life will change forevermore.

Wedding Goddess Exercises

*I*n addition to the legal license, there are other documents that celebrate the emotional and spiritual bond of your union, as well as your responsibilities as marriage partners. In Judaism they call it a *Ketubah*. Muslims have a similar contract given after the couple has a traditional ceremony. And Quakers have a spiritual document that the whole congregation signs.

Whether you include a contract from your faith tradition or create your own, it is important for you to spend some time focusing on what marriage truly means to you. "There's so much craziness that comes up around planning a wedding," says Rev. Diane Berke, Spiritual Director of One Spirit Interfaith Seminary and veteran wedding officiant. "Couples can get so lost in the small details. I think it's important to take time to think, *Why do I want to spend the rest of my life with this person?*" She says you should also look deeply at what you each want to bring to the relationship—not just what you want to take from it.

Each marriage is unique and so are the goals, desires, and hopes of each bride and groom. Before the ceremony, it will be a blessing on your marriage if you and your beloved sit down and create your own personal wedding contract, agreement, or outline of your intentions for married life. Creating a personal marriage contract of your own is a beautiful way to clarify what you both anticipate, and what you would like to experience and create in your marriage. It can include everything from being kind and thoughtful every day, to having children, to building a dream house and growing old together. This is not your legally binding document; rather, it is a spiritually binding document. It can be a very nontraditional format, as long as it suits your needs. Here are some ways you can both express the spirit of the relationship you want to create:

1. **Create a Mission Statement for Your Marriage.** The first step of any new enterprise is to create a mission statement. This can apply to your marriage as well. Brainstorm, discuss, process, and bat around ideas until you come up with a marriage mission statement. This is your mutual intention for marriage; it is what you want to *be* and *build* together. It can be one sentence or reflect a number of ideas. For example:

Our union gives us strength, power, and fortitude to deal with all of life's ups and downs, and it empowers us to contribute to others and to the world. We are best friends, confidantes, and partners, and we have many close relationships with people we consider "spiritual family." We are a couple who inspire others with our love and who model what it is to be in a great relationship.

2. **Wedding Scrolls.** Together, create a list that spells out your intentions, aspirations, goals, hopes, and dreams for your wedded life. Turn it into your official "Wedding Scroll." Write neatly or type it. It can be on pretty parchment-like paper, or any attractive paper. Consider having it written in calligraphy and framed, or simply roll it up and tie it with a gold ribbon. No one need see it but you two. However, take it to your ceremony and keep it at the altar so it will be blessed by the expressions of love and commitment shared at your ceremony, and energized by the vows you exchange.

3. **Write letters to each other.** Both of you can take the time to craft a beautiful letter to each other, stating what you love about each other and what your promises for married life are, and you can place them in a sacred spot in your home, or even include them in the ceremony. Rev. Vic Fuhrman, MSC, R.M., an interfaith minister, saw this carried out in a very meaningful way when he co-officiated a wedding with a father of the bride. During the ceremony, the bride and groom were handed the letters they had written to each other. As the reverend explains, "The bride's dad said, 'I know you two are utterly in love right now, but take my word for it, there will come a time, be it ten months or ten years from now, when you will have a fight. That's when you will open these letters and remember the spirit of the commitment you made here today.'"

4. **Define what you will bring to the relationship through your names.** In the Cabbalistic tradition, as taught by Rabbi Joseph Gelberman, author of *Kabbalah As I See It* and founder of The New Synagogue, you can imbue a new meaning into a name or word if you take each letter and embellish it with a fuller definition. Write both your names vertically, and take each letter and use it to explain a quality that you intend to bring to your relationship. For example:

L: Love

A: Affection

U: Unity

R: Renewal

I: Inspiration

E: Excitement

V: Valor

I: Insight

C: Compassion

T: Tenacity

O: Openheartedness

R: Responsibility and Romance

WEDDING GODDESS VOW

*We vow to appreciate and remember the power of
the day we get our license to marry.*

Arlene Sandler/Lensgirl.com

CHAPTER ELEVEN

Release, Prepare, Purify

Ride the cleansing waves of closure and completion with the old. The salty sea and the rivers offer cool waters for purification. Stand by the ocean, and let the waves cleanse you for your life together.

—Yemaya, the great goddess of the African Yoruban tradition,
known as "Mama Watta"

When you are ready to embrace a serious love, you are generally very anxious to come into your marriage with a clean slate. On a very basic level, marriage is a rite of passage that calls you to release parts of your past that no longer serve you, merge your lives into a more unified partnership, and bond in a deeply soulful and spiritual way.

This is not a task for the faint of heart. While it gets more natural as you go along, you better believe that on the way to the wedding, the emotions can kick into high gear for you both. It will be very natural to have questions, doubts, and plenty of fears. This is a big step, and big steps are not without a certain amount of emotional upheaval. A step like this requires you to transform, to grow into your new lives, to become more of who you are meant to be. Ultimately, marriage is the opportunity to go places—physically, emotionally, spiritually—that neither of you have been before. It will take some releasing, preparation, and purification to get ready for the big day.

A Wedding Goddess knows that in-

> ## WEDDING GODDESS RULE #11
>
> **A Wedding Goddess seeks a fresh start on all levels.**
>
> You lovingly support and motivate your man to release excess emotional, physical, and spiritual baggage. And you lead the way toward purification and renewal together as you ready yourselves for married life. You seek ways to creatively release the past as you look forward to your future, together.

herent in the commitment to marry there dwells a magical potential for a new beginning. She also understands that it is important to accelerate change by helping it along—through mundane actions such as cleaning house, as well as practices and rituals that will prepare and purify you both.

How to Prepare and Purify Yourselves, and Each Other, for Marriage

*I*n a beautiful wedding ceremony that appears in her book *Illuminata*, Marianne Williamson tells brides and grooms: "I congratulate you on the journey of your lives, on the strength and the courage it has taken for each of you to make your way to this place. Both of you have found a way to put away childish things and embrace a very serious love. You receive on this day the blessings thereof, for yourselves and all the world." She goes on to say, "We live in times that are beset with problems. This marriage is not to be an escape from the world, but indeed it is to be a commitment to greater service to the world. You shall not exclude the world but include it in your love. Together, in this marriage, you shall contribute more fully, for you shall be more full."

The concept of such fullness in marriage is what leads so many people to the altar. It is the ideal of being so full of love, so ripe with possibilities, so bursting with happiness, and so complete because you have found your "other half." It is the promise of this fullness, and your pursuit of it, that helps couples survive their pre-marital days of planning. Yet part of the process of attaining such fullness in marriage is in part, to empty out the parts of your past that will not serve your marriage. (See Chapter One.) The first year of marriage can be bumpy as you both adjust to a new way of being. Now is the time to help your beloved do some releasing of his own; next, you can both move on to preparations and purification of yourselves and your relationship.

Many of the world's traditions have ways to cleanse, purify, and prepare for marriage—from prescribed rites of holy purification to ritual blessings of many kinds. There's the Jewish *micvah* for purity, and the Hindu fire ceremony to ward off evil. There's the tradition of release from sins in Sudan where brides and grooms bend to kiss the knees of their parents, asking for forgiveness and blessing. There is the ritualistic participation of the clan, such as the Thai ceremony of washing the couple's hands with holy water. There is the Pre-Cana marriage preparation course in the Catholic Church. In America, the custom for emotional purification is a course, a workshop, or counseling with a therapist or clergyperson who can help you begin to resolve nagging emotional or spiritual issues in your relationship before the big day.

The Wedding Goddess and her mate should create and select practices and rituals that allow a sense of completion with the past and a cleansing of anything that she does not want to take into her new marriage. Here is advice from some experts in various disciplines that can provide a range of insights for your journey.

> We both moved out of our homes and bought a new home together in a new town. We got mostly new furniture, dishes, everything we could new. We saved only treasures, and threw out or gave away the rest.
>
> —*Julie, who married Leonard on July 21, 2003*

> I had to kind of put my foot down, but ultimately Russell let me pack up all of his ex-wife's belongings and return them to her family. His house was still filled with her stuff. She had moved far away, and he didn't want to deal with it. There was so much of it around him that he didn't realize how much it affected him and how much it was coming between us. It was like living in a museum of his past. A good spring cleaning and a paint job helped a lot. We became much closer after that. We were so much freer.
>
> —*Terri, who married Russell on November 22, 2003*

A ritual of release—helping him release some of his "stuff." Physical release of things that are no longer needed or wanted is always a good start for clearing some space for new things in your marriage. You've already rampaged through your closets. The trick now is to enlist your fiancé in the same. There's a terrific commercial where a man and woman, apparently engaged, are sitting at his place. The bride says, "We won't need this place once we're married. My place is nicer." The groom, seeming a bit lackadaisical, says, "What about my stuff?" Then the screen cuts to a fantasy image of the bride burning it all. The groom suddenly realizes: He needs storage. That commercial is a great enactment of many a female fantasy—the desire to ditch all of her fiancé's premarital belongings, especially those that contain memories of old loves. Once you have gone through your own spring-cleaning rituals, you will probably be itching to motivate your man toward a little healthy tossing, releasing, and purifying. Keep in mind that merging two lives means merging two households—you may have to go slow in that department and give your man some space.

"For most men, just the act of getting married feels like he's merging his stuff with her stuff plenty!" says Charley Wininger, a Brooklyn-based psychotherapist and dating coach. "If a man feels the need to hold on to his past stuff, it shouldn't be taken as a lack of caring or commitment. Territory is a very real issue for men. If he resists letting go, it could be because he perceives a threat—although he may not articulate it in that way."

You might find that your mate has little interest in this form of purification and that he will be glad to let you take charge and rummage through his belongings and history as if you are his mom cleaning his room. On the other hand, he might feel invaded if you start steamrolling into his closet, looking for items to trash. The best option is to work on this together, so he feels supported and motivated and you experience a sense of progress. Wininger advises:

- If he's hesitant to begin, ask: "Is there any part, or aspect, of the past you'd be willing to let go of as a symbolic gesture on your part?"
- Whether he offers something tangible (to toss that big, worn-out chair) or something emotional (to delete his ex's phone number from his phone's memory), accept whatever it is and try not to analyze him.
- Thank him for what he gives, and he'll feel more comfortable with the entire process.
- When it comes to releasing physical stuff, you may have to repeat this process a few times before the wedding day.
- If he's simply a pack rat (and many men are) and puts up a lot of resistance, don't push it. If he feels he can keep his stuff for now, he'll feel better about possibly parting with it later.

2. **Spiritual divorce—closure with the ones who came before.** In the Jewish faith, it's called a "Ghet," or "Get," and it is granted by a rabbi. In ancient times, it *was* the divorce; today, it serves to help couples feel spiritually free of their former partner as well as legally unbound. While it is little more than a piece of paper written in Hebrew and signed by a rabbi (in the *Talmud*, it's referred to as a *Sefer Keritut*, scroll of cutting off), some couples seek it as a decree that separates two souls from the holy union they agreed to on their wedding day. In some indigenous cul-

tures, marriage is in spirit, and thus divorce is as well. Among one tribe in Mexico, a chief will bless a couple's decision to separate if a new home and husband has been found for the wife. If that requirement is met, then the couple is absolved of financial and spiritual obligation to each other.

In any language and any culture, a spiritual divorce is as important as a legal divorce, and is as relevant even if you never married the person who played an important romantic role in your life. Before you can fully connect to your beloved, and before he can fully give himself to you, you both must commit yourselves to a spiritual cleansing of the imprints of relationships past. "Spiritual divorce calls us to reconnect to the highest aspect of our being," says Debbie Ford, author of *Spiritual Divorce: Divorce as a Catalyst for an Extraordinary Life.* "It is here that we can reclaim our power, our joy, and the limitless freedom to create a life of our dreams."

> We did a spiritual divorce ceremony before we became engaged. We wrote down the names of our ex-spouses, and all our most important loves, and we put the list under a seven-day candle. For seven days, we would visit with the candle for a few minutes together, stare at the flame, and say a prayer for those we once loved. On the final day, as the flame blew out, we said, 'We set you free now. . . . Thank you for all you have given.' Knowing we had blessed the people, we felt they were okay. To symbolize our independence from them, we put the paper with their names in our paper shredder. It may seem harsh, yet it was powerful for us to do that together.
>
> —*Charlotte, who married Avi on March 6, 2003*

The life of your dreams, now, is the life you will be creating together, and Ford says it is especially important for engaged couples to spiritually divorce their former mates. If you are negatively or inappropriately connected to an ex—through a dysfunctional relationship, bad memories, anger, or upset related to child-rearing—it is important to find peace for yourself and to free your ex as well. By the same token, even a good relationship with a onetime love requires a spiritual divorce, so that you can take *all of yourself* into your new relationship. Everyone you have ever loved leaves their imprint, and it is best to disconnect from them spiritually before your wedding day. If you and your fiancé both work on this together, it can bring powerful results. Here are some steps you can take over time to fully move on from an ex-love.

• Acknowledge what the relationship was about for you. For better or for worse, how did it change your life?

• Look at the best parts of the relationship(s) and how they contributed to where you are now.

• Look at the worst parts, all the lessons learned, and at how these contributed to where you are now.

• Look at ways to bring completion to any relationships that remain an open book, and that can interfere with the new chapter you are writing with your new marriage (letting go of old wedding gifts, giving to charity the sheets you once shared, working to let go of anger and discord, etc.).

• Remember the happy memories, let them stay forever in your heart, and honor them as part of the growth that brought you to the great relationship you have now.

• Seek to ritually relinquish spiritual ties to that person, and to lessen the connection to that person through symbolic gestures. Karen Weissman, who with Tami Coyne authored *The Spiritual Chicks Question Everything*, once held a divorce shower for a friend to help him let go of his ex and move on to new love. They gave him kitchen gifts, she says, and "We made him play silly games, and his sister had us all sing the theme song from *The Mary Tyler Moore Show*, and we tossed a beret in the air at the end."

Spiritual divorce rituals can be done with the help of friends, or you can do them individually or as a couple. The process will move your relationship to the next level by acknowledging where you've both been and what you've been through. It can help show you that all your relationships were the building blocks that brought you to this moment in time, and it can help you relinquish unfinished relationship issues that could get in the way of your happiness and commitment.

3. **Marriage preparation course for couples.** Through the ages, most cultures have offered some form of preparation for marriage. In our fast-paced society, however, there is lots of preparation for the wedding but very little preparation for the marriage. In fact, some couples don't realize that it will take more than love to make a marriage work, or they choose to avoid dealing with relationship challenges while planning the wedding.

This all too often means that important issues are pushed to the future, to be wrangled with at another time.

"Most couples could benefit from some assistance and more awareness," says Arizona nondenominational minister Paul Michael, developer of the Engaged Couple's Class, an e-mail course in four weekly sessions. "There is a universal law that says you must know what you are dealing with in order to be able to deal with it. Every relationship has issues, and a good marriage-education course will bring these issues to the forefront so they are able to be dealt with." Taking a course together will allow you to dip below the surface of things for a clearer view, and you both stand to learn many new things about each other along the way. Michael also suggests that a good marriage-preparation class will sharpen communication tools as it helps couples:

- Learn to accept and resolve their relationship issues (acceptance is the first law of spirit)
- Learn a simple skill for how to find the golden opportunity in any challenge
- Become graceful in dealing with even the most sensitive issues
- Let go of fears of the unknown as they realize it's never about the issue itself but about *how* you relate to it.
- Relax and begin to settle into their relationship
- Achieve the highest potential in marriage

"Life's unknowns can be challenging enough for an individual, let alone two individuals who—coming from two unique worlds—are aiming to succeed in a cooperative, mutually beneficial effort called marriage," says Michael. "In this day and age, with so much on their plates, many engaged couples perceive that they don't have any time for the relationship part. So taking a class can serve as a way for them to carve out time for this. And it can root their connection to each other deeper and make it harder to be interrupted. The most painful part of any relationship is when the connection is not felt, but as a couple improves their skills of communication, they can enjoy the forever feeling that 'No matter what comes, we are prepared (and will stay connected).'"

4. **The counseling option.** Some couples need some *extra* help to clear cobwebs from their emotional closets before they marry, and some need

to take a good look at spiritual or religious challenges that keep coming up over and over again, with the help of an impartial observer. "Most people, unfortunately, often wait until they've reached the breaking point in a marriage to seek counseling; at that point, it is hard to recommit because of the deep-seated pain and anger," says Rev. Vic Fuhrman, MSC, R.M., an interfaith minister and spiritual counselor. He says that couples who know they have some issues to cleanse should consider using counseling as a way to enhance their marriages before they begin. You can seek pre-marital counseling as a couple with a therapist or a spiritual counselor such as a minister. Fuhrman says the benefits include:

- A balance of spiritual and practical support that facilitates a way for you to learn more about each other's likes and dislikes, patterns and points of view.
- It helps you mark the problem spots and find creative solutions for dealing with conflicts.
- It is a tool by which you can address the issues that you will be facing together.
- Rather than a means of repairing a troubled relationship, it is a way for you to enrich your bond and deepen your channels of communication.

"Not every couple will require this, but you should be prepared to consider it if you need any support whatsoever," says Fuhrman. You might be pleasantly surprised and relieved to find how helpful it is to explore issues related to marriage by communicating openly with each other in a safe space, with a skilled practitioner to support you through.

5. **Become a Hero and Goddess—together.** Many couples dream of sharing a higher love. Ray Bergen, Ph.D., is at the forefront of an effort to awaken couples to the divine within and help them go beyond a great relationship into the realm of the sublime relationship. Along with his wife and partner, Akama Bergen, he offers workshops, programs, and counseling through the Hero Goddess Institute. "Marriage is an invitation to transcend the human condition," he says. "In stepping beyond the self-focus of wanting to have only our own needs met, and in schooling ourselves in the experience of putting another human being and his or her needs in the position of equal value to our own, we touch the presence of the divine."

The idea of Hero and Goddess as a working model in a relationship gives couples a chance to tap into their truest nature. Bergen says that behind every nagging woman is a man who has abandoned his Hero presence, and behind every reactionary man is a woman who has lost her Goddess voice. "They are ancient, universal patterns already encoded in our DNA," Bergin explains. "You don't have to be endowed with great strength, courage, or beauty to be a Hero or a Goddess. Think of them as roles. When two people want to create love, they learn to step into these roles. Most couples refine these roles enough to get to the altar—then they stop! Thinking they've crossed the finish line, they relax, not realizing they are merely at the starting gate."

In his approach, Bergen places the dance of initiation in the hands of women, and he counsels men on how to surrender and quit resisting. "Every man's challenge is to empower the feminine in his woman, and every woman's challenge is to guide them both to connect. It is the woman who puts out the call and says it is time to drop our preoccupations and come together. Join me. Let's step out of practical concerns and touch souls." The Bergens offer a couples retreat, "The Courage to Move into Love," as well as audiotapes to get you started: *When Heroes and Goddesses Love* and *Turning Tyrants to Heroes and Dragons to Goddesses*.

6. **Seeking insights from the stars and planets.** In many Asian traditions, it is customary to consult an astrologer on all major issues related to marriage. For example, Hindu and Buddhist families often assess the compatibility of a bride and groom before the official engagement through insights provided by an astrologer (respectively via the traditions of Jyotish and Buddhist astrology), and then they plan the wedding, and all events and rituals related to the wedding, according to auspicious times. In recent years, many Westerners are following suit and doing the same. Astrologer and Beliefnet.com columnist Shelley Ackerman strongly suggests that engaged couples have an astrological reading with a professional astrologer. "An astrologer can cast either a chart comparison between the bride and groom [known as 'synastry'], a composite chart, or a relationship chart, as well as select an all-important wedding chart," says Ackerman. "This would help you to understand why you are together in the first place and clarify what the real strengths are in the relationship; it will also provide language and tools to better grasp the challenges and obstacles that

need to be overcome. The reason this is invaluable is that once you have language to understand the specifics of what each person has brought to the relationship (background, ancestry, intimacy requirements, etc.), that's half the battle in resolving those issues early on, thereby insuring a more peaceful and enduring marriage."

This kind of astrological assessment is much deeper than the surface kind of treatment astrology gets in magazine and newspaper columns. "Purification has to do with clarity. And getting clear is empowering. This kind of clarity—understanding *why* you are together and *why*, and even *if*—you are ready for marriage at this time is much more desirable than entering into this kind of commitment unconsciously. Astrological insights can help you go into the marriage *grounded*. It will deepen your readiness and enhance, through understanding, the next part of your journey together."

7. **Rituals of purification.** Purification rituals before marriage are as common as marriage itself in many of the world's cultures. Couples today can adapt the best of tradition, or even the essence of ancient customs, and personalize it to their needs. A purification ritual can take five minutes or five hours. It can take five days or five months. It depends on the customs to which you adhere, what kind of rituals you choose to take part in, and how deep you both want to go.

A purification ritual can be as brief as lighting a candle and saying a prayer, or it can be ongoing. You can even consider your entire preparation for marriage to be one long, ongoing ritual. The point is, you are engaging in activities that in some way will give you the experience of releasing, letting go, shedding old skin, and preparing for the new. International ritual expert and author of *The Joys of Everyday Ritual* and *The Joy of Family Rituals*, Barbara Biziou explains it best. "A ritual is a consciously designed set of behaviors meant to evoke certain feelings and experiences that are needed to effect change in one's life," she says. "It works on many levels. It influences the subconscious mind. Part of the psyche doesn't know the difference between performing a ritual and actually experiencing an event. When you complete a ritual, you are telling yourself you have completed whatever you have symbolically enacted. For example, if you take a ritual bath for purification, part of you literally believes you have released the past. And so it becomes true in your life."

8. **Cleansing your auras.** Energetic healing has long been practiced by clergypersons, nurses, and healers who practice laying on of hands to heal people, and by practitioners who work with the energy fields that surround the body (called the *human aura*, these energy fields have been documented by science and Kirlian photography). Many believe that people carry karmic imprints in those energy fields, as well as the imprints of their ancestors and imprints from recent experiences. These imprints, called "energetic signatures," can be anything from an illness or emotional malady passed through generations, to negative relationship patterns that are repeated through every generation, to energy patterns from heartbreak and aches from your last relationships. Every little bit helps to clean the karmic slates for your marriage. To derail some of these patterns you can strive to clear your auras—and keep them clear—using energetic healing, cleansing, prayer, and rebalancing techniques.

"Marriage is the beginning of a new life where you leave your old self behind and become a new person," says Roy Anthony Shabla, Ph.D., a California-based healer and creator of blesstheworld.com, a network of websites that offer spiritual services and products for energetic cleansing, including remedies called Aura Spritz and Karma Cleanse. He says it is important that a couple do whatever they can to clear patterns that do not serve their highest good in this new life. "Do whatever you can to remove the issues, the blockages, the patterns of fear and disappointment that held you to disharmony in your old life so that you will not be bound to disharmony in the new."

There are literally particles of energetic junk or energetic signatures of events and emotions past that can get caught in your auric field. For example, you may feel as if you have healed an old pattern of abandonment that began with your father and was reinforced by your first few boyfriends, but a residue could still cling to the field of energy around you and get activated in your marriage. It might be reactivated when your new husband goes on a business trip and could suddenly cause you to get that old feeling of being left behind; by the same token, if your beloved once had a girlfriend who cheated on him, there could be a fearful part of him that gets reactivated every time he sees you talking to another man. Although deep-seated emotional components may require therapeutic help, it is always useful to clear patterns from the subtle energy around you. This allows the emotional issues to surface so they can be explored and healed.

9. **Pray together.** There is an old saying that "the couple that prays together stays together." In your own way, every day, pray *for* each other and pray *with* each other. Pray that you each gently release, prepare, and purify for your new life together and that you are supported in this in all ways.

Wedding Goddess Exercises

1. **Spiritual divorce.** A very simple way to say good-bye to the ones you have loved before is to go together to the ocean and partake in a simple ceremony using sand, surf, and the power of Mother Nature. All you need is a stick, a couple plastic bags, a prayer in your heart, and the intention to have a spiritually clean slate for marriage.

- First, walk down to the water and look out to the vastness of the sea. Let the cleansing waters, salty sea air, and ocean sounds wash over you and calm you. Feel yourself centered on the sand. Say a prayer, such as:

> *Mother, Father, Divine Spirit of All There Is,*
> *please fill us with your holy presence and guide us in this rit-*
> *ual of release.*
> *May all we do here today serve to set us free spiritually.*
> *May it also serve to spiritually set free [say your names] with*
> *love. And so it is.*

- Using your stick or your finger (cover your hand with the plastic bag so that you don't get sand in your nails), write the name of the first person you need a spiritual divorce from. Write it in a spot close to the point where the sand meets the shore (where the sand is just about mud) and the next wave is likely to wash it away.
- Watch as the wave comes to claim the spot on which you have written the name. Notice how nature so beautifully fills in the dents in

the sand and smoothes over the name with water. And allow yourself to feel that person released from you spiritually, with love.

• Say this prayer: *"I surrender my attachment to [name], and I release her/him to the universe, with love and with blessings. I forgive [name] and ask that all be forgiven between us on the highest levels. I thank [name] for all he/she has given me. May [name] be blessed in all ways. [Name], you are free now and I am free now."*

• Go on to the next person. Most of us have a few significant others to release. Repeat this process for the most significant, and then do one final release for all the others. You and your beloved can alternate, each doing a release after the other. Or you can do yours and then he can do his.

• When you feel you have spiritually released your former loves, stand again and gaze out at the ocean, and allow yourself to feel the calming power of the Mother healing you and your fiancé, and healing all those loved ones you said your spiritual good-byes to.

• End with a prayer: *"Mother, Father, Divine Spirit of All There Is, Thank you for your divine presence. Thank you for your healing waters, and for the sand that shows us that everything in life can be smoothed over and harmonized. Thank you for your blessings and for your light. May all those present and all mentioned move on with love and blessings in a way that harms none. And so be it!"*

2. **Ritual bathing and a little Karma Cleanse.** A ritual bath is a widespread custom in many European countries. For centuries, it symbolized the purification of the bride from evil influences. In France, it was meant to remove thoughts of a woman's former boyfriends and the influences from her former life before marriage. It is an old Scottish custom to begin marriage on the eve of the ceremony, with some singing and dancing followed by a ceremonial foot wash for the bride. On the wedding day, it is a custom for Moroccan women to bathe in milk before they are ritually painted with henna. Any ritual bathing with intention can help purify you both. You can:

• Share a swim in the ocean and feel yourselves purified by the natural saltwater, take a dunk in a natural lake, find your way beneath a waterfall for a sacred shower, take a bath together in sea salt, or shower together.

• As you do any of these, imagine that the heartache and the pain, the challenges and the disappointments of the past, are washing away, cleansing you both for your new life together. Water has a natural power to cleanse on so many levels. Your intention to release is what counts—let the water do the rest.

• As an added cleanser, once you are done, step out of the purifying waters and gingerly spray the outline of each other's bodies with Karma Cleanse from Bless the World. Don't forget to spray between the legs and around raised arms and armpits. (You can also do this ritual with burning white sage in an abalone shell and a feather to fan the smoke around the body. This is an ancient Native American cleansing technique. The smoke grabs on to negative particles in the aura and neutralizes them.)

• Look into each other's eyes and know that as you spray (or sage), you are helping the one you love subtly release some of the issues of the past that could otherwise interfere with married life. It is especially powerful when you do this for each other, because you relay so much love to each other in this ritual. Say the following prayer:

Because I love you, I am helping you cleanse. Because I love you, I want you to be free of the patterns that have caused you disharmony in the past. Because I love you, I cherish our relationship and will cherish our marriage. I want us both to be energetically free to love each other fully. And so it is.

• Pat each other down with towels and take some sacred time to sit and look at each other, soaking it in, or to lie down and cuddle.

3. **With a little help from your friends.** In a Thai wedding custom, a bride and groom visit a monk for the religious ceremony on the morning of their wedding. They are given a sacred string ("Sai Monkol") and blessed water to utilize in a ceremony later that day. The bride and groom kneel on throne-like kneeling cushions for a blessing that will be offered by everyone in their party who is older than they are. A chosen elder will place the sacred string over the heads of the kneeling bride and groom to symbolize that they are tied together in marriage, and the assembled guests then pro-

ceed with what is known as *rod nam*. You can adapt this as a prewedding purification ritual that can include the blessings of loved ones.

- Using a decorated conch shell, guests pour holy water over the fingertips of the bride and groom and offer them a blessing for a happy and fruitful marriage.
- In the Thai tradition, only guests who are older than the bride and groom are asked to participate, which means the bride and groom receive the blessings of the elders.
- Other good-luck symbols may also be offered, such as peas and sesame seeds as symbols of fertility, and gold coins as symbols of wealth.

This is a powerful ritual, because as the guests pour the holy water from the conch shell onto the hands of bride and groom, they can look them directly in the eyes and offer a blessing. Also, the water purifies, and the blessings offered set forth a new intention; water also purifies you as individuals, readying you for marriage, and the blessings unite you.

For an interfaith feel: Use Lourdes water from the healing waters of Lourdes, France, holy water of any kind, accumulated rainwater, or water from the ocean. The conch shell is also sacred to the Hindu God Vishnu. He and his beloved consort Lakshmi are considered to be the perfect couple.

WEDDING GODDESS VOW

I will ensure that my beloved and I do everything we can to release the past, prepare for our future and purify ourselves for a soulful marriage.

PART FIVE

Celebrating Your Union in a Personalized Ceremony

As we begin our new life together as husband and wife, I am amazed at our love. It is an invisible thing—our love—and yet, it is a force so strong, so durable that it will hold our lives together for all the years to come. Our past is over; our future is new, and as we take our vows today, we will be changed forever. I take them gladly and without reservation.

—from *Diane Warner's Complete Book of Wedding Vows*

Arlene Sandler/Lensgirl.com

CHAPTER TWELVE

The Ceremony
Is the Wedding

Pay close attention to the messages of the heart. Take care to define the
right wedding path for you Let your desires to impress and placate others
fall away. Choose the sacred ceremony that will marry you well.

—Maat, Egyptian Goddess of Balance, patron of truth, law, and universal order

*I*t used to be that a man would propose, the couple would pick a date, the
parents of the bride would pay for and arrange a wedding in their hometown house of worship, and the bride and groom would be married by the
family priest or rabbi. No one ever asked about the form or content of the ceremony. Who even thought to—or would
dare—question a religious leader about
his area of expertise? More likely, the
bride and groom would simply go along
with whatever they were told to do, often
standing there dazed at the wedding altar.
Many brides and grooms can't even remember what happened between the
processional and recessional. As one
woman told me of her wedding two de-
cades ago, a time before couples sought
the kind of personal touches that brides
and grooms can hope for today, "We got
married by a rabbi who did the entire service in Hebrew. We had no idea what was

WEDDING GODDESS RULE #12

A Wedding Goddess gets married in her own way.

Although you are respectful of the traditions
of your parents, your in-laws, and the ancestors
who came before them, you select a wedding ceremony style and tone that is truly suited to you and
your beloved. You explore your options and together choose the way you will wed. You never fold
under family pressure but, instead, seek to blend
the treasures of tradition with the contemporary.

being said, or what it all meant. To this day, we still have no idea what really happened during our ceremony."

The Wedding Goddess is not a likely candidate for a cookie-cutter wedding ceremony. Even the most traditional Wedding Goddess bride and her groom will find that there are many options for personally tailoring their ceremony. It's important that you both figure out the general tone that you would feel most comfortable with—religious, nondenominational, civil, offbeat, humorous, solemn, etc.—as well as decide on the kind of wedding officiant you would most like to work with.

Unless you choose to be married in a religious ceremony that will follow a time-honored religious protocol, you can be as creative as you like. We live in a new age of weddings. With so many couples marrying outside their faith, and physically marrying in a location other than a house of worship, an entire world of possibilities exists. Explore the many kinds of ceremonies that you can choose from long before the wedding day, so that you have time to put together all the right components for your sacred event.

How to Decide What Kind of Ceremony You Want

*M*any brides and grooms are surprised to know that there are so many ways to approach a wedding ceremony; it is almost overwhelming when they discover that they can blend aspects of many different kinds of ceremonies into one uniquely loving, expressive, and personal wedding. The range of options is vast—from super-religious and traditional to a stunning ceremony that includes everything they are, yet is unlike anything they have ever seen before. Here are *some* of the possible flavors of weddings today.

1. **Traditional religious.** If you are both of the same faith and have decided to marry in a traditional house of worship and/or select a traditional clergyperson to officiate at an outside venue, you are signing on for a traditional religious ceremony. Your clergyperson will speak, offer prayers, and include rituals from the holy books of your faith. This kind of cere-

mony generally follows a specific form and has very specific content. You can request the inclusion of personal vows; depending on the clergyperson, you may be able to try for other unique touches. Like it or not, you can't expect to edit religious protocol—you wouldn't tell a Catholic priest to leave Jesus out, suggest that a Buddhist monk chant in English, or tell a rabbi to skip the seven blessings over the wine. You can certainly ask to see the ceremony beforehand or be advised of what it contains, so you are aware of what to prepare for.

2. **Nontraditional religious.** If you are both of the same faith but do not relate to the traditional ceremonies you've witnessed or gone through, or if you have been precluded from marrying through traditional channels, you might want to have a ceremony that honors the faith you were both raised with but that goes easy on religion. You can have a lovely ceremony that celebrates your love and your belief in God, and can include only the parts of the ceremony that are personally meaningful to you. For example, one Catholic couple I married had a double challenge. She'd been divorced (and not annulled), and he never completed all the sacraments required before marriage. So they opted for a restaurant wedding that included Catholic vows, a scriptural reading, and prayers in the name of the Father, Son, and Holy Spirit, but they decided to modify the language, and make the ceremony more about their commitment to each other than their commitment to God.

3. **Interfaith.** If you and your beloved are of different faiths, you might choose a ceremony that honors both. This can be done in a number of ways: co-officiated by a clergyperson from each of your faiths, or by a single interfaith or nondenominational minister. If one or both of you is religious, or if either of your parents are, you might want to have a religious ceremony that includes a balance of prayers and rituals that both you and your families will recognize and feel comfortable with. If you are not terribly religious but would like to *honor* aspects of your faiths or heritage, you can *blend in* symbolic traditions from each faith. For example, a Jewish groom and a Catholic bride might have a reading of I Corinthians and unity candles from the Christian side, and the breaking of the glass along with a Hebrew prayer from the Jewish side. If your wedding is officated by

> We had a special concern in creating our ceremony. I was raised Christian, and my husband was raised in a Jewish family. We wanted to have a ceremony that would make everyone feel comfortable and wouldn't exclude anyone. So we decided to have a mainly nondenominational ceremony with a central theme of love. It was a sweet, spiritual, loving ceremony, and it helped set the tone for the evening and our marriage
>
> —*Laura, who married Erez on July 11, 2002*

two clergypersons from different faiths, they might want to structure a more traditional format or each do their own ceremony, one at a time. With an interfaith or nondenominational officiant, you can choose the level of religion included. For example, a Buddhist bride who did not consider herself very religious had a prayer, written by her dad, read at the ceremony, and also asked her mother to ring a sacred bell, while her Christian groom decided to include vows from his own faith, without the ritual aspects. On the other hand, an atheist Korean groom and a somewhat spiritual American bride I know ended up with two officiants doing two distinct ceremonies. One was a nondenominational minister who did a *slightly* spiritual ceremony in English, and one was a Korean minister who did the service in Korean.

4. **Nondenominational.** If you consider yourselves spiritual but not religious, and you are not marrying in a house of worship, you might want a beautiful ceremony that honors marriage and honors God or Spirit but does not include *any* aspects of any religion. You might not even want to use the word *God* and might prefer to personalize the prayers to "Divine Spirit" or "Creator," or even "Mother, Father, Great Spirit." The idea is to honor your spirituality and celebrate your relationship in a sacred yet secular way. Many brides and grooms—interfaith, of the same religion, and nonreligious—love the nondenominational option because it seeks to honor the most common denominator and takes a middle ground, which makes *everyone* feel comfortable.

5. **Multicultural and culturally inclusive.** In addition to interfaith ceremonies, some couples are from very different cultures, or perhaps from the same faith, but literally from different worlds. Other couples have simply adopted many traditions along the way in life and would like to include them. A multicultural approach to a ceremony can be interfaith, re-

ligious, or nondenominational. It means including customs from more than one culture—sometimes from several. For example, I officiated for a couple in Brooklyn with the New York City skyline as the backdrop, and included the Native American custom of calling in of the directions and a dream-catcher ceremony, an adaptation of the seven steps from Hinduism, a Hawaiian sand ceremony, and the Jewish custom of the breaking of the glass. Another American bride and her beloved, born in Spain, had a nondenominational ceremony that included readings in both English and Spanish.

6. **Civil.** Typically, this is a "no frills" ceremony that includes just the legal aspects of solemnizing vows—a question of intent, free will and the pronouncement of you two as husband and wife. It usually contains no religion or religious references. A traditional civil ceremony is performed by a justice of the peace, a judge, a notary public, or a mayor, for example; it might be in a judge's chambers, a town clerk's office, City Hall, or a restaurant. "Civil" is sometimes interchanged with the word "nonreligious" and used to describe a ceremony that has no mention of God or religion yet has a creative or romantic spirit. An interfaith couple who married in Central Park in New York City insisted on a traditional civil ceremony but asked for a slight cultural twist. He was Australian and she from Sri Lanka. They included the Sri Lankan customs of tying strings around their fingers instead of exchanging rings, and they ended the celebration by eating Sri Lankan wedding cake.

7. **Spiritual marriage or sacred love ceremony.** Here, the emphasis is on an even greater spiritual connection between the couple. Rather than relying on "God above" to create and strengthen their union, the couple is empowered to see their own divinity and the divine light within each other. This theme is common in ceremonies in some of the pagan traditions, such as Celtic hand fasting, and also in some Hindu or Tantric traditions, where the bride and groom come to the altar as God and Goddess, to declare their love. The sacred love ceremony gives marriage an extraordinary start. It doesn't have to look like a Hindu or pagan ceremony. It can be a groom in a tux and a bride in white who walks down the aisle, or a shoeless couple on a beach in Maui.

8. **Contemporary, creative, personalized**. Every wedding is a sacred event that holds profound meaning and potential for the two who step to the altar in the name of love. This kind of ceremony is the ultimate Wedding Goddess ceremony because it can pull together elements from *any* kind of ceremony and be personalized and unique from start to finish. In this style of wedding, you as the Wedding Goddess and your mate can literally create your own wedding.

Finding the Right Officiant

*A*s you can see, in order to select the right kind of wedding for you, you have to also select the right officiant for you. Obviously, I am biased here and will always recommend a loving, caring, supportive wedding officiant. You want the person who facilitates this important milestone in your life to be someone you *both* feel comfortable with and confident about.

You may not have a family minister or even feel that you want to use a clergyperson from your own faith. There are many kinds of clergypersons and officiants available to serve modern couples, including Unitarian and Humanist ministers, as well as former Catholic priests. Perhaps you were hoping to have your best friend ordained, like Joey, who presided over Monica and Chandler's wedding on *Friends*. (That's a possibility, but keep in mind that while it made for good TV and it is legal in California, in New York, where *Friends* was set, his Internet ordination would not be legally recognized.) For a civil ceremony, you might prefer a retired judge or a justice of the peace. There is also a growing new profession of independent officiants and interfaith ministers who are trained to create *any kind* of personalized ceremony for couples of all backgrounds. Many of them are hip, open-minded, and willing to cocreate the ceremony you truly want.

> Creating a meaningful ceremony was one of the most important considerations when we were planning our wedding. Choosing an officiant who was spiritual, down to earth, and open to alternative ideas was paramount. We were lucky to find someone who imbued these qualities and was able to help us create a ceremony that was unique and wholly ours. We choose readings that spoke to us as well as rituals and blessings from our cultures and other cultures that were meaningful to us.
>
> —*Jackie, who married Brian on July 27, 2002*

They are often very glad to co-officiate with other clergypersons and even your friends or relatives.

The Wedding Goddess and her mate should seek someone who makes them feel so at ease on so many levels that they can relax on their wedding day, knowing they will be taken care of—and that there will be no surprises or unwanted preaching. One bride had a clergyperson who unexpectedly launched into a tirade of religious political commentary between the vows. "I found him offensive," she says, "and could barely focus on the ceremony. It was so distracting."

Always insist on meeting with potential officiants beforehand, and ask some key questions. The initial consultation should be free. Find out what this person is truly able to offer you—a canned ceremony or a personalized approach to helping you create the wedding of *your* dreams?

Wedding Goddess Exercise

*T*he Wedding Goddess usually seeks ways to blend tradition with creativity and romance. Yet, you might be surprised to find yourselves yearning for or leaning more toward tradition. Even nonreligious people tend to "get religious" when it comes to a wedding; you might look forward to a ceremony based on your faith tradition. These traditions are pleasantly familiar because you've seen them so many times at the weddings of friends and family members. Tradition is a wonderful thing, and it is important to assess, together, how much of it you want in your ceremony.

1. **Ask yourselves, "Where does religion fit in?"** For example, if you've not stepped into a synagogue since a childhood Chanukah party, would you want a Jewish ceremony in a temple with a rabbi or a cantor? Or would you perhaps like to include just a symbol of the religion, such as the breaking of the glass or a Hebrew prayer?

2. **Would a traditional ceremony be most suited to the two of you—or not?** Would that fit with you? Or would you rather blend in *aspects* of your traditions in a nondenominational ceremony? Or would something romantic and offbeat be more your style? On the spectrum between a for-

mal and traditional ceremony and the wackiest exchange of vows you can think of, where are you? Somewhere in the middle, or somewhere on the edge, wanting to be different?

3. **What are your special needs**? Think about the requirements each of you may have. Is one of you more religious than the other? Is one of you atheist or agnostic? Are you an interfaith pair? Do you hail from different cultures? How much do you want to honor your heritage and the traditions of your parents and family, etc.? Is there anything you abhor about those traditions and would never want in your own ceremony?

Tim and I knew we didn't want our ceremony to be *too* religious, because we are both of very different faiths. We knew we wanted this to be a celebration of uniting our families. This is where having a terrific and intuitive minister is so invaluable. She allowed us to have our individual personalities show through during the ceremony, which made it fun for all of us.

—*Patti, who married Tim on April 25, 2003*

4. **What do you two truly want?** Most important, be completely honest with each other (and then with your officiant). Honor your heritage and your parents, but make sure you are creating this ceremony for the two of you—not just to please others.

5. **Agree to take a stand.** No Wedding Goddess (or her mate) has to settle for a ceremony that is completely controlled by someone else. Even if you two decide to go the traditional route, ask to make adjustments to any language that you cannot live with. (One bride couldn't bear the idea of being pronounced "man and wife," and asked her clergyperson to make sure he said "husband and wife." Another asked her minister to replace the phrase "till death do you part," because "it was too negative-sounding.") Even in traditional settings, look for the most open-minded clergypeople, and at the very least, insist on knowing exactly what will be said in the ceremony and what you will be asked to do.

WEDDING GODDESS VOW

We will create our wedding ceremony our way.

Arlene Sandler/Lensgirl.com

CHAPTER THIRTEEN

Crafting Your Dream Ceremony ... Together

Create, together, the ceremony that will herald your joining as one. Let it speak of the love you share ... and the life you are choosing to lead together. Fill it with the blessings and personal intentions for married life. Let it be the foundation of all that will come.

—Juno, the Roman Goddess of marriage, the home, and childbirth, whose name inspired the month of June, a favorite time for weddings

When planning the biggest day of your life, it is completely natural to get wrapped up and sometimes carried away with the details of how you will eat, drink, and be merry. The Wedding Goddess knows it is also essential that she and her beloved partake in the process of exactly *how they will be married.*

Beyond selecting the level of spirituality and the general tone of the wedding, you and your beloved can put your imprint on every segment of your ceremony. *The ceremony is the wedding,* and the wedding is the start of the most intimate relationship of your lifetime. When you work on the details of the ceremony together, and you each take the time to add input and ideas, it will draw you much closer and enhance your wedding experience in so many ways.

This is the part of the wedding day that allows you both to step up to the plate and formally declare your love, commitment, and intentions for marriage before family, friends, and the world. The

> The fact that we wrote the ceremony ourselves, including our vows, reinforced our investment in the actual event. We included two poems that reflected exactly how we were feeling. We loved creating our own special day!
>
> —*Courtney, who married Ray on October 26, 2002*

language of the ceremony literally lays the foundation for your life together. The experience you share can truly awaken you both to a new depth of commitment and a new sense of power—the power of two who unite in oneness.

How to Personalize Your Ceremony

*E*very couple's relationship is unique, so you want to make sure—whenever possible—that the words, readings, and vows expressed in the ceremony uniquely represent the two of you. The language of the sacred is very subjective. I believe every couple should have the opportunity to choose (or at the very least review) all that will be spoken and relayed at their wedding, as well as the opportunity to write and speak their own vows.

Personalizing your ceremony. When planning a traditional ceremony based on religious protocol, you will not have as much freedom to "tweak" or personalize your wedding—but just asking your clergyperson questions and seeking ways to make the ceremony more meaningful will be a wonderful shared experience for you both! If you and your beloved have opted for a creative contemporary ceremony, the sky is the limit. Whether you write it yourself or work with a loving officiant who will help craft your dream wedding, it is a very powerful and enlightening process!

What the law requires. The requirements for a ceremony outside of a house of worship are minimal—similar to the requirements of a civil ceremony. Other than following the state laws of whatever locale is home to your wedding, you are free to create the wedding of your dreams. Check the requirements state by

WEDDING GODDESS RULE #13

A Wedding Goddess personalizes her wedding ceremony.

You know that the true foundation of your new life together lies in the words, promises, and intentions evoked in your wedding ceremony. Therefore, you ensure that your ceremony reflects the two of you, the love you share, and the life you are choosing to create together. Even if you elect to include aspects of religions or family tradition, you make sure the heart of the ceremony is about the bond you share with the man you are marrying.

state. New York, for example, requires a valid marriage license, a witness over age eighteen, and an ordained or otherwise legally empowered officiant who can sign the license, ask a question of intent, and pronounce you husband and wife.

Anatomy of a wedding ceremony. You will be well on your way once you understand the essential segments and structure of a wedding ceremony. You need a form and format to wrap your brain around; until then, the ceremony can seem vague and ethereal. A well-versed officiant will be able to help you fill in the blanks by getting to know your style, showing you sample ceremonies, and feeding you many ideas.

> What was most important to me was to focus on our life together. One element I chose to have was remembrance of those who couldn't be there—grandparents, my husband's mother, my dog Phoenix, who I had always planned on having as my ring bearer. It was a moment that brought tears to my eyes and to the eyes of the others who had known these beautiful souls. I enjoyed every moment of my ceremony. The rain that fell around us couldn't do anything to ruin the wonderful feelings I had inside.
>
> —*Deborah, who married Chris on July 15, 2000*

Wedding Goddess Exercise

Your most important tool will be an outline of what *can* be included in a wedding ceremony. The following will help expand your awareness of the possibilities as you two begin to formulate ideas, including where to place rituals, readings, and vows. Sit down with your beloved and go through these elements in an organized, step-by-step manner. Discuss the ideas you both have for the ceremony. You will learn a lot about each other in the process!

This basic structure and outline can be used for a nondenominational, interfaith, or any contemporary creative wedding ceremony. It was adapted from the standard ceremony format used in *Sacred Threshold* by Gertrud Mueller Nelson and Christopher Witt, and from Daphne Rose Kingma's book *Weddings from the Heart*, course materials from The New Seminary, and other sources.

- **Processional.** Decide the order and plan the music that will bring the relatives and bridal party down the aisle and, then, something special for the bride to walk to. In the Jewish tradition, the groom's parents walk with the groom first, and the bride's parents walk with her last. Many modern couples like this touch, regardless of their religion. Some couples plan a more informal start of the ceremony and have their officiant simply call their guests to order or ask them to gather around.

• **The greeting.** This is where the minister on TV typically says, "Dearly beloved . . ." At your wedding, he or she can simply welcome everyone and thank them for being there on this special day.

• **The opening prayer/invocation/convocation.** A sacred space is created by a prayer to God (the Creator, Spirit, the Divine), and a petition is made for a strong, loving marriage filled with good fortune. This can also be offered as a general blessing, without evoking the Divine. Buddhists and nonreligious couples can instead open with a moment of silence.

• **Wedding reading.** A favorite poem or scriptural passage (or even a song you love) is read by the officiant or a friend or family member. (There can be more than one reading. Additional readings may be placed here or elsewhere in the ceremony.)

> What made our wedding so special was how our minister told the story of our relationship, including how we met, our time together, and what we love about each other. It was special for us, and our guests also enjoyed it. It reminded us how special our relationship is and the fun times we had together.
>
> —*Jessica, who married Michael on September 13, 2003*

• **Minister's message.** The officiant offers loving advice for a long, strong marriage. This is a great place to include insights into your relationship, your love for each other, and your intentions for marriage. It's also a good place for the offciant or one of your friends to share a story about your relationship.

• **A special wedding ritual or tradition.** You may light a unity candle, do a wine ceremony, or a sand ceremony, or include some religious traditions. The ritual might also be placed elsewhere in the ceremony, such as a hand wrapping and blessing after the exchange of rings.

• **The declaration of intent.** This is more commonly called the "I do's." This can be done in the form of a question ("Do you, Jane, take . . ."), or you can declare your intent to each other ("I, Jane, take you, Jim, to be my lawfully wedded husband. I promise to . . ."). They can be classic, traditional, or hip and modern. As long as you essentially say "I do," it's a done deal. This is a legal declaration that must be included.

● **The Vows.** These are optional but highly recommended. Writing your own vows is a special way to declare your loving intentions for marriage. You can borrow from existing vows, or even read a poem that fits. You can read them to your beloved, or do this in repeat-after-the-minister style. (See Chapter 15 for more details.)

● **Blessing and exchanging the rings.** There are a million ways to do this. You can include audience participation—such as asking people to silently bless the rings by filling their hearts and minds with good thoughts for you two—and you can include a ring vow, such as "With this ring, I pledge my love" or the classic "With this ring, I thee wed."

● **Pronouncement.** This is where the minister formally declares you husband and wife. This is a legal requirement.

● **The kiss.** You know what that's about! But you may not realize that it doesn't always have to be encouraged with the statement "You may kiss the bride!" You can also ask you officiant to say, "Please share your first kiss as a married couple" or "You may kiss."

● **Closing cultural tradition.** If you are including the Jewish tradition of breaking the glass, this is the time. Also, the jumping of the broom, an African custom, comes now.

● **Or first act as a married couple (optional).** Many guests are used to the wedding being over with the kiss, but you can choose to include another meaningful moment or two. You can exchange a rose or a gift, or you can invite the community to shower you with personal blessings, called out from the crowd. Hindus throw flowers, and orthodox Jews sometimes throw candy. Some couples hand out cones or bags filled with rose petals to be thrown as they go up the aisle.

● **Benediction or closing prayer.** If you want to end the wedding with the kiss, this can come before the pronouncement. A beautiful prayer or poem will bring the sacred ceremony to a close and send you on your way with love and blessings. Many couples like the "Apache Wedding Blessing" or the scriptural "May God Bless You and Keep You." It can be very short, even just one line.

● **Recessional.** Congratulations! You're married. You head up the aisle with your Mister in tow, and the bridal party follows. It's a nice touch if the clergyperson allows your moms and dads and even grandparents to step out from their seats and head up the aisle as part of the recessional.

• **Receiving line.** After this, you will likely want to consider having a receiving line, or figure out a different way to greet your guests and let them congratulate you.

WEDDING GODDESS VOW

Our wedding will be an expression of who we are as a couple and of the future we choose to create.

Jason Groupp/www.JasongPhoto.com

CHAPTER FOURTEEN

Choosing Rituals, Customs, and Rites

We are all children of the same earth. All paths lead to the same truth, the same light that lives in us all. Let us each celebrate and be enhanced by rituals from around this world.

—Gaia, Greek mother goddess of all things, who represents the world, nature, humanity, and personification of the earth

Special rituals, woven into the wedding ceremony, offer you and your beloved the chance to affirm and celebrate your love, as they seal the union between you two and acknowledge the family ties that are established on your wedding day. Many brides and grooms have gone along with the rites of the wedding ceremony, sometimes not knowing much about what they meant. The Wedding Goddess knows it is essential that she and her beloved have a hand in choosing the rituals for their special day, or, at the very least, that they understand the meaning of those rituals.

"Ritual lifts us from the mundane into the sacred," says ritual expert Barbara Biziou. Thus, the rituals in your ceremony will serve to move you from your everyday state of being to a higher state of love and partnership, and toward deeper family bonds. These rituals are also meant to symbolically take you from singlehood and engagement into the

We had a Bahai ceremony on the beach at Lanai, Hawaii. The Bahai officiant chanted in Hawaiian at the end, and that was really wonderful. On the day of the wedding, my groom's brother had ordered special leis and had them sent over from Maui. We were stacked with leis. I felt like a Kahuna.

—Jill, who married Leonard on July 21, 2003

realm of marriage. Just think about it: You start your journey down the aisle single . . . and you leave a married woman! How cool is that?

Search for the rituals that truly sing to you and that you are comfortable partaking in. In this chapter, you'll find a sampling of ideas.

How to Select Rituals That Are Right for Your Wedding— and Your Marriage

*I*t's very important that we embrace rituals, because they make our wedding experience so much richer," top event planner Colin Cowie told me, at the Association of Bridal Consultants' Ninth Annual Asian-Pacific Bridal Summit. "Ritual brings us together; it helps us to understand where we come from and where we are going. The whole idea of a wedding ritual is to have a little reflection."

Wedding rituals and customs are typically symbolic markers of the occasion and of the intention of marriage. They may be religious or spiritual in nature, or they can be nondenominational and creative rites. Essentially, they celebrate union and commitment, as well as acknowledge the transformations that marriage brings—going from single to married life, from one family to the merging of two.

The rituals and customs you choose to include in your wedding ceremony will depend on how you choose to honor the

---

WEDDING GODDESS RULE #14

A Wedding Goddess embraces empowering rituals.

You choose rituals, customs, and rites that make you both feel that your special bond is being honored and empowered. You feel free to choose rites from the tradition you were born into, as well as those you have adopted along the way. You recognize that the rituals in your ceremony must empower you as individuals—whole unto yourselves—as they also strengthen your partnership and union.

tradition you were born into—if at all—and what rituals feel right to you and your beloved. Here are some of the religious and cultural rituals and customs that modern brides and grooms might choose to honor their heritage, organized by faith or ethnicity.

1. **African American.** Jumping the broom takes a couple from single life into the land of matrimony. This custom honors the tradition begun by slaves. At a time when they were not allowed to legally wed, couples would jump over a broom holding hands to signify their commitment to each other.

2. **Chinese.** The Chinese red goblet ceremony gives the couple a chance to take a sip from either one goblet or two goblets tied together by red or gold ribbon. It symbolizes unity and blessings for shared good fortunes.

3. **Christian.** The lighting of the family unity candle brings the light of two separate candles together to light the one candle that represents the new union. (Can also be adapted as a non-denominational ritual.)

4. **Hindu.** Satipati or the Seven Steps is one of the most important Hindu rituals, where the bride and groom take seven sacred steps to seal their marriage covenant.

5. **Japanese.** The saki ceremony symbolizes the fusion of two lives and offers blessings for long life and good fortunes as bride and groom alternate sipping from three different-sized cups.

6. **Jewish.** The breaking of the glass reminds us that while we are joyous, there is still suffering in the world, but that the love of the couple adds to the healing of the world.

7. **Native American.** Calling in the directions is a way of praying for blessings from the east, west, north and south. It honors the ancestors and calls in the support of the spirits from all corners of the universes.

8. **Pagan ritual**. Hand fasting is an ancient Celtic tradition of literally tying the couple's hands together to signify their bond.

NONDENOMINATIONAL RITUALS

Here are some popular traditions with nondenominational interpretations.

1. THE LIGHTING OF THE UNITY CANDLE

The mothers typically light two separate tapers and pass the candles to the bride and groom. Then the bride and groom join their lights to light one central unity candle. These are usually secured on a unity candle holder, or on separate candle holders.

> OFFICIANT: *It has been said that "From every human being, there rises a light that reaches straight to heaven. When two souls that are destined for each other find each other, their streams of light flow together, and a single brighter light goes forth from their united being." (This is a quote from the great Hasidic Master Bal Shem Tov.)*
>
> *The lighting of the unity candle symbolizes the light of two individuals coming together as one brighter light. It symbolizes the promise to merge two lives as one, And it honors the family ties that are created by marriage. As a gesture of unity between the two families that are united on this day, I ask the mother of the bride and the mother of the groom (anyone can represent the two families, or the bride and groom can light the tapers on their own) to step up here and light the solo candles from the one light that already burns on the altar. This light represents the light within us all.*
>
> Parents/Family come to either side of the bride and groom. They light the candles. Then the clergyperson asks them to pass the light to the bride and groom.

> "Our wedding ceremony included two important rituals: Breaking the glass and the lighting of the unity candles. We made it very clear that although we didn't want religion to be a part of the ceremony, we did want spirituality and family to be the main theme. To us, the breaking of the glass really honored my mother and father's beliefs. While the lighting of the unity candle represented our two families coming together to *help us* join together. We also used my grandmother's wedding topper (also my mother's) and her wedding knife to cut the cake, which I thought was pretty cool."
>
> —*Randi who married Christopher on August 9, 2003*

To the bride and groom: *Please hold the candles for a moment. These two lighted candles represent the two of you, as well as your families, ancestors, the source of who you are. These two distinct flames represent your lives up until this moment. (Pause.) Please bring these two separate candles together to light the unity candle. The bride and groom bring candles together with unity candle.*

Closing blessing: *May the loving light of Divine Spirit, family, community, and good friends always bless this marriage!*

2. Wine Ceremony

The bride and groom share a sip from one chalice. (Grape juice can be used instead of wine.)

Officiant, to bride and groom: *This cup represents your new life together. It contains your hopes and dreams, your fears and concerns, and all the possibilities that lie before you. Sharing a sip from this cup symbolizes that your two lives—once separate—are now joined. Now, take a sip to celebrate your sacred union. May you never thirst for love!* (The couple shares a sip.)

> For our sand ceremony, we each had a container of different colored sand that represented ourselves as individuals. To symbolize our individual selves merging in marriage, together we poured our containers into a large glass vase. The two colors of sand formed a beautiful pattern in the vase—a meaningful tribute to our marriage that we still have in our home today."
>
> —*Amy who married Bart on May 18, 2002*

3. Sand Ceremony

The bride and groom select two different colors of sand and pour the sand from two separate containers into one central container.

Officiant: *We are all made up of millions of molecules, facets, possibilities, points of view, experiences, desires, hopes, and dreams. Our very beings are as vast as a beach that stretches on forever, and our makeup as complex and complete as the many tiny particles of sand that when joined together make the beach such a stunning sight. In the modern tradition of the sand ceremony, a couple acknowledges their individuality, and their desire to merge their lives in marriage, by pouring two separate containers of different colored sand into one empty vessel. This symbolically unites the many aspects of their individual selves, and also brings together the families that are united by marriage.*

To the couple: *You come to this day as individuals, whole and complete unto yourselves. Bringing the many tiny aspects that represent the two of you together into one vessel represents a joint venture that is a stronger, fuller, more powerful expression of your love. These two containers of sand represent the two of you, as well as your families and your ancestors, the source of who you are. These two distinct containers represent your lives up until this moment.*

The couple pours the sand simultaneously, and when they are finished, the clergyperson says: Your newly formed union is represented by the intertwined pattern of sand you have created together. It represents all that you both are, all that you both bring to your marriage, and all that you will become together. May this union be blessed in all ways.

4. Hand Wrapping and Blessing of the Hands
This nondenominational blessing of the hands can be done after the ring exchange or even as part of the pronouncement. The bride and groom can use their own sacred cloth.

To the bride and groom: *an ancient Celtic tradition to join two lives as one through the rite of hand fasting. The couple joins hands and is literally tied together to symbolize their unity. Today we will use the slightly modern tradition of hand wrapping.*

If you choose to become one with each other, please place your right palms together, and then place left palms over them, to create a figure eight, or infinity symbol, with your hands. It signifies hearts that will love forever. I will wrap them with a sacred cloth, also in an infinity symbol. This will signify a relationship that lasts forever. (The clergyperson lays the cloth or scarf across clasped hands and brings the ends up over each other, also creating a figure eight or infinity symbol, and places a hand on the couple's hands and offers this blessing.)

BLESSING OVER THE HANDS:

> *Shakespeare said, "Now join your hands, and with your hands, your*
>   *hearts."*
> *As your hands are bound together,*
> *imagine also that your lives and spirits are joined.*
> *Choose a union of love, trust, and mutual support.*
> *Heart to heart, soul to soul, body to body . . . and so it is.*

5. THE BONDS OF MARRIAGE

Many cultures include customs that create a bond in marriage by literally binding the couple. You might want to adapt some aspect of these customs to symbolize a bond that will go on. In a pagan handfasting, the hands of the bride and groom are literally tied together with individual ribbons of different colors that each represent a certain quality or blessing that the couple hopes for. In some Buddhist traditions, the bride and groom's hands are wrapped with a prayer shawl. In the Hindu Seven Steps (*Satipati*), the bride's sari or sari shawl is often tied to the groom's coat in what is known as "the wedding knot," as they take seven steps around a sacred fire. In the Greek Orthodox Church, the bride and groom each wear a crown of flowers. The crowns are tied together as they take their first steps as husband and wife around the altar. In Thailand, an elder ties a "sacred thread" like angel halos around the heads of the bride and groom, joining them by a long thread that connects them in a symbol of unity. In the Native American tradition, the couple cozies up under a blanket that is wrapped around them during the ceremony.

> Our wedding was made special by candle lighting and hand wrapping. The candle lighting allowed us to include family and friends and the hand wrapping really sealed our commitment to each other.
>
> —*Monica, who married Simon on December 8, 2003*

Wedding Goddess Exercises

There are many different ways you can strengthen your union and seal your commitment. First, you both have to get a sense of how much ritual you would like to include in your ceremony, and from how many different traditions.

Some couples prefer a very low-key and ritual-free wedding, and some vote for "Wedding Theater," which includes more fanfare and more participants coming up to read and offer blessings. Before you decide which rituals you want, ask yourself these questions:

1. Do you both love the idea of the ritual aspects of weddings—such as candles, wine, small ceremonies within the ceremony, etc.—or do one or both of you find yourself turned off by it?

2. Would you prefer something simpler, or would you prefer to express your love mostly through the words spoken by the officiant?

3. Do you want to honor your religious backgrounds and heritage by choosing rites that your parents had at their wedding?

4. If the wedding will be interfaith or intercultural, do you want to combine rites and rituals from your different backgrounds, or would you rather not call attention to your differences?

5. Would you be most comfortable addressing the most common denominator in your wedding ceremony and choosing rituals that are completely neutral?

6. Would you consider including rites from traditions that are not your own, simply because you like them?

7. Would you feel comfortable asking mothers and grandmothers to share any family traditions that might be fun to include?

WEDDING GODDESS VOW

*We choose rites and rituals that honor who we are
and reinforce our special bond.*

Arlene Sandler/Lensgirl.com

CHAPTER FIFTEEN

Creating and Speaking Vows Together

If you speak from the heart, words of love will flow like a great river.
Meditate on all you mean to one another, and your vows will be revealed.
Never struggle for words; true love can never find language in striving or
pain. Open to love's wisdom and remain fluid, ready to catch the flow.

—Saraswati, Hindu Goddess of Wisdom and Learning whose
domain is language, writing, poetry, and music

Personal vows are a wonderful way to express your love on your wedding
day. Although your whole ceremony can be an expression of love and
commitment, a Wedding Goddess knows that the promises she and her
beloved make to each other are the hallmark of a sacred ceremony.

Public speaking may not be your or your groom's thing, so it is important you
do not stress yourself out over your vows.
But it is so helpful to give the vows some
thought together and be willing to speak
them from the heart and soul. Contained
within those vows are the seeds of
dreams to come true, intentions for marriage, and deep declarations of love.

Tony and I wrote rather long vows. Each part of
the vow was clear, self-contained, and to the
point. In general, I encourage couples to keep
their vows short and pithy, going right to the
heart of what they want to promise each other.
That way, the vows can be something you can
tuck into your heart and pull out in those moments when you need to remember them most.

—*Diane, who married Tony on May 19, 1996*

How to Decide the Kind of Wedding Vows That Are Right for You

While you may have a certain preconceived notion of what a wedding vow is meant to be, there are many different options for expressing your love and commitment in the form of vows and promises. You and your beloved should pick the kind of vows most suited to the two of you, taking the following into consideration.

- Whether or not you desire to write you own vows, and if you would truly enjoy writing them or would rather adapt vows from a book or from someone else's writing.
- How comfortable you both are about speaking in front of friends and family, or if you would rather "agree" to certain promises than express them out loud.
- If you would prefer to read vows to each other or have your officiant support you in repeat-after-the-officiant fashion.

WEDDING GODDESS RULE #15

A Wedding Goddess includes heartfelt vows in her ceremony.

You know that words and promises of love, adoration, and commitment are an important part of your ceremony. You want to pay tribute to the man you love and the relationship you have built together, and you also want to receive the same from your beloved. You look forward to making your promise to love, honor, cherish, and more for the entire world to hear.

SO MANY UNIQUE COUPLES, SO MANY VOWS

Using examples of vows written and selected by couples I've married, here are some of the different ways to include your personal vows in your ceremony. You and your beloved should have input on and approval of what you decide to share and how you decide to share it.

1. **Question-of-intent vows.** In every ceremony, there is a question put forth by your officiant that gives you a chance to declare that you freely choose to marry the man standing beside you. It's called the "question of intent." If you two feel that you do not want to speak much during the ceremony, because you are shy or because the thought of it makes you too nervous, you can have an extended "question of intent" that satisfies the legal requirement for a question (such as, "Do you, Colleen, take Art to be your husband?") and gives you a chance to agree to certain declarations. The question will be asked by your officiant. For example, this is a traditional vow that many people are familiar with:

> *Do you, Colleen, take Art to be your husband,*
> *To have and to hold from this day forward,*
> *In sickness and in health,*
> *In good times and bad times?*
> *Will you love, honor and cherish him,*
> *All the days of your life?*

Here's a more modern approach to the same kind of vow format. To this or the above, you will, of course, answer "I do."

> *Do you, Jane, take Adam to be your husband?*
> *Do you promise to grow with him in mind and spirit,*
> *To always be open and honest with him,*
> *And cherish him for all the days of your life?*

2. **Repeat-after-the-officiant individual vows.** You can also have a set of vows said individually *in addition to* the question of intent (right after or before), or spoken as part of your ring vows (during the blessing and exchange of rings). These vows should be of a manageable length and "fed" to you in bite-size segments so that you don't have to memorize anything and so that the vows will be easy for you each to repeat. Here's an example from Sophia and Zvonko's ceremony:

> *I, Sophia, promise*
> *To trust and respect you,*

Be patient and understanding,
Openly share my thoughts,
And share my fears and dreams,
Watch after your well-being,
Nurture your growth,
And bring lightness and joy to our lives.
I will be a loving and supportive partner.

Or, if you have a vow that is on the long side, instead of having you both repeat the same lines, you can speak a part, your beloved can speak a part, and then you can repeat the final lines together. This can also be done in repeat-after-the-officiant fashion. Chris and Lori adapted this vow, in part, from Roy Croft's classic poem "Love."

Chris says:
Lori, I love you
Not only for what you are,
but for who I am,
when I am with you.
Not only for what you have made of yourself . . .
But for what you are making of me.

Lori says:
Chris, I love you . . .
For helping me to see
the dreams I have for Life
more clearly than ever before.
One of those dreams is becoming realized,
right now,
As we come together as a family.

Lori and Chris say together:
I promise to you today . . .
that I will forever fulfill my role . . .
as your partner . . .
in the life we are building together.

If you prefer to speak your vows along with the exchange of your rings, which is common in the Christian tradition, you might have a vow like this, used by Liz and Robert.

Take this ring
As a sign of my devotion
And my commitment to our marriage.
Today we begin anew.
I look forward to all our tomorrows.

3. **Simultaneous vows.** One way to do something different is to speak the same vow simultaneously. This is like a stereo vow—you hear it consciously and subconsciously—and it is a really nice touch to share your sentiments and promises to each other at the same time. It represents partnership and working in the spirit of harmony and cooperation. For example, you might recite a vow like this one:

On this day,
our new adventure begins.
I promise you that
I will stand by your side,
As your partner in life.
I look forward to sharing
Laughter and tears,
Comfort and challenges,
Great joy and triumphs.
I want to inspire you,
And be inspired by you,
Be your best cheerleader
As you follow your dreams.
And hear your cheering
As I achieve mine.
Let us grow together,
In heart, mind, and spirit,
And stand together to face the world.
I will cherish you always.
You are my one and only true love.

4. **Alternating line vows:** If you have a lot to share with each other, it may be a little too unwieldy to do in repeat-after-the-officiant style; and perhaps it is redundant to read the same long vow to each other. You can instead divvy up the lines and alternate reading them. This is a very creative and somewhat theatrical way to share your vows. It's very special. Here are the vows Tony and Summer wrote and read to each other.

> SUMMER: *My darling Tony, you are the magic of my days.*
>
> TONY: *My darling Summer, you help me to laugh and teach me to love.*
>
> SUMMER: *This I promise to you: I will always be honest, kind, patient, and forgiving.*
>
> TONY: *This I promise to you: I will encourage your individuality, because that is what makes you unique and wonderful.*
>
> SUMMER: *I will nurture your dreams, because through them your soul shines.*
>
> TONY: *I will help shoulder our challenges, because through them we'll emerge stronger.*
>
> SUMMER: *I will share with you the joys of life, because with you they will be that much sweeter.*
>
> TONY: *I will be your partner in all things, working with you as a part of the whole.*
>
> SUMMER: *I will be a true and loyal friend to you.*
>
> TONY: *I will cherish you, hold you, and honor you.*
>
> SUMMER: *I will respect you, encourage you, and cherish you, in health and sickness.*
>
> BOTH: *Through sorrow and success, for all the days of my life. I will love you with all of my heart. These are my sacred vows to you, my equal in all things.*

5. **Writing and reading your own vows.** Of course, the time-honored way to share vows is to each write your own separate vows and read them to each other at the wedding altar. Some couples like to coordinate their vows, and some choose to share them for the first time on the wedding day. Either way, it is always a beautiful touch when the Wedding Goddess and her mate share what they love about each other and what they promise to each other on this day. Some couples opt for completely

unique vows, and others choose to also add some traditional sentiments, such as these vows from Katerina and Xingmin. They printed their vows on beautiful scroll paper, for an elegant touch.

KATRINA:

Xingmin, I love you for being gentle, kind and tender.
I love you for hearing my thoughts, sharing my dreams.
I love you for filling my life with joy and loving me without end.
I love you for accepting me as I am.
With you, I can be completely happy and completely myself.
From this day, I promise to love, honor, and cherish you,
in sickness and health, in good times and bad.
I pledge myself to be ever faithful to you, with my body, my mind,
and my heart.
I freely take you as my husband.

XINGMIN:

Kaca [her nickname], I consider my decision to learn ballroom
dancing the best decision I ever made in my life. That's how I
met you, got to know you, and fell in love with you.
I love you because you are beautiful, intelligent, and kind.
I love you because you make me happy and you make me whole.
From this day, I promise to love, honor, and cherish you,
in sickness and health, in good times and bad.
I pledge myself to be ever faithful to you, with my body, my mind,
and my heart.
I freely take you as my wife.

6. **Other ideas for vows.** Be as creative as you like! If you would rather select or adapt vows from poetry or a song, go for it. For example:

• Tim and Patty adapted their favorite songs. Tim read the lines from Chicago's "Inspiration," and Patty shared sentiments found in "From This Moment" by Shania Twain and had a guitarist and singer play it live immediately after she and Tim exchanged vows.

• Maria and Michael used poetry. The bride was shy about speaking, so Michael read Oriah Mountaindreamer's stirring poem "The Invitation."

● Steven and Deborah chose not to speak vows themselves, and instead had their officiant read their favorite song, "My First, My Last, My Everything" by Barry White.

7. **Speaking from the heart—and from the hip.** Some brides and grooms prefer to speak without a piece of paper. It is not recommended that you try to memorize your vows—it's too stressful on your wedding day—yet by all means if you or your beloved prefer to simply "share" what is in your hearts, do so. If one of you needs to have a piece of paper at the altar and the other feels more comfortable just speaking freely, that's fine, too.

Wedding Goddess Exercises

Obviously, there are many ways to celebrate your relationship, promise your love, and affirm your commitment. The most important thing is to make sure your vows are truly meaningful to you both, and that you select a way to express them that is comfortable. Neither of you should feel forced to speak or pressed to write vows if writing will stress you out. By the same token, if one of you would love to speak and the other is super-shy, find a way to make it work for you both! The following are some ways to create the perfect wedding vows.

Questions to ponder. The first thing I give brides and grooms is a writing exercise to help them bring out their feelings of love, friendship, and appreciation. They know they love and adore each other, but they don't always have the language to express it. It would be so helpful for you and your beloved to take some time to ponder and answer these questions, together or individually. Your answers will give you insights on ways to personalize your ceremony, as well as inspiration for things to express in your vows.

> The part of the ceremony that most strengthened our union was when Ron started to speak from his heart. It wasn't planned, rehearsed, or read from a card. It was just from the heart.
>
> —*Kelly, who married Ron on October 26, 2002*

1. How did you meet, and what first attracted you to each other?

2. What do you love about each other?

3. What does getting married mean to you?

4. What are some of your dreams and intentions for married life?

5. What story do you want to share about your love?

Utilizing other people's ideas for vows. Borrowing from other sources is completely acceptable in weddings. It could be that the perfect vow already exists out there, that someone else wrote it as if they were reading your heart and mind. So feel free to pore through favorite songs, poems, and other people's vows for ideas. There are many sample weddings and vows posted on the Internet, in places such as theknot.com and beliefnet.com. Here are some terrific books on vows, or that include vows, to consider.

Words for the Wedding: Perfect Things to Say for a Perfect Wedding Day by Wendy Paris and Andrew Chesler (Perigee Books, 2001)

Weddings from the Heart: Contemporary and Traditional Ceremonies for an Unforgettable Wedding by Daphne Rose Kingma (Conari Press, 1995)

Wedding Vows: How to Express Your Love in Your Own Words by Peg Kehret (Meriwether Publishing Ltd., 1989)

Diane Warner's Complete Book of Wedding Vows: Hundreds of Ways to Say "I Do" by Diane Warner (Career Press, 1996)

The Everything Wedding Vows Book: Anything and Everything You Could Possibly Say at the Altar—and Then Some by Janet Anastasio and Michelle Bevilacqua (Adams Media Corporation, 2001)

Your Special Wedding Vows by Sharon Naylor (Sourcebook Casablanca, 2004)

> I think I wrote the perfect vows. I was inspired by a set of inspirational candles given to me by a friend. They read: Gratitude, Safety, Joy, Faith, Truth, Growth, Healing, Love. I decided these were the principles I wanted to live by and to be part of my marriage, so I made sure to include each in my vows. I remember Bob thinking he wanted to add something to them, and my panic, since I thought they were totally perfect. The best could not be improved. But in the sprit of sharing, I gave them to him to change as he saw fit—a test of faith. He finally agreed that they *were* perfect!
>
> —*Susan, who married Bob on July 3, 1999*

The Knot Guide to Wedding Vows and Traditions by Carley Roney and the editors of The Knot, (Broadway Books, 2000)

Joining Hands and Hearts: Interfaith, Intercultural Wedding Celebrations by Rev. Susanna Stefanachi Macomb (Fireside Books, 2003)

WEDDING GODDESS VOW

*Our wedding vows are our unique and authentic expression of our love,
our commitment, and the life we choose to live together.*

Jason Groupp/www.jasongphoto.com

CHAPTER SIXTEEN

How to Involve Friends, Family, and Children in Your Ceremony

Remember, you are not just merging families, you are merging worlds. Call upon the spirit of all living things to help celebrate your dear ones. We are not as separate as we may seem. Good intentions and thoughtfulness will create unity at your wedding altar.

—Patchamama, the South American Earth Mother Goddess, considered the personification of fertility and growth

Many brides grapple with ways to include family and friends in the ceremony. You might be seeking a way to honor your heritage and family traditions, to acknowledge specific loved ones, or to merge into the new family that is formed by your marriage. The trick is to do this in a way that doesn't make anyone feel pressured, that doesn't make anyone feel excluded, and that is true to the spirit and the tone of your ceremony. The ideal, in fact, is to make *everyone* feel included and welcomed.

Unfortunately, the ceremony can be a hot potato, especially if you and your

WEDDING GODDESS RULE #16

A Wedding Goddess seeks to blend families and traditions together.

You recognize that marriage is not just the coming together of you and your mate, but the merging of two families, two life stories, and perhaps even two different traditions. You aim to cast a circle of love that includes the whole family—and to do this in a way that honors your relationship and the spirit of your wedding.

beloved hail from different backgrounds, or if your families try to impose their own beliefs and needs on the two of you. Some inclusions take a little more finesse than others because you want to avoid any tricky religious issues or family politics. For example, it might be easy to honor both of your mothers, or to pay tribute to the best friend who introduced you two; yet if you or your beloved have a child or children or if one or both of your families is super-religious and you're not, it may take a little creative thinking to appropriately include the kids or honor the parents.

The Wedding Goddess understands that the key to including loved ones is to blend these tributes into the ceremony with love. If you have loving intentions that come from the heart—and not from pressure or wedding politics—it will ultimately work.

How to Include the People You Love in Your Wedding

There are many ways to include the people you love. Mothers can light unity candles or read prayers. Siblings and friends can offer blessings and readings. If a relative has a great voice or plays an instrument, that person can sing or perform. Your children can light candles, participate in a modern-day sand ceremony, sip grape juice while you sip wine, and be included in the rituals and prayers. You can also lovingly remember those relatives who have passed on, as well as those who cannot physically be present.

If you want to give everyone something to do, you can have a group candle lighting, an organized time for calling out blessings, or a tossing of flower petals at a designated moment (as the Hindus do), or hand out candy (as Hasidic and Muslim folks sometimes do to celebrate a joyous event). You can also choose to assign certain blessings to a group of people,

> My younger brother was an usher, and I was so proud of him doing such a good job. One of my favorite memories from the planning process was when I had written William a letter to ask if he would be usher and he telephoned me and said, "Thank you for trusting me," and I just broke down.
>
> —*Jodie, who married Andrew on July 1, 2002*

such as having seven friends offer the seven blessings (a Jewish tradition) or speak the intentions of the Seven Steps (a Hindu tradition); or have four friends call in the four directions (Native American and Goddess traditions).

Wedding Goddess Exercises

Consider some of these suggestions for including loved ones in the wedding ceremony, and see which are most appropriate for you. These ideas come from dozens of brides and their grooms, who have walked the path before you.

1. **Using symbolism.** You can have something that represents the family or a particular member on your person or at your wedding altar. In the famous phrase "something old, something new," the something old is meant to be something the bride carries or wears that is passed on by a relative. For example, Sue carried her grandmother's handkerchief when she married Joshua. At Jackie and Tom's wedding, the bride carried a bouquet of eight calla lilies that represented eight important people in her life, including her mom and dad, her groom's mom and dad, her grandparents, her uncle and her best friend. She made note of this on her wedding program and added that "the bouquet was tied by the groom . . . as a symbol of the love and unity that brought them here today."

> I got my mother and my mother-in-law to search through the family photo albums so that I could create a family photo tree of both of our immediate families. We set up a memory table outside the chapel and then moved it into the reception. I had photos of us together, us as kids with our siblings, and our parents, grandparents, and my great-grandparents on their wedding days.
>
> —*Mimi, who married Mark on March 7, 2004*

2. **Unique walks down the aisle.** Some brides use the processional to include the whole family, giving everyone a place of honor. Nikki and Eric had fourteen family members come down the aisle to a medley of the bride's favorite Disney tunes. When Jane married Adam, she made sure all of her groom's family were represented, and also her posse of *five parents*

(Her mom, dad, ex-stepmom, ex-stepdad, and current stepdad) walked down the aisle. At Tim and Patty's ceremony, the bride wanted to have her former in-laws *and* her two uncles give her away. Her parents and her first husband were deceased, and she was very close to her first husband's parents as well as her uncles. So the in-laws walked her to one point down the aisle, and the uncles brought her the rest of the way. (See more on going down the aisle in chapter 18).

3. **Having loved ones at the wedding altar.** It is traditional to have the bridal party at the wedding altar with you, or, when it's a tight space, just the best man and maid of honor stand. Yet you don't have to stand on tradition; in fact, you can adapt tradition to suit your needs. At Xiomara and Brian's Hindu-African ceremony, the bride and groom skipped having attendants and instead had the groom's parents and the bride's parents at the altar throughout. This fit in with their theme of honoring their ancestors. When the bride or groom hails from the Jewish tradition, they can honor family and roots with a huppah, a canopy on poles that represents your new home. It can be set up to stand on its own or might involve at least four people to hold the poles. At Dan and Amy's wedding, the groom built a special huppah to honor his bride's heritage. He asked everyone at the wedding to sign it in lieu of a guest book. It was then attached to the poles. With the loving blessings of friends and family just over their heads, this symbolically brought the love of all the people they care for into their marriage and their new home.

4. **Opening or closing with a musical performance by a loved one.** If you have a talented relative who is willing, by all means include a personalized musical offering. At Safia and Kenneth's interfaith and multicultural ceremony, the bride's younger sister opened with a stirring rendition of the Andrew Lloyd Webber's piece *"I'll Go with You."* At Michael and Amanda's ceremony, the groom's sister rocked the house when she ended the ceremony with the soulful sounds of *"I'll Always Love You."* At Mary Anne and Barry's nuptials, the bride's family heritage was honored by having a dear friend sing "Ave Maria" for the processional. When Elizabeth married musician Glenn, they used a beautiful piece of music written by a member of the bridal party. Musical couple Jake and Suzanne had a

friend—a professional recording artist—sing while they walked down and back up the aisle.

5. **Rituals that merge the families.** There are many lovely rituals that can include the family. A sand ceremony that includes parents and/or children of the bride and groom is a creative way to symbolically blend families together. (See more in the chapter on "Choosing Rituals and Rites)."

> • **Unity candles as the common ground.** Unity candles originated with the Christian tradition, yet they also serve to bring light and connection to families of any faith and any culture, who speak any language. Moms usually help light the candles and then take their seats. But if your moms hail from different faiths, or if one or more of them is very religious, it is a nice touch to invite them to offer prayers from their faith traditions or special blessings just before they light the candles. At Martin and Jana's wedding, the bride's mom offered a Hebrew prayer of celebration, and the groom's mom, who was Catholic and hailed from Quebec, offered a Christian blessing in French as part of the candle-lighting ceremony.
>
> • **Family welcoming/rose ceremony.** There is a nondenominational tradition of offering flowers to the moms or to significant family members. Usually, the bride and groom give a red and white rose—colors that represent unity—to each to their moms. It is particularly nice if bride and groom each give one flower to each mom, followed by a hug. This would also be a good time to publicly acknowledge your moms and thank them. Here is the rose ceremony from AnaMaria and José's wedding.

> *As this bride and groom come before us to be married, they wish to acknowledge and thank their families for their love and support. As a gesture of unity between the families that are united on this day, and as an acknowledgement of the special people who have loved and nurtured this bride and groom, they will present a very special gift of flowers to their mothers. (AnaMaria presented to her groom's mother, and José presented to his bride's mom.)*

With these flowers, they welcome each other's families into the new family that is created by their marriage today. These flowers symbolize the love José and AnaMaria feel for each other extended to their loved ones, and they are also symbolic of the merging of two families in love and unity.

• **Ritual blessing from elders.** You can adapt blessings from earth-based traditions and ask your family to participate. At Jackie and Brian's wedding, the four parents of the bride and groom called in the four directions, a Native American custom of praying for blessings from the east, west, north and south. Dawn and Dominick wanted to bring a blessing of elements to their marriage, so they asked their parents to each bring a small item up to the wedding altar that represented the elements—water, air, fire, and earth—as the officiant read a blessing on behalf of each parent.

> OFFICIANT: *Marriage is more than the coming together of two individuals. It is the joining of two families. To honor the family ties that are created by this marriage, and bless the union of their children, the parents of the bride and groom will perform a blessing for new beginnings.*
>
> *I will ask the mother, father, and stepmother of the bride, and the mother and father of the groom to step forward as they are called. They each have a special offering to place on the wedding altar. Let us all join them in blessing this marriage with the elements of our common being, with earth, air, fire and water. (Parents come up one at a time, except for the bride's father and stepmother. After placing item on altar, they stand off to the side.)*
>
> AIR: *The mother of the bride brings a feather that represents air. "We bless this marriage with the element of air, which represents intelligence and spirit. We ask that this union be granted gifts of communication, wisdom, and understanding."*

FIRE: *Father and Stepmother of the bride, please bring a candle that represents fire. "We bless this marriage with the element of fire, which represents illumination and passion. We ask that this union be granted gifts of vitality, passion, and creativity."*

EARTH: *The father of the groom brings a crystal that represents earth. "We bless this marriage with the element of earth, which represents a strong and solid foundation. We ask that this union be granted gifts of stability, strength, and abundance."*

WATER: *The mother of the groom brings a vessel of water. "We bless this marriage with the element of water, which represents the clear and holy spirit of purity. We ask that this union be granted gifts of love, intuition, and trust."*

Thank you, moms and dads. You may all be seated.

6. **Inviting loved ones to offer readings and blessings.** Your officiant can read poems, readings, and blessings that you select, but it is always nice to ask a loved one or two to participate. There are many creative ways to do this. Typically, a wedding will have one or two readings. You can select readings that you love and then consider who you might like to read them; or you can ask people you love and trust to select or write a reading. It can be your siblings, best friends, or the person who introduced you. Here are some of the creative ways couples have asked people to partake in their ceremony.

• **Shared readings.** If you want to keep the number of readings down, you can have two or more people each read a stanza or two. When Jane and Adam married, they invited their three siblings to each read a portion of one poem. They came to the front of the room, read the poem, and then took their seats again.

• **Very personal tributes from friends.** For her wedding to José, AnaMaria asked two close girlfriends to come up with readings. The results were both hysterical and poignant. The bride gave them carte blanche and did not ask to know the content beforehand. One friend, Reshma, told the story of this couple's love like only a friend could. She highlighted how this couple had been best friends for years, when they finally professed their love for each other. Here's an excerpt.

You realized that the One, the guy you've been waiting for, the one who has been waiting for you, is right in front of you. He's your best friend. Why didn't you see him before? He tells you that he's been waiting for you all along, and you're speechless. You are struck mute in your kitchen. He holds out a handful of flowers, and you check your pulse. You cannot move. Your fuzzy slippers might as well be made of concrete. And suddenly, the heavens seem to open up and the opera of "no more dating" rises to a rushing crescendo. You fall back onto your refrigerator door, slide to the floor, cup your hands to your face. And that's it. You came for friendship, but somehow you take away love. It's not a science, and it's not predictable. . . . The rest is history, as they say.

• **The whole gang.** When Jackie and Brian married, they were intent on having their ceremony be a multicultural community event. They had seventeen readers! The way this was accomplished in a ceremony of thirty-five minutes was to give each person just one or two lines. A number of the prayers and blessings were divvied up among participants, who sat in the audience and stood only when it was time to speak, passing the microphone from person to person.

> We had our families and friends call out blessings at the end of our ceremony, right before the pronouncement, so they would all feel included.
>
> —*Annie, who married Alexander on April 3, 1999*

For example, drawing from the Hindu tradition (although neither were Hindu), the final blessing was shared among seven friends.

OFFICIANT: *Culling from the Hindu tradition, where man and woman are married as God and Goddess, we conclude this ceremony with seven blessings. These are adapted from the ancient rite of Satapadi, whereby the bride and groom take seven steps around a ceremonial fire and agree to seven vows that will make their marriage strong. This ritual is said to seal the marriage forever.*

We capture the essence of that soulful commitment in these blessings upon this union. I ask you, Jackie and Brian, to concentrate on these seven blessings as they are spoken and allow them to formulate the foundation of your new life together. The blessings will be offered by seven loved ones.

VICKI: *May this couple be blessed with an abundance of food and comforts, and be helpful to each other in all ways.*

KIM: *May this couple be strong and complement each other.*

PHOEBE: *May this couple be blessed with prosperity.*

DEBBIE: *May this couple be eternally happy.*

ERICA: *May this couple be blessed with a happy family life.*

PAM: *May this couple live in perfect harmony.*

DENISE: *May this couple always be the best of friends.*

OFFICIANT: *Your two lives are now joined in one unbroken circle.*

• **Having a special friend or family member co-officiate.** When Andrea and Patrick married, they wanted the groom's dear friend to play an important role, so they hired a local ordained clergyperson who could write a ceremony, co-officiate, and sign the license. When John and Dana wed, they had their heart set on the bride's father, a deacon, officiating. Since the bride's dad was not authorized to sign the license, they also were able to find a flexible clergyperson who could co-officiate and make the ceremony legal. Jodi and Dennis looked for ways to include *all* their siblings, including having Jodi's brother, an interfaith minister, officiate, along with his wife, also a minister.

7. **Honoring family traditions.** Sometimes it is extremely important to acknowledge your parents and family by honoring your heritage. There are many ways to do this subtly, so that is does not dominate the ceremony.

- **Duplicated readings in different languages.** If the family members of the bride or groom speak different languages, you can translate your favorite reading or scripture into their native tongues and have family members read it. At Stephanie and Javier's wedding, one of the bride's family members read I Corinthians in English; to honor the groom's Costa Rican family, the groom's brother was invited to read the Spanish version.
- **Blending in traditional elements.** Don and Deb wanted a non-religious ceremony, but Deb's parents were devout Buddhists from Vietnam. They were concerned that family members would be insulted if there was not at least a bit of Buddhist tradition included. The bride's mom was invited to step up to the altar and ring a Buddhist chime three times to create a sacred space for the wedding, and the bride's Dad wrote a prayer that the officiant read. Also, a friend read a poem by the Vietnamese monk Thich Nhat Hanh.
- **Blessings from the elders.** It is always quite beautiful if parents or grandparents offer a special blessing and if symbols of family tradition are woven into the wedding. Just before Sophia and Zvonko's ceremony, the mother and father of the bride offered the couple a traditional Ukrainian blessing with a holy icon that belonged to Sophia's paternal grandmother. Several ritual cloths, embroidered by Sophia's relatives in the Ukraine, were used to decorate the altar. The bride and groom stood on one through the ceremony and used another for a hand-wrapping ritual.

7. **Including children.** If you or your beloved come to your new marriage with children in tow, it is important to acknowledge the new family that is

formed on your wedding day. If you have all been together for a while, you might already feel like a family—which is great—so your ceremony can reinforce that. If there are tricky issues with being a stepparent, the ceremony can serve to begin to soften them.

• **Candle lighting.** When Tina married Jim, his two children from his first marriage were going to be living with them part of the time and with their mom the other part of the time. The bride's sons,

My daughter, Juliana, had to be included in the ceremony. We both felt that way. I wanted her to feel like a bride. Juliana escorted me down the aisle, and we met my parents halfway. During the ceremony, she said some brief vows of her own, and Kris and I presented her with a locket. We had a sand ceremony to blend our new family together, and we were pronounced a family at the end of the ceremony. It was the joining of this family that was most important to all three of us.

—*Lori, who married Kris on July 26, 2003*

though older, also still had a relationship with their dad. So Tina and Jim sought to mention the new blended family without negating the kid's relationship to the other parents. They opted for a family unity candle ceremony with a special candelabra :

OFFICIANT: *Ordinarily, we have three candles . . . one for each partner and the one they light together. On this occasion, as a gesture of family unity, we have five candles. The top candle represents the bright light of Tina and Jim's love. The four candles around it represent their children and the new family that they form on this day.*

We ask Janie to please, on behalf of herself and her brother Ryan, light two candles. We now ask Keven, on behalf of himself and his brother Paul, to please light two candles.

It is important to mention here that people who are meant to be together do not always begin *as blood relatives, but they share a common bond that helps them grow into a family. May the lighting of these candles represent the kindling of the divine light within each of you and the joining of a loving family.*

• **Family Medallion.** Kelly and Bill sought to include his daughter Janey in many ways, including with the gift of a family medallion. This involved presenting her with a piece of jewelry as part of the ceremony.

> OFFICIANT: *Bill and Kelly, you have made a special place in each other's hearts, and your love for each other now creates a circle of love that gathers in the whole family, especially Janey.*
>
> *Just as your wedding rings are the gifts you give each other on this day, the family medallion is a special gift you give to your daughter, to show her how much you love her and how happy you are to be a family—together. (The bride and groom give Janey the medallion.)*
>
> *Please look at Janey and repeat after me:*
> > *With this medallion,*
> > *We pledge to you,*
> > *Our love and support.*

• **Vows to the children.** For Patti and Orlander's wedding, it was all about kids—his two daughters and the bride and groom's baby son. The groom's daughters each read poems, such as "The Owl and the Pussy Cat." And Patti made special efforts to offer her love and commitment to the girls, as well as asking them to pledge to nurture their family life together. She did this through vows that they each agreed to.

> OFFICIANT: *In this ceremony, we are joining more than just a man and a woman; we are bringing together a family. So we have some very special vows for Patti and the girls.*

> PATTI'S VOWS TO GIRLS:
> > *Patti, do you promise*
> > *To accept Meagan and Zaena as your own,*
> > *To love and support them,*
> > *To be patient and understanding,*
> > *To watch after their well-being,*

> *To nurture their growth,*
> *and to be there for them always?*

PATTI ANSWERS: *I do*

GIRLS' VOWS TO PATTI:
> *And now, Meagan and Zaena,*
> *Do you promise to love and respect your dad's new wife?*
> *Do you promise to support their marriage and your new family?*
> *Do you promise to accept the responsibility of being their children?*
> *And to encourage them and support them in your new life together?*

THE GIRLS ANSWER: *"We do."*

OFFICIANT: *May you all lovingly keep the sacred promises that have been spoken today.*

• **Special offerings.** When Jill married Paul, the well-being and happiness of their kids was foremost on their mind. They created a unique ceremony that gave starring roles to Paul's eight-year-old twins and Jill's nine-year-old daughter. The kids were the only members of the bridal party. They walked down the aisle, they stood at the altar the whole time, and they all danced back up the aisle together when the ceremony was over. During the ceremony, they lit candles, and Jill's daughter read two very special poems that she had written for the bride and groom. It was a truly unique moment.

9. **Honoring those no longer with us.** There are many poignant ways to do this. You can ask the officant to call for a moment of silence. Have family members (siblings or surviving parents) come up and light a remembrance candle, or light one yourself. Keep flowers on your wedding altar to represent the ones who have passed on. Create a memorial table or some physical remembrance. (At Ally and Jim's wedding, the groom placed the

folded American flag from his dad's coffin on the front-row seat next to his mother; another bride had the wedding picture of her deceased parents on a nearby table.) You can make the remembrance just a moment or two and move on quickly to a more uplifting part of the ceremony, or you can memorialize someone more extensively.

At Deborah and Steven's wedding, the groom honored his mother—who had never met his bride—by coming down the aisle with his two brothers, to a piece of music his brother had written for his mom, followed by the three of them lighting a candle for her. The officiant paid tribute to his mother immediately following the opening prayer, and shared what she was like and how much she was loved. From then on, the ceremony was quite upbeat and funny, so the remembrance did not create sadness—just reflection.

You can also choose a more general remembrance. Here's something your officiant can include at the start of the ceremony:

OFFICIANT: *None of us comes to an important moment like this without the love, support, and nurturing of the special people who help shape us and prepare us for love. We begin with a moment of silence for the souls that have touched this bride and groom, and have brought them to this moment in time.*

Let us remember (speak the names)

(Then hold a moment of silence.)

In loving memory, let us all light a candle in our hearts and our minds. We know on this joyful day that their love continues to live on in our hearts.

And let us also include in our circle of love those who could not physically be here today. Amen.

10. **Including those who cannot be present.** Many brides and grooms these days have to face the reality that some friends and relatives just cannot make it to the wedding. During Summer and Tony's wedding, there

was an acknowledgement of the bride's grandparents, who were unable to travel. Since Monica and Simon came from England to New York to marry, they had only their best friend, along with the bride's sister and father, at their wedding; a candle was lit for all the folks back home who wished them well. One bride and groom made a point of holding a moment of remembrance and prayer for a military friend who had just shipped out to Iraq for active duty.

The idea is to just take a moment at the start of the ceremony in which you symbolically "invite" these loved ones to be part of the ceremony by acknowledging them. When Katerina married Xingmin, her family in the Republic of Yugoslavia and his family in China could not be there, so they arranged for everyone to tune in at the time of their wedding. Here's one way to include loved ones from afar.

The bride and groom would like to begin the ceremony by taking a moment to include those loved ones who could not physically be here. They have asked their families to send good wishes at the hour of their wedding. We light this candle to represent the light and love of their families. Symbolically, the light of the fire acts as witness and brings illumination to the ceremony. (Moment of silence.)

• **Other ways to honor loved ones who are far away.** Warren's Dad couldn't make it to Warren and Kathy's wedding due to illness, so Warren's sister read a prayer his dad had written for the couple. The mother of another groom, Orlander sent along a scriptural verse. Although the wedding was not religious, the couple asked their officiant to read the verse to honor the groom's mom. They sent her the videotape. Sunee and Christopher eloped, but set up a computer remote of their ceremony for friends and family in Sri Lanka and Australia to see.

WEDDING GODDESS VOW

*I will include the ones I love in my wedding in a
very personalized and delightful way.*

PART SIX

The Big Day

BE A GODDESS
ON YOUR WEDDING DAY

Most beloved of the sacraments is the one of marriage. It symbolizes the fulfillment of earth's sweetest dream. Almost any sensitive person can testify to the emergence of power that is broadcast during a marriage ceremony. This force is created by the beauty and intent of the rite itself. The spiritual fusion of two individualities into a duad of love generates an energy and luminosity that reaches even the most impersonal onlooker.

—Rev. Flower Newhouse, from *The Symbolic Meaning of Marriage*

Arlene Sandler/Lensgirl.com

Transforming Jitters to Joy

Your special day has arrived. This is your moment to blossom fully. Gather yourself together, like so many flowers in your bouquet, and take this moment to revel in the delights that surround you. This is a joyous day. Allow yourself to feel the pleasure that is yours.

—Flora, the Roman Goddess of flowers, gardens, and spring, known as "the flourishing one," the embodiment of nature and of the flower of youth

One of the greatest challenges of being a bride is *enjoying it*—nervousness and all.

In the days before the wedding, many brides find themselves in a state of chaos and panic, worried about so many little details that it skews their perspective. They focus so much on the external that they negate and miss the extraordinary and precious internal experience that occurs just before, and on, their wedding days. Inside you a transformation is taking place on a subtle level, unseen if you are bogged down with busyness. It is the start of a powerful, significant initiation. With it comes a host of emotions, yet the experience also brings a very soothing, very natural sense of balance and calm that will wash away the nervousness—if you let it.

Many brides do not realize that freak-

> ## WEDDING GODDESS RULE #17
>
> **A Wedding Goddess embraces all her feelings.**
> You recognize that trying to avoid being nervous is not the peaceful path to the altar. Rather, you do what you can to center yourself, and then embrace all the feelings that arise and let them flow through you. While doing this, you release tension by not resisting it, and you allow for a state of joy.

ing out about how they will look, sound, feel, and be perceived by their guests, or despairing about final details and last-minute glitches, is a way to avoid the deeper feelings of the moment. You're getting married to the man you love. After months of planning a wedding, you are about to enter into a marriage. This is what you've wanted, since you were a little girl perhaps! The moment is here. This is a very big deal in your life, and the very nature of it can stir up big emotions.

The Wedding Goddess understands that in order to fully embrace all the powerful feelings that come with this initiation, as well as embrace the calm that is at its center, she must find a point of stillness within and allow the magic to take over. On your wedding day, you can have an experience of heaven mingling with earth. All you need to do is plant your feet firmly on the ground and open your arms to the winds of heaven. These winds will soothe and comfort you, and they will uplift you.

Remember, when all is said and done, into the arms of the man you love you will go. You may as well start to enjoy the journey now.

How to Embrace Wedding-Day Jitters

The nervous jitters of the wedding day may keep some butterflies fluttering in your stomach and distract you, even if you have prepared for this day in many ways. This is natural. It's all new to you and you feel a little nervous; okay, maybe you feel very nervous. But you don't want to feel *too* nervous. Nor do you want to be detached or numbed of all feelings. The Wedding Goddess aims to embrace it all.

It is important to recognize that on this very significant day, in this amazing moment in time, every emotion of the entire wedding journey may surface—and that's okay. "I tell all brides I work with that on their wedding day, they should expect and prepare for feeling all the emotions that came up during their engagements," says Allison Moir-Smith, a psychotherapist who operates Emotionally Engaged, a counseling service for brides based in Brookline, Massachusetts. "If a bride anticipates that her wedding day will be full of many emotions—the joyful and the difficult—she'll be better prepared to deal with them."

The trick is, you don't want nervousness to overpower your experience. Some brides get nervous and overwrought about their nervousness! Whatever you do, *do not* alter your consciousness by drinking alcohol or taking nonprescription medications. Here are some simple ways to treat yourself to some natural, calming relief and remedies in the days before the wedding and on your wedding day.

I had a natural calm. No details to fuss over other than whether the sunset would be good enough for pictures, which was out of my control. My hair was too curly, but what the hell. I did have the thought: *How could I have done this if we had a big wedding? Or any guest to see my hair so curly?* Seeing him so happy and excited made my nervous thoughts go away.

—*Julie, who married Leonard on July 21, 2003*

1. **Go to sleep with a warm bath, and awaken to a cleansing shower.** Before you go to bed on "W-Day" eve, take a warm, relaxing bath and use a scented candle or aromatherapy oil and wonderful music to help you relax and reflect on the journey you have been on. Tomorrow marks a new start in your life, a grand initiation into the female experience.

2. **Do a little yoga when you rise.** Yoga is the gentle stretching exercise that hails from the Hindu tradition and centers the body and mind. "A few minutes of conscious breathing and stretching can help release the jitters," says Barbara Kizner, Certified Kripalu Yoga Instructor and founder of Imagine YogaWorks in Queens, New York. She suggests these postures:

A. **A simple "Sun Breath."** Stand with feet hip width apart. Just inhale with your arms up, and exhale, putting your arms down. Repeat this several times to help center you, to clear your mind, and to give you a little stretch. Use the inhalation as an opportunity to breathe in relaxation. Use the exhale to release, with a sigh, fears, anxiety, and tension. Allow your heart to expand with joy and excitement.

B. **Do a "Swan Dive."** It's perfect for loosening up on your wedding day, says Kizner.

• Stand with you feet hip width apart, firmly connecting to the earth.

- Tuck in your tailbone just a touch and bring a gentle squeeze to your thighs.
- Acknowledge how your legs are strong and supportive.
- Be sure your shoulders are relaxed, away from your ears.
- Be sure your chest is gently lifted up to the sky, keeping your heart center open and receptive.
- Inhale and bring your arms slowly overhead, breathing through your nostrils.
- Once you've come to the top of the breath, wiggle up out of the waist and exhale through your mouth.
- Bring your arms down slowly, with resistance.
- As if you were gracefully diving down, begin to fold your body.
- Keeping your knees soft, allow your belly to rest on your thighs.
- Stay there for three breaths and notice the nice stretch and release of the lower back. It brings very small gentle movements to your neck and head, loosening up any tension that might have settled in your shoulders.
- Try sighing; it can feel great. With each sigh, release tension, anxiety, and fear.
- Slowly roll your body back up to standing position, allowing your neck and head to come up last.
- Repeat two more times.
- Think of the swan, so graceful and always going with the flow. Also, swans mate for life!

3. **Center yourself.** Before you get dressed, take one last look at yourself in the mirror. Feel your feet firm on the ground—and feel that firmness beneath your feet—and put your hands right under your belly. Kizner explains that the Japanese call that part of the body the "Hara," which means center. Then take a moment to once again feel your feet connected to the earth below, as if you are a tree. Know that the leaves may sway in the wind, but your trunk will stay upright and strong.

4. **Eat light, but eat something.** Although in some religious traditions the bride and groom fast, which is symbolic of starting fresh, consider a light

meal before the ceremony. High-protein foods will fill you up, give you strength, and keep your blood sugar balanced. Stay away from excessive caffeine, sugar, and overeating—which can all make you shaky. For an easy and tasty protein treat, try Goddess Granola. It comes in snack size bags that can easily travel with you.

5. **Stay organized.** It is important to curtail chaos by having a game plan and timeline for the day's events and sticking with it as closely as possible. This should include everything from the time you awaken, shower, and stretch, to getting to the chapel on time, to events in between and at the reception. "Brides tend to be on the planet Zippety Doo-Dah," says New York–based and internationally known makeup artist and hairstylist Filis Forman, who often serves as a beauty coordinator for brides on their wedding day. "If a bride keeps very organized, she will be so much calmer coordinating her day."

6. **Anchor yourself in the love all around you.** Focus on wedding-day bliss and the happiness and joy of the moment. Realize that everyone at your wedding is there to support you, that it is a day when you can do no wrong; everything you say and do, every tear you cry, will be adorable to those who've come to celebrate. Trust and lean into the love you share with your mate and all the love in that room.

7. **Stay present, yet keep your eye on the prize.** When motivation guru Tony Robbins used to do his famous "Coal Walks," leading groups of people barefoot over hot coals, he'd say before they walked: "Think of it as walking on cool moss" and, before you walk, "Imagine how you will celebrate on the other end." Although you want to be present for your ceremony, it is likely that you will feel very uplifted and relieved when you are finally pronounced husband and wife. Think about that moment in time, and celebrate it in your imagination— a beautiful ceremony has united you in marriage and you are walking back up the aisle to applause as Mr. and Mrs., a married couple, months of

> I wasn't really nervous . . . more excited, really. When it comes to handling the stress, you've got to learn to let things go. Don't get so caught up in the small details that you forget to enjoy your special day.
>
> —*Kelly, who married Ron on October 26, 2002*

wedding planning behind you. Allow the anticipation of that fill you with joy. Smile. A smile will help you feel it in your heart.

8. **Give yourself some good energy.** Reiki, pronounced *ray-kee*, is an ancient form of gentle healing that has its roots in the Asian Buddhist tradition. It's a noninvasive natural transfer of energy that promotes well-being, reduces stress, and leaves you feeling rested. There are many Reiki practitioners who offer sessions, and you can also Reiki yourself. "Reiki means 'Universal Energy,'" says, Rev. Vic Fuhrman, MSC, R.M., a Certified Reiki Master. "It is the life force that permeates the Universe and flows through all of us. One need not be a trained Reiki practitioner to enjoy the benefits." He suggests this simple technique, known as "Universal Position," which is effective for wedding-day grounding, centering, reducing stress, and creating a sense of well-being and self-love.

> The bliss is already there . . . bumps are bumps . . . move forward. Anything can happen. A wedding is interactive theatre. You can only set it all up. What happens once the curtain goes up is the magic. As long as the bride and groom are there, that's all that matters."
>
> —*AnaMaria, who married José on January 24, 2004*

• While either sitting, standing, or lying down, simply place one hand over your heart chakra (the center of your chest at heart level) and the other over your solar plexus chakra (just above your navel). Use whichever hand, left or right, feels comfortable in each position.

• With your hands gently over these areas, close your eyes and take several deep breaths to your level of comfort.

• Allowing your breath to return to normal, imagine a loving, gentle, glowing light flowing down from the top of your head through your neck, to your shoulders, and out through your arms to the palms of your hands.

• Visualize that energy circulating through your heart and soul, removing stress and discomfort and leaving you feeling very safe, centered, and loved. Know in this moment that you are loved, perfect, and whole just as you are.

• Dwell in this delightful place for as long as you can, and when you are ready, express gratitude for this gift from the universe and

gratitude to yourself for taking the time to enjoy it—and for knowing that you are worthy to receive it.

• Take a few deep breaths to seal in the benefits, and then release
your hands and open your eyes. You will find yourself refreshed, renewed, and ready for everything the day will bring!

9. **Try a flower essence.** Since flowers are so much a part of the wedding
day, flower essences may offer a natural path to relaxation and peaceful-
ness. One of the most famous brands is Bach Flower Remedies, developed in 1934 by medical doctor and homeopathic physician Dr. Edward
Bach. The sight of water glistening on a flower petal inspired him with
the possibility of extracting the essence of a variety of flowers known to
help with a range of emotional issues. He believed that in order to heal
an imbalance, "a change in outlook, peace of mind, and inner happiness
is needed," says Connie Barrett, flower essence practitioner, teacher and
coproprietor of Beyond the Rainbow, at www.rainbowcrystal.com.
"Flower essences are generally recommended on the basis of individual
personalities, and they work in a subtle way to dissolve emotional
blockages." Remedies can be taken a few drops at a time, under the
tongue, or rubbed onto the skin. While Barrett suggests that each bride
consult with a flower essence specialist to see which essences are most
suited to her, she says the following are some of the common issues
related to wedding-day stress that might be alleviated with specific
flower essences.

Rescue Remedy: the all-purpose emergency remedy.

Larch: for the bride who lacks self-esteem or feels insecure.

Walnut: for easing the transition from a single to a married state.

Beech: for the bride who is excessively critical of her spouse, her
future in-laws, the job her caterers have done, etc.

Honeysuckle: for those who look nostalgically back at their
blissful, single state.

Aspen: for the bride who has vague but troubling fears about
getting married.

Centaury: for the bride who lets others make the major decisions
about the wedding and thereafter.

Vine: for the need to be in charge of every aspect of preparation.

Elm: for a state of feeling overwhelmed and unable to do what's necessary.

9. **Aromatherapy—how sweet it is.** Special healing scents can bring a lot of lightness to your wedding day. Polarity Wellness Educator Michael Edan, RPP, of Healing Touch Services offers a special bridal blend of essential oils called Essential Wedding. It combines soothing, calming, and uplifting scents that are empowering for you and your female attendants—Ylang Ylang, Lavender, Geranium, Bergamont, Neroli, and some secret ingredients. He also consults with brides on how they can create their own wedding-day aromatherapy signature blends using several scents.

If you would like to try one or two scents on your own, he suggests that you seek therapeutic-grade oils, which have the greatest purity and distillation process (Young Living Oils is a reputable company that offers wonderful oils and a powerful diffuser for the oils; see chapter 2). You can take a bath with five to seven drops of oil in the bathwater (adding fresh flowers, soft candles, and music is always a nice touch) or diffuse the oils into the air while you are getting ready, once you arrive at the wedding venue, or even at the wedding altar. You can also wear a scent as perfume or carry the scent on a tissue or hankie. Here are Edan's picks for calming wedding-day jitters.

- **Lavender:** Probably the most universally used oil. It has been clinically evaluated for its relaxing effects. It is useful for a broad range of physical, emotional, and mental concerns. Its benefits for skin care have long been recognized. There are various lavender oils to choose from. Tasmania Lavender is particularly exquisite to smell.

- **Geranium:** Has been used for centuries for skin care, and it is excellent for skin conditions and hormone imbalances (so if you get hives or have PMS, this is for you!). It's both sedative and uplifting. Its fragrance is floral and refreshing. It is a gentle stimulant of the adrenal cortex, whose hormones are essentially regulating and balancing in nature.

- **Bergamont:** Comes from the rind of a fruit that grows in Italy, and is one of the most widely used essences in the perfume industry. The scent is sweet and citrus-like, but it has a warm, floral quality and is truly unique. The scent and effect can be very uplifting, which is why it is often used as an antidepressant.

• **Neroli (Orange Blossom):** This is one of the most exquisite and distinctive scents to inhale. Orange blossom has been a sacred wedding flower in many cultures—Queen Victoria wore them in her hair on her wedding day, and the Chinese cultures believe them to bring great luck. Neroli was apparently loved by the Egyptian people for its great attributes of healing the mind, body, and spirit. It is very helpful with anxiety, depression, digestive spasms, fear, headaches, hysteria, insomnia, nervous tension, PMS, stress-related conditions, and skin care in general. This is a "high-end" essential oil, meaning it is expensive, but it's worth it. It blends particularly well with bergamot.

• **Ylang-ylang:** It means "flower of flowers," and has been used in Asian cultures to cover the beds of newlywed couples on their wedding night. The scent is exotic, rich, and sweet, and it blends well with other oils. Its effect on the nervous system is euphoric and sedative. It reduces tension and anxiety and is also used as an aphrodisiac. It may help to balance male-female energies for greater spiritual attunement. (Your groom will love it, too!)

Wedding Goddess Exercise

YOUR IDEAL WEDDING DAY: A MEDITATION FOR W-DAY EVE

*T*he night before your wedding, try to take some time out *alone* to do this meditation.

Set the mood. Light two candles—one for him, and one for you. This will symbolically bring the light of grace to your experience and illuminate your path to the altar.

Include *everything*. If you truly want a soulful wedding experience, see it in your mind's eye. Be as specific as you can, and include details on the physical, emotional, and spiritual (and any other) dimensions of the experience.

Open with an empowering affirmation. Meditation begins with this positive affirmation in the present tense: "I am ready, now, to marry my beloved. I am cherished, loved, honored, and adored by the man of my dreams. I am beautiful, graceful, confident, and radiant."

Now reflect on these points. Give each of the following points some time, visualizing and "feeling the responses" when possible.

1. See yourself beginning that walk down the aisle. Hear the processional music, and let it move you along. How does it feel to be so beautiful, so graceful, so confident, so radiant?

2. Imagine how secure you feel, holding your dad's arm (or however you will be walking and whomever you will be walking with), walking down that aisle—beautiful, graceful, confident, radiant.

3. See the smiling faces of the people you love most in the world. They are there for you, feeling love for you, sending love to you, filling the room with love and good energy. How does it feel to be surrounded by such good energy and love as you walk down that aisle feeling beautiful, graceful, confident, and radiant?

4. How does it feel to receive the loving attention of others? All eyes are on you, yet those eyes are filled with love and hope and joy. They look at you and see a woman who is beautiful, graceful, confident, and radiant— a Wedding Goddess!

5. Now begin to get closer to him—your beloved. Look at him. He is so handsome and beautiful. He is so filled with love for you, and you are so filled with love for him. This is the man you have chosen and who has chosen you. Look at the way he looks at you—such love in his eyes. He is blown away at the site of his bride. How do you feel as the man you love looks at you, takes you in with his eyes, loves you with his eyes. He sees his beloved, beautiful, graceful, confident, and radiant. He sees his Wedding Goddess coming to him.

6. You are at the wedding altar now, the altar of your hopes and dreams. He steps forward to greet you. You kiss your dad. He and your father hug, and then you are all his, at the altar together, ready to express your love. You are holding hands now: Feel the joy, feel the love, feel the promise of

the moment, let the love fill you heart and soul, and let the energy take you. You feel it all, and you feel so beautiful, graceful, confident, and radiant.

7. The music has stopped now, and so has the rest of the world. It is that moment when time stands still because you are the only place you want to be. You are with your true love; he is with you. You stand in awe of the moment—a good awe, a great awe, an awe that allows you to feel the power of the commitment you will make today. As you stand there, you feel you are firm on the ground. You feel the earth beneath you. You are centered, clearheaded, congruent, present, there. *So right there*. And he is right next to you. You are so beautiful, graceful, confident, and radiant.

8. The officiant begins to speak. You hear. You listen. You know these are the words that unite you in holy, sacred, amazing matrimony, yet your eyes are on your groom. You devour each other with eyes that kiss and reach out into each other's souls. You are so close that you begin to breathe in harmony and you both feel it—that feeling of "I am in you and you are in me," that oneness, that coming together of two hearts, two souls, two lives. Can you embrace this new feeling, and through it, can you feel your beautiful heart, your graceful heart, your confident heart, your radiant heart connecting to the man you love? Can you embrace it now?

9. Something wonderful is rushing over you. Can you feel your heart opening? Can you feel your soul expanding? Can you feel the doors of the heavens opening because you are professing your love to each other and making it known to all the people you care for and to the entire world? Something is lifting you both higher and higher and higher in a bubble of love. It's the most amazing feeling in the world—so safe and so delightful.

10. Feel how it feels to be so loved—loved by those who are there to support you, loved by your bridal party, loved by your beloved. How does it feel to be loved by him? How does *he* feel to be loved by you? What's it like to be so in love?

11. What does love smell like to you? What does he smell like as you stand together, hearts entwined? What does your own skin smell like? What scents fill the air?

12. What does love sound like to you? The rhythmic beating of his heart, and yours, in harmony? The soft sound of his breath and yours? The sounds of quiet all around you?

13. What do you sense about life, about yourself, about your relationship, when you are in this state? Where does the journey take you? Deeper into your heart? To a place of the awakening of love, where the world feels so delicious and you feel so overwhelmingly wonderful?

14. Now you are being pronounced husband and wife. What is the kiss like? How does your mouth feel? How does his mouth feel on yours? Is there anything you want more than to be here, in this moment, with the one you love? How open can you be? How intimate do you truly want to be? How much do you want to give? How much do you want to receive? Feel the energy that runs between you, from your heart to his, and surrounding your both.

15. And now you are married. Mr. and Mrs., God and Goddess, enraptured in Divine Love. Hooray! Relief! Celebrate! Your heart leaps with joy as you walk back up the aisle as husband and wife. Finally! You are so happy, so beautiful, so graceful, so confident, so radiant, so loved—so married!

Close with this affirmation. Say it out loud and give it energy and life. "I am beautiful, I am graceful, I am confident, I am radiant, I am loved."

Go to sleep right after this meditation, and awake refreshed. This can raise your energy so that you begin to lift yourself into your wedding vision and live it more fully. Also, send your wishes out to the universe, asking for support in gracefully experiencing *all* the fullness of your big day. You might even want to make a list of things that you hope for, and sleep with it under your pillow.

WEDDING GODDESS VOW

I am beautiful, I am graceful,
I am confident, I am radiant, I am loved.

Arlene Sandler/Lensgirl.com

CHAPTER EIGHTEEN

The Walk Down the Aisle

Just as winter turns to spring, you'll change from bride-to-be to married woman. Spring is the time when the length of day equals the length of night. This is symbolic of the Goddess meeting her God. Today you are both renewed as you merge as one at the altar of your love.

—Eostre, the Germanic Goddess of springtime,
who brings new beginnings and fresh starts

*S*ymbolically, life as it once was ends and new life begins as the bride comes down the aisle. This one short walk may seem longer than it really is, because it brings you from your life, up until that moment in time, to what will hopefully be the longest part of your life history.

This is the part of the wedding that is *all about the bride*. The other people in the processional serve to lead the way for your entrance—the entrance that everyone in attendance is eagerly awaiting. This is your moment to shine. You may be wondering; *How will I handle it if I have quivering lips and cheeks twitching with tension? Should I greet the eyes of my guests or look straight ahead? How can I be sure I will not fall or step on my train or trip over my vows?* There are a million concerns that may run through your

I was ecstatic! I was so happy and excited when I got to the front of the room that I started jumping up and down with joy! I was overjoyed to be looking at this man who I love so much and who loves me so much. I couldn't believe how wonderfully gleeful I was at that moment. I couldn't have imagined a more perfect feeling than the moment that I took his hand. We were ready, we had made it, we were getting married.

—*Laura, who married Erez on July 11, 2003*

> ## WEDDING GODDESS
> ## RULE #18
>
> **A Wedding Goddess is graceful.**
>
> You acknowledge your nervousness and your elation, and no matter what emotions arise on the wedding day, you are radiant. You feel yourself *inside your body*, centered and grounded, and you walk like a Goddess. You walk down that aisle in a state of grace and claim your place as the bride you have dreamed of being.

mind. You've got to just let them run through your mind and walk on. If you focus on those worries, you will give them power and you'll miss out on the glorious experience of walking down the aisle. A Wedding Goddess knows that her greatest gift awaits her on the other end of the aisle—and *he* will be there to hold your hand if you get a little shaky.

As you walk down the aisle, you are embarking on the ultimate rite of passage, the big moment in time when you join the special sorority of *married women*. It is a big club, and many women have come before you, paving the way for you to be a beautiful, lovely bride of your own making. Prepare for this moment the best you can by organizing your processional and ceremony logistics, and by familiarizing yourself with the lay of the land before the big day!

How to Walk Down the Aisle Like a Goddess

When you walk down the aisle on your wedding day, everyone's attention will be on you. But it is the most adoring, nonjudgmental attention you can imagine. In the eyes of all who love you and who have come to celebrate your big day, *you are a Goddess*. The moment you enter the chapel or ceremony site, you will be uplifted and awed by the presence of love. It will make your walk so much easier.

People await the entrance of a bride the way they look forward to a movie star stepping onto the red carpet at a premiere. They will admire you and won't be able to take their eyes off you because you will be so radiant. In order to be as natural and comfortable as possible, make advance preparations that will allow this experience to be smooth and joyful.

1. **Pick music that truly inspires you.** Beautiful, heart-opening music is the hallmark of the wedding procession. Usually there is music played for the "rites of gathering," as people begin to come in and take seats. Then, to signal the start of the ceremony, there is a piece of music for the bridal party and a special selection for the bride. The days of piped-in organ music are gone, and these days brides hire string quartets, classical guitarists, pianists, or have a DJ play the music their way. Some couples just use a technically adept friend with a boom box. Lovely and soul-stirring choices for music, selected by Wedding Goddesses who truly wanted to be surrounded by the right sound for them, include: the classic and quite beautiful Pachelbel's "Canon in D", "Prayer" by Celine Dion, "She" by Elvis Costello, "At Last" by Etta James, "I'll Cover You" (the slow version) from the soundtrack of *Rent*, and "Stairway to Heaven" by Led Zeppelin. You can pick any music that inspires and uplifts you!

> I was overcome by joy—on the brink of tears—and as I made the walk, escorted by my mother and father, I looked into my fiancé's eyes and soaked it all up. I remember being startled that everyone stood for me and giggled a bit at the thought. The moment I took my fiancé's hand, I knew everything was as it should be and that I was going to hold it together.
>
> —*Summer, who married Tony on September 20, 2003*

2. **Organize your wedding processional long before the wedding day.** The procession and who is in it is of great concern to most brides—they aren't sure who to include, and sometimes they feel they must include everyone, lest anyone feel left out. There is a "traditional" form, and also many alternatives. The first step is to figure out who will be in your processional and how you want to organize it. Think of it this way: Who would you like to pave your way on your big day? The following are some things to consider.

- **Have an awareness of the typical setup.** In a traditional processional, the lineup goes something like this: the officiant leads or comes in from the side door, the groom and best man follow, the ring bearer trails behind, and then the groomsmen come down the aisle in pairs with the bridesmaids. Then the maid of honor walks down. The bride's runner is rolled down the aisle, and the flower girl walks down first, symbolically paving the bride's way with the purity of her youth and the flowers she tosses. Then the bride walks with her dad. However, outside of a house of worship, you are free to "tweak" tradition. The only thing you might not want to tweak is saving the best for last—the bride!

• **Find out if your groom wants to walk down the aisle, too.** Or would he rather just take his place there and await you? The sight of the groom, standing by the altar, awaiting his beloved, is classic. He and his best man can get in place, and the other groomsmen can escort the bridesmaids. Or you can send all the men to the altar before the procession. That is what Summer did when she married Tony. Her seven bridesmaids walked single file, each holding a candle in an old-fashioned holder, paving her way with light.

> I opted to organize the processional as is done in a traditional Ukrainian wedding—the bride and groom walk down the aisle together. I was adamant about not being "given away" to my groom. The walk down the aisle was wonderful— a beautiful sunset, the New York City skyline in front of us, and my best friend by my side.
>
> —*Sophia, who married Zvonko on October 11, 2003*

• **Consider any traditions you might want to honor.** African American weddings sometimes include traditional African dancers and drummers who come down the aisle before the wedding party. In Thailand, three exotically dressed female dancers wind their way down the aisle. In the Orthodox Jewish tradition, the groom is walked by both of his parents as the first in the processional; the bride, who comes last, is also is escorted by both of her parents. In some aspects of the Eastern Orthodox tradition, both bride and groom walk together with the priest.

• **Decide whether you will have little ones in the processional.** At Suzanne and Jake's wedding, the nine flower girls in different sizes, with their fairy wings, were a big hit. It really set forth the energy of playfulness, purity, and innocence, and started the wedding off with humor because they all sort of went off in their own directions.

3. **Consider how, and with whom, you want to enter.** The processional has an inherent poignancy and drama to it. You can choose exactly how

you would like it to flow. And you can set it up in a way in which you feel most comfortable and supported, which could mean coming down the aisle in a traditional way or adapting tradition so it fits your style. Here's how some couples—including those I have officiated for—have done it:

• **Being "given away."** It is tradition that the bride is usually walked, or "presented," to the groom. This comes from the days when women were considered property of their fathers, and when marriages were arranged, and it was the dad's responsibility to literally give his daughter away. The walk down the aisle symbolized leaving your father's home and going to your groom's home and family. Despite the roots of the tradition, even the most untraditional Wedding Goddesses continue to enjoy following that form, or some aspect of it. Many brides today ask both parents to "escort" them down the aisle. It takes the charge off of the idea of being "given away," and it gives brides a chance to include and honor their moms. Even if your parents are divorced, it is still appropriate to ask them to walk with you. When Jane married Adam, she didn't want to choose between her father and her stepfather, so she had both of them walk her. Joanie had her thirteen-year-old son walk her down the aisle when she married Paul. When Lori married Kris, she came down the aisle with her nine-year-old daughter, who was donned in a matching dress and flower garland in her hair. It was quite a stirring sight to see them escort each other, but they did not completely forsake tradition. The two then met Lori's parents at the foot of the altar, and the parents escorted them both to the groom.

• **Giving yourself away.** Some modern brides, especially those who've taken the walk before, like the idea of making a solo journey down the aisle. They feel they are independent women and want to reflect that in their walk to the altar. Some brides do it because their dads can't be there. When Elizabeth married Ross, she decided to walk down the aisle herself because her father had passed away and she did not feel she wanted to replace him. At the same time, she was concerned about being nervous and a little lonely. The solution: Ross met her halfway and walked her to the wedding altar. This kept her company and also symbolized a wedding of equals, meeting each other halfway. Some brides don't even come down an aisle.

"I did not walk down the aisle," says psychotherapist, interfaith minister, and recent bride Susan Turchin. "It was my nontraditional, non-compromise. We greeted our guests at the door, and when it was time for the ceremony, we all proceeded outside together. Bob, myself, and our rabbi and huppah holders went to the front, and everyone else sat down."

- **The balance of partners.** The walk down the aisle is a rite of passage that is an initiation into the deeper rites of womanhood through partnership with your complement, teammate, and true love. Some couples like to consider the bride as a Goddess coming forth to join her God or Hero. In Hindu ceremonies, the bride and groom literally come to sit on throne-like chairs and are considered Lakshmi, Goddess of fortune and beauty, and her consort, Vishnu, and they are treated like divine beings in human bodies on that day. In Ukrainian ceremonies, the bride and groom walk down the aisle together to symbolize their equality in the marriage. In Celtic handfasting ceremonies, the bride and groom often walk from different directions and merge at the altar; the ceremony is conducted in a circle, where they are surrounded by the love of friends and family.

4. **Make sure all the logistics work for you.** For a large wedding, you will generally walk down a center aisle of theatre-style seating, with chairs on either side. You can choose to be a little more intimate, or creative, with the logistics. Set it up in a way that you feel most comfortable and supported.

- **Gather around.** Jodie and Andrew married in a garden with a beautiful fountain. There were no chairs, save for two benches made available to any elderly or pregnant guests. Most people gathered as close as they could to the wedding altar, surrounding the bride and groom with a bubble of love.
- **Coming home.** Monica and Joshua had nine of their siblings, cousins, and friends hold a huppah made of sari material and held by four bamboo poles and five long ribbons. In the Jewish tradition, the huppah represents the new home of the bride and groom. The intimate participation of the nine huppah holders made the bride feel that she was being welcomed by representatives of both families, and of both their lives.

- **Wedding in the round.** Monica and Simon together spread out a circle of rose petals and then stepped into it together, representing a joint effort to surround themselves and their marriage with protection, beauty, and love. At Patty and Orlander's wedding, the couple and their three kids stood together surrounded by a circle of family and friends. The circle has always represented unity, togetherness, and eternity. It's also believed that the circle can better contain the energy of love.

- **Face-to-face.** Whether in a circle or theatre-style, it's nice if the couple faces each other so all can see them (and it's best for the wedding pictures!) or if they face the guests. Many clergypeople are willing to stand with their backs to the audience or off to the side so the couple can be viewed easily. At Len and Alice's wedding, the bride and groom stood where the minister would typically stand and were able to enjoy gazing out on their loved ones and seeing all their beaming faces.

5. **Have a wedding rehearsal.** No matter how you choose to set up your processional and logistics, it is always a good idea to have your officiant and everyone in the wedding party do a run-through of the processional a day or so prior to the wedding date. (The night of your rehearsal dinner, a different time, or even the day of the wedding will do, if you and your beloved will be seeing each other before the ceremony.) Even though getting down the aisle may be a no-brainer for all your experienced attendants, you (and they) will feel better knowing exactly how it will go on the big day. There are subtle wedding-day logistics—such as where exactly you will stand, how close you will be together (as close as is comfortable!), what to do with your flowers during the ring exchange—that are best answered and resolved at a rehearsal. On the wedding day, there is always bound to be a little tension and nervousness, and the brain is not functioning in a normal way. Preparing for the processional in a very organized and clear way will make your walk all the easier. You will also feel more comfortable about what will be happening during the ceremony. "We didn't have a rehearsal ahead of time, so when I finally made it to the altar, I wasn't sure where I needed to stand and if I could hold Michael's hand," says Sharon. "I would suggest that everyone do at least one dry run beforehand so that any questions you have—such as can I hold his hand?—

can be addressed." (Of course you can hold hands, and should, but sometimes you just don't think of these things unless you can run them by your officiant in rehearsal.)

6. **Embracing the emotions of the moment.** Allison Moir-Smith, M.A., a psychotherapist who runs Emotionally Engaged, a premarital counseling service in Brookline, Massachusetts, says it is unfair to suggest that a bride *not* be nervous during that walk down the aisle. "There are many reasons why," she points out, including the following.

- It is one of the big moments of life.
- It is a grand entrance.
- It is silent.
- It is ceremonial—guests stand to honor you.
- It is transformative: It marks the ending of one life and the beginning of another.
- It is sad—just look at your dad.
- It is happy—just look at your husband-to-be.
- It is epic and ancient—think of the millions of brides through the ages who have walked this walk before you.
- It is the most photographed walk of your life.
- It is life-changing and profound.

"The tension is *supposed* to build, so don't fight it," she suggests. "In fact, do the opposite: invite the nervousness and tension to accompany you during your walk." This worked for Allison and her bridal party at her own wedding. "Before we walked down the aisle, I gathered my maid of honor and flower girls in a huddle and said, 'Listen, we're all supposed to be nervous. I'm about to change my life in a huge way, and you guys are picking up on my feelings, kind of feeling some of my feelings for me. Plus, you're all walking alone, with all eyes on you—that's stressful! So it's appropriate to be nervous. Let's not fight it; let's let ourselves be nervous.'" She says that

> At the beginning I thought, *Don't trip and make a spectacle of yourself falling down.* But after a few seconds I felt wonderful. He was standing there, looking so handsome and happy, and I just thought, *I want him—us—to be happy all our lives. I love him so much.*
>
> —*Katerina, who married Xingmin on January 6, 2000*

once she gave in to the nerves, anxiety, and jitters, the uneasiness in the pit of her stomach was gone and the butterflies had disappeared. She was ready.

Wedding Goddess Exercise

For a smooth walk down the aisle:

1. **Handle logistics in advance.** Make sure your attendants, the venue, and the photographer know your game plan and have a timeline for the wedding. Attendants should be standing right at the ceremony site at least fifteen minutes before the ceremony is scheduled to start. The venue should have processional support to help round up everyone in the bridal party and line them up. If they don't, assign this task to a friend or family member, and ask your officiant to help line everyone up. You don't want to be hunting down a flower girl—or your groom, for that matter—at the last minute.

2. **Take a few minutes to yourself.** Leave yourself time on your wedding day to have a few moments to cool out and breathe right before your processional. This means that if you are taking photos, stop at least a half-hour before "showtime." If you are chatting with guests, that's the time to stop. Go to the bathroom, fix your makeup and hair, take care of last-minute self-care, and then sit quietly by yourself and breathe. If you are seeing your groom before the ceremony, spend a few moments with him, and then take your leave for a moment alone.

3. **Ground yourself.** As you get ready to take your walk, stand for a moment, hands on your belly, and feel your feet firmly planted on the ground, the strong earth beneath you. Imagine you are as strong as a tree yet as flexible as the branches and leaves that blow in the wind. When you feel centered, it is time to walk.

4. **Remember the gift at the end of the aisle.** If you feel confused at any time or concerned that your lips are quivering as you try to smile, or wor-

ried that you seem too stiff or are walking too fast, or wondering if you will be so overwhelmed by the attention that you will falter, just look up and he'll be there. Every bride says that nervousness subsided when she realized that true love awaited her, and when she saw that love in the eyes of her husband-to-be as he awaited her at the wedding altar.

5. **Take these words to heart.** This truly can be the happiest moment of your life! Savor it.

WEDDING GODDESS VOW

I will flow down the aisle with the grace and confidence of a Goddess . . .
because I am a Goddess.

Arlene Sandler/Lensgirl.com

CHAPTER NINETEEN

Understanding the Nature of Wedding La-La Land

Your Precious Moments at the Altar

Call upon the divine feminine energy that dwells within and allow yourself to feel fully connected to the moment. You are standing in the dwelling place of Love. Let Love's blessing in. Let Love lift you to the highest state of wedded bliss.

—The Shekinah, considered the indwelling presence of God in the
Hebrew tradition, seen as the "bride of God," the feminine soul
that merges with Him to become one

*I*n the days before the wedding, it is not uncommon to find yourself pulled into a wedding fog, where part of you feels as if it is someplace else. By the time you get ready to walk down the aisle, until after you are pronounced husband and wife, things may seem somewhat surreal.

Some brides feel they are being escorted to the altar by an energy much larger than themselves. They feel oddly safe. They may experience a wild array of emotions and behaviors—giggling, crying, nervousness, shakiness—yet simultaneously, they feel an amazing calm. This is all completely natural.

While making your approach to the altar, and while standing there, you are literally in an altered state of mind: Wedding La-La Land. It is as if you and your beloved are surrounded by a protective bubble, or encircled by a ring of light, and you are uplifted by a rare, extraordinary energy. The energy is love: Your love, the love of all those who came to witness your ceremony and who surround you with their open hearts, and divine love.

Whenever two people come together in the space of love, whether they consider themselves spiritual or not, there is a spirit of love that fills their wedding place with a holy presence. The Wedding Goddess knows this is an extraordinary moment in time—a moment meant to be fully experienced, embraced, and cherished.

How to Surrender to Wedding La-La Land

*T*here is an extraordinary energy that becomes available when two people in love literally step up to commit themselves to sacred union. Whether in a traditional religious setting or in the most offbeat of venues, a holy temple can be created *anywhere* love is present.

All wedding ceremonies have a rhythm, and a life, of their own. The energy begins to percolate as the processional starts, it comes alive as the bride makes her silent walk to the altar, and it builds like a symphony with each segment of the ceremony. There is a unique anticipation that fills the hearts of every bride and groom, and the hearts of those who come to witness their sacred union. While it has been experienced by so many people in love throughout the ages, it is a moment in time that is unique unto itself. Your wedding-ceremony experience will be your unique moment in time!

Because it is so soulful and so profound, it is not uncommon to feel as if you are being pulled along, even when you are feeling focused and calm. It just sort of takes you on a journey, one that just keeps flowing and getting better with each moment. The world seems to disappear, and all the people seem to fade, and you two engage fully in the experience of *getting married.* The Wedding Goddess and her beloved can seize this opportunity to unite not just their hearts, lives, and families, but to unite their very beings.

From the moment you two set eyes on each other at the altar, it is as if your souls connect and you both begin to gently swirl in a slow, steady ascension into a higher state of love. It is important that you surrender to this sacred moment in a profound and meaningful way. Just go with it, wherever it takes you. By the time your vows or "I do's" are exchanged, it will feel as if the universe has cracked open its heart to you and is embracing you. Once you reach the kiss, it is as if the

> I remember standing under the huppah, which was a sheer white fabric held up by birch branches. The sun was filtering through the trees. I heard birds chirping and the wind slightly rustling the leaves. And I remember thinking that I wanted to take it all in, breathe it all, not to miss a single magical moment. It was an otherworldly experience. Absolutely everything was magical and perfect.
>
> —*Arielle, who married Brian on August 9, 1998*

heavens are raining love on the gathering. There is a sense of pure joy in the air. You both are so open-hearted in this moment that you feel as though you can hug the whole world.

The dynamics of Wedding La-La Land. It kicks in a few days before, when life feels slightly out of balance, and it comes on full-fledged just before the wedding. You feel, in some ways, as if you are outside of yourself, and yet present. Your focus seems very specific, yet your mind wanders. This is because your soul is already being called to spiritually get ready for your wedding day, and sometimes your soul has to grapple with your personality, which is still so busy with little details. Part of you is already there, at the altar of your love. So when you walk down the aisle and join the man you love, you are also rejoining a part of yourself. You will get the feeling that "this is where I am meant to be" at that moment in time. You will both get that feeling as spirit steps in and lifts your two hearts and souls toward the heavens and weaves them into each other in love. When the ceremony is over, you will feel a major release. It is the letting go of tension and unexpressed excitement, and letting loose for the big celebration. You are now married, joined. You said I do—and so now that part is done!

Trusting what is. Many emotions will emerge. Some brides are very nervous about crying; they worry that they will fall apart. Yet the emotions that emerge on

> As I walked down the aisle, I thought, *Wow, this is my life. I've done good.* When I saw him there, he looked amazing—and nervous. When the ceremony began, I felt very focused and very happy. I radiated happiness. I felt beautiful inside and out. We cried a little. We both felt that wave of big emotions. I let myself feel everything.
>
> —*AnaMaria, who married José on January 24, 2004*

> You'd better believe I cried. I tried not to, but tears of joy are a wonderful thing.
>
> —*Kelly, who married Ron on October 26*

the wedding day are like the weather—you cannot control them. They emerge from deep within. They flow naturally from your open heart. They are stimulated by the love that fills the air that day. Allow yourself to feel safe enough to express yourself freely that day, and don't worry that you will fall apart. You will not fall apart. But you may feel emotions rise from the pit of your stomach, the depths of your heart. Some will be followed by tears. Let them flow.

Resist and they will persist. When you try to choke back emotion or squinch back tears during your ceremony, it is like cutting off your circulation. Your emotions will come from such a deep, primal place that day—and trying to cut them off only makes them stronger. Once you release them, it is like a tremendous release of energy. So it might mean that you cry for a moment and then it passes. Or there could be a lot of waterworks. Many brides say their most beautiful wedding pictures are the ones of them when they are teary-eyed, because the shots are so honest. Others say the weirdest shots are of how their faces scrunched up when they tried to hold back tears. Underneath all the emotions of the ceremony is an extraordinary, huge, uplifting energy just waiting to carry you away. A unique euphoric feeling takes over as the ceremony ends and the wedding celebration begins.

Spreading the love. As Kahlil Gibran writes in *Spirit Brides,* "The oneness of each of them was a pair of lips declaring their unity, an ear listening to the revelations of their love, and an eye dazzled by the splendor of happiness." You two are *so* open-hearted as you stand there in the embrace of your love, you are essentially sitting on a love volcano. An open heart means you've let down your defenses and your shields so love can come in and be expressed. Make this energy available to everyone at your wedding—and beyond. When the room fills with love—yours and your guests'—it will just keep multiplying itself. During the course of the day, take a moment to send a prayer out to the world—to all those who need some love and all places bereft of love. This energy is powerful on your wedding day. Share it with the world.

Wedding Goddess Exercises

*A*dvance and practical preparation will allow you to get lost in Wedding La-La Land and fully enjoy the spirit of the moment.

1. **Decide how you will *be* with each other.** Knowing, in advance, where you will stand and how close together you want to be will help you both feel more comfortable at the altar. During your wedding rehearsal, or even at home, practice standing there together, and decide what feels natural. People of different cultures and personalities have different ideas about what they are "supposed to do" at the altar. Many of us have seen so many weddings where bride and groom stood with their backs to the audience, seeming stiff as boards. A Wedding Goddess doesn't have to adhere to formal etiquette, yet you may not know what is appropriate for you personally. Ask yourselves these questions:

• Do you want to face each other the whole time and look at each other, or will you be more comfortable looking at your officiant for part of the time and at each other during certain parts, such as the vows, "I do's" and the pronouncement?

• Do you want to hold hands? One hand or both? Or do you want to link arms and huddle close together, leaning into each other?

• How close do you want to stand; what will be most comfortable?

• How do you feel about kissing each other before the big kiss at the end? Some couples can't help themselves from sneaking a few, because it's natural.

If you put a tad of time into assessing your most comfortable stance at the altar, you can just flow right into it when you arrive

> I had a mixture of feelings running through my head. I felt delighted and empowered by the words of the minister. I was thankful for the activities in the ceremony with specific actions. When Michael and I read our vows to each other and he couldn't speak, that was a huge moment of "we are perfect together." I knew I would have a hard time getting the words out, and when he did, too, it was the biggest comfort to know he felt the same way. I was taking deep breaths to help him through his vows. I was smiling, laughing, and crying, and was relieved when it was complete.
>
> —*Sharon, who married Michael on March 20, 2004*

there on your wedding day, and you will avoid any awkward feelings, such as, "How am I supposed to stand and be up here?"

2. **Anticipate your marks and camera angles.** In movies and TV, the actors have marks they must stand on. The marks let them know exactly how to stand for the best camera angle. Wedding photos are always important—whether they are shot by friends or top photographers. Give some thought to the kinds of ceremony photos you want, and make arrangements for them in advance so you do not have to think of them when you are in the moment of your ceremony. Once you decide where you will stand and how you will stand there together, give directions to photographers and videographers in advance. Make sure the photographers know which rituals and special moments will be in the ceremony, and make sure your clergyperson approves and is aware of the arrangements for how these shots will be taken. (It's good if clergypeople and photographers chat just prior to the ceremony.)

3. **Take care of creature comforts.** Remove or arrange for any physical barriers or issues before the ceremony begins.
- Visit the bathroom.
- Make sure you have your glasses or contacts on.
- Do a last hair and makeup check so you are not distracted with "Do I look alright?" worries.
- Make sure you are warm enough (outdoor brides should always have a small jacket or shawl, just in case).
- Make sure your dress and veil are organized and that your maid of honor or a helper is standing by to do any necessary "fluffing" or arranging of the dress at the altar.
- Give your bouquet to an attendant or rest it on the altar so you don't have to worry about holding it during the ceremony.
- If you are going to speak your vows into a microphone, make sure it is logistically arranged beforehand and ready to go.

Ultimately, when the moment arrives, you will forget you have to go to the bathroom and the love will truly warm you, but it is always a good idea to take care of your needs or arrange for them before the ceremony begins.

4. **Let your mind be free.** If you can avoid it, don't try to memorize anything for your ceremony. Put your vows down on paper, or say them in repeat-after-the-officiant style. If you are sure you want to speak free-form vows or statements, organize your thoughts well in advance, and don't be afraid to take some cue cards (in the form of index cards) up to the altar, just in case. Know what is in your ceremony in advance, but let your officiant lead you through it the day of the wedding. As I said before, the brain does not function normally in Wedding La-La Land—and it is not meant to! You don't want to break the Wedding La-La spell by forcing your left brain to be focused and be ready to speak from intellect. This should be a moment of speaking from the heart.

5. **The great surrender to Wedding La-La Land.** There is a place in the Niagara River that they call "the point of no return" because if you step into the water at that place, it will sweep you into Niagara Falls. There comes a time just before the wedding when you have to settle yourself and be ready. Once you get down the aisle, there is no turning back. It's showtime. Even if you are distracted by relatives or upset with a vendor, all that must be put aside so you can give yourself to the moment. This is what it is all about! You've done all your preparation, and now it's time to trust that everything is perfect, including tears, giggles, nervousness, and the occasional un-planned-for event—such as a microphone not working or a cell phone going off in the audience. Trust that it is all okay, as it is meant to be.

ADDITIONAL SPIRITUAL SUPPORT

Set up of the wedding altar. Everyone uses the term "wedding altar" frequently, but not everyone knows what it is, what it should contain, or who is responsible for bringing each item and setting it up. It is in many cases a table provided by the venue, covered with a tablecloth. Making sure the wedding altar is set properly in advance is the key to smooth sailing with no interruptions. This is something you usually work on with your officiant and/or wedding planner. Always connect with your officiant prior to the ceremony. Make sure you both have a checklist of what will be needed for the wedding altar, and make sure you are clear on who is bringing what. Once you decide what is needed, you might leave some of those supplies at the venue in advance, or bring some with you the day of the wedding. Store them all in one place, along with your wedding license, so you can give all the items to your officiant before the ceremony. If you are setting it up yourself, make sure you have all your ceremonial and ritual items, as well as any special spiritual tokens you would like on the altar. For example:

- If you are doing a candle lighting, sand ceremony, or wine ceremony, make sure all the elements you need are out of their packages and ready for use on the altar (candles out of boxes and plastic, wine bottle opened, or already poured, etc.)
- If you are reading vows, make sure the vows are on the altar.
- If you are breaking the glass, see that there is a wineglass or lightbulb in a napkin.

You can also use your wedding altar for spiritual support and extra blessings.

- If you have a wedding scroll or Ketubah, you can keep it on the altar, to be blessed.
- You can have items representing the elements of nature on the altar, honoring the ancestors and spirits of the four corners. In the east, you can honor air with a feather; in the west, honor water with a small cup of blessed water; in the south, honor fire with a candle; in the north, honor mother earth with a crystal or stone, such as blue lace agate, which also gives off a cool, healing vibration.
- You can scatter rose petals on the altar to represent love and new beginnings.

WEDDING GODDESS VOW

*I will fully enjoy this sacred moment in time with my beloved
as we stand here, soul to soul, and pledge our love.*

PART SEVEN

After the Wedding

KEEPING THE SACRED ALIVE AS A MARRIED COUPLE

When a man and woman blend the inspiration of love
with the hard work of putting that inspiration to practice,
their marriage becomes a sacred alchemy, joining heaven and earth.

—John Welwood, Ph.D., from *Journey of the Heart*

Jason Group/jasongphoto.com

CHAPTER TWENTY

After the Wedding

Sweetly Keeping the Promises You Made

May your partnership stay sweet and filled with everyday graces. May your home be a sancturary, vibrant with love, passion and beauty. May your marriage be blessed with loving family and good friends. May you together experience good fortune, material and spiritual. May marriage be your greatest blessing and highest achievement. May you always be thankful for the love you share.

—**Lakshmi, Hindu Goddess of Fortune and Beauty,**
also considered the perfect wife

After the wedding, you two will probably be ready for some time alone—to privately celebrate your love, relax, and enjoy reviewing the many new memories you have to share from your ceremony. You might be thinking about catching a plane, getting out of town, and enjoying your honeymoon. You should feel great—you had a fabulous wedding! Mission accomplished . . . congratulations . . . you're married!

It is sometimes a jolt, *after all that wedding planning*, when the day actually comes and goes. For so long, it was this *huge part of your life*, yet it was just sort

---

WEDDING GODDESS RULE #20

A Wedding Goddess keeps the sacred alive.

You know that the ceremony is the foundation of your life together, and you want to ensure that the promises made, the loving energy exchanged, and the energy received live on. You set out to savor those moments when two become one, spread them out over time, and find new ways to express your love to one another, become closer, and continue to allow your commitment to deepen with each season of your lives together.

of sitting on the horizon of your lives and seeming so far off in the distance. It was a time in your life so filled with activity, energy, and promise. Now it is part of your history together, another chapter of your personal love story.

The great part is that you can take all that is sacred about your wedding day and extend it into your new life as a married couple, and build on it as time goes on. As you move forward into this new chapter of your life, I offer you one of my favorite blessings, adapted from Daphne Rose Kingma's *Weddings from the Heart*: May you sweetly keep the promises you have made.

How to Keep Your Vows and Promises Alive

*T*here is a famous and classic quotation from theologian, scholar, and Unitarian Minister Theodore Parker that is often used in modern wedding ceremonies to encapsulate the essence of a true marriage. Originally published in 1865, it makes complete sense for couples today: "It takes years to marry completely two hearts, even the most loving and well assorted. A happy wedlock is a falling in love. Young persons think love belongs to the brow-haired and crimson-cheeked. So it does for its beginning. But the golden marriage is part of love which the bridal day knows nothing of. . . . Such a large and sweet fruit is marriage that it needs a long summer to ripen, and then a long winter to mellow and season it."

And, as the song goes, *you've only just begun!* Marriage will hopefully be a long and fruitful journey. To keep it fresh and keep it vibrant, look for ways to continually renew your commitment and to acknowledge the sacred promises you made. Over time, your marriage will need a tune-up here and there, when you must make sure you are both still aligned with your vows; in addition, your vows themselves may need some enhancement. As time goes on, you will both change and grow, and your married life will evolve. Yet the vows you made on your wedding day remain the starting point and the foundation of married life.

One of my favorite ways to suggest that couples sweetly keep their promises alive is to continue to share their wedding vows into married life. I first heard one of the most creative approaches to this idea from Rev. Diane Berke, who is now Spiritual Director of One Spirit Learning Alliance and One Spirit Interfaith

Seminary in New York City. She shared her own experience of renewing her wedding vows *every night* with her husband. "We wrote our own vows and decided we were going to say them every night for a month to really give them a chance to take root in our consciousness and our hearts," she recalls. "At the end of that time, we were finding it to be such a meaningful practice that we decided to continue for the first two years we were married. It very much kept in the forefront of our awareness what we wanted to bring to the marriage. Repeating our vows was particularly helpful in the times we weren't living in alignment with what we were promising each other; it became very clear and it gave us a chance to shift."

> We redo our vows every year on our anniversary. I like to see how I feel about these words each time we do it. It a good barometer for how I am doing in the relationship. I have an informal video of the ceremony and have watched it a few times. It definitely brings back that lovin' feeling.
>
> —*Susan, who married Robert on July 3, 1999*
>
> We always dance to our first-dance song whenever we hear it, anywhere, even if for just a minute. We call each other husband and wife a lot, like when he does something very sweet I will tell him, "You're such a loving husband," or when he's happy about something, he'll exclaim, "I love my life and I love my wife!"
>
> —*Jessica, who married Terry on November 15, 2003*

As she points out, the vows offer both a way to connect to each other and a way to have a checks-and-balances system in the relationship, letting you both know when things are out of sync and giving you a chance to get back in sync with each other.

Wedding Goddess Exercises

1. **Sweetly keeping your promises alive—the first stage.** You will be pretty high on love and life after your wedding—that's why they call it the "honeymoon" period!—yet remembering the promises made at the altar can help you both maintain the energy of your very special day, every day.

• **Exchanging vows every night.** Take your vows with you on your honeymoon, and every night, before you go to bed, take some time to look deeply into each other's eyes and repeat them. Keep it going by continuing this nightly ritual at home. Do this for at least thirty days. As Berke points out, thirty days gives the vows a chance to take root in both of you.

● **Surround yourself with reminders of your sacred day.** Get some beautiful paper, print out your vows, and frame them. Keep them in your boudoir, next to your favorite wedding photo and any other mementos from your wedding that fill your senses with happy memories.

2. **Expand your vows—the second stage.** The vows you speak at your wedding may be on the short side, or they may be romantic. There may have been some things that you felt were too personal, or too practical, to add in. And once you have a little experience with marriage under your belt, you may find that there are additional sentiments you would like to add to your vows. These are very personal statements the two of you can come up with together. You can add them to your existing vows and repeat them to each other, frame them, or just keep them in a sacred place— such as a holy book or even in a frame behind your wedding photo, sym- bolically making them the foundation beneath your marriage. For example, about six months into marriage, Jan and Peter discovered by trial and error, that there were a few more agreements they needed to make with each other, so they expanded their vows to include these promises:

● We treat our love as sacred, and we are responsible for managing our relationship.

● While we include others in our circle of love, we never take our issues outside the relationship, or talk negatively about each other to relatives, because this dissipates our sacred bond.

● We consult each other on all major life issues, purchases, and plans, and yet give each other freedom and space to be individual and to do our own things.

● We make each other's well-being a priority!

Over time, you can add anything that you desire as you learn more about what you both hold dear in married life.

3. **Regularly recommit to your marriage—third stage and beyond.** Re- member, you can celebrate and recommit to your marriage at any time.

Your legal marriage is a onetime deal, yet there is no law that says you cannot renew your commitment at any stage.

• **Renew your commitment in a ceremony.** Recommitment ceremonies, or renewal-of-vows ceremonies, are a great way to restimulate and relive your original wedding vows—long after you've taken that walk down the aisle. You can have a catered affair, just invite a few friends over to celebrate, or simply hold a private ceremony between the two of you.

• **Read each other love poems.** Collect romantic readings and poetry that reflect your feelings for each other and set aside a special "love ritual" evening when you can read to each other with candlelight and soft music in the background. Or read passages that speak what is in your heart, anytime—before bed, on anniversaries, during special moments, or while you are both relaxing. Any time is a good time to declare your love!

• **Share a simple expression of love.** This excerpt from Song of Solomon, in the Old Testament, is a beautiful example of selecting words that are simple yet powerfully honor and express your love. You can just look each other in the eyes, hold hands, and say: "I am my beloved's, and my beloved is mine" or "Let him kiss me with the kisses of his mouth, for thy love is better than wine." Seal it with a kiss. And so it is.

Every time you experience a ritual that declares your love, it's like giving your love, your life, and your marriage a new infusion of energy, or even a fresh start. Dr. Ray Bergen of the HeroGoddess Institute reminds us that the wedding ceremony should be one of many in your lifetime together. As he puts it, "Every relationship ceremony is a call to connect as lovers."

WEDDING GODDESS VOW

I am my beloved's, and my beloved is mine—forevermore.

Experts Interviewed and Products Mentioned

CHAPTER 2: BRIDAL BEAUTY AND GRACE

Aromatherapy
Young Living Essential Oils
http://www.youngliving.us/

Barbara Biziou, author
The Joy of Everyday Rituals (St. Martin's Press, 2001)
The Joy of Family Rituals (Golden Books, 2000)
creator of *Momentary Meditations* DVD
http://www.joyofritual.com/dvds.cfm

Dr. Patti Britton, relationship and sex coach and author
The Complete Idiot's Guide to Sensual Massage (Alpha Books, 2003)
http://www.yoursexcoach.com/

Goddess Lipstick
Tony & Tina Herbal Aromatherapy Lip Gloss
Available at www.sephora.com

Laura Norman
Author, *Feet First: A Guide to Foot Reflexology* (Fireside Books, 1988)
Reflexology sessions:
The Laura Norman Reflexology Center

1-800-FEET-FIRST or 1-212-532-4404
www.lauranormanreflexolgy.com

Dr. Linda Olson, America's Love Doctor, clinical psychologist, radio host and Imago Relationship Therapist
www.americaslovedoctor.com
Creator of The Wedding Series Collection, the True Love Collection, and *The True Love Bridal Journal*
http://www.americaslovedoctor.com/lovegifts/wedding/index.shtml

The Bridal Survival Club™
BridalSurvivalNY@aol.com
www.nywg.org
www.bostonweddinggroup.com

CHAPTER 3: FINDING *THE* DRESS

Arielle Ford, author
Hot Chocolate for the Mystical Lover (Plume Books, 2001)
Partner, The Spiritual Cinema Circle
http://www.spiritualcinemacircle.com/

Irene Shack, Vice President and Managing Director at The Wedding Channel.com, Founder of Independent Visions CE (Courture Exhibitions)

Kathryn Weber, feng shui practioner and consultant
The Red Lotus Letter, free feng shui e-zine
http://www.redlotusconsulting.com/Index.html

CHAPTER 5: BUILDING YOUR BRIDAL DREAM TEAM

Arlene Cronk, MSW, founder, The New York Wedding Group, The Boston Wedding Group, and The Bridal Surival Club, and owner of Invitations & Company
www.bestinvite.invitations.com

Donna Henes, Urban Shaman, ceremonialist and author
Queen of Myself (Monarch Press, 2004)
www.donnahenes.net

Sharon Naylor, author
The Ultimate Bridal Shower Idea Book
http://www.sharonnaylor.net/books.htm

CHAPTER 6: A BRIDAL SHOWER FIT FOR A GODDESS

Rev. Paul Michael, nondenominational minister and founder of Wedding Officiants.com, contributed the title "Goddess of Honor"

Phyllis Curott allowed us to adapt her beautiful "Aphrodite Ritual"
author of *The Love Spell* (Gotham, 2004)
Witch Crafting: A Spiritual Guide to Making Magic (Broadway, 2001)
Book of Shadows (Broadway Books, 1999)
www.templeofara.org and www.phylliscurott.com

CHAPTER 7: DEALING WITH WEDDING DYNAMICS

Judith Orloff, MD, author
Positive Energy: 10 Extraordinary Prescriptions for Transforming Fatigue, Stress, and Fear into Vibrance, Strength & Love (Harmony, 2004)
Guide to Intuitive Healing (Three Rivers Press, 2001)
Second Sight (Warner Books, 1997)
www.drjudithorloff.com

Virginia Rachmani, CSW, MA, psychotherapist
50 East 89th Street,
New York, NY 10128
212-996-9000

Kathryn Weber (See chapter 3)

CHAPTER 8: STAYING CLOSE TO THE MAN YOU WILL MARRY

Dr. Patti Britton (See chapter 2)

Dr. Judy Kuriansky, clinical psychologist, sex therapist, and author
The Complete Idiot's Guide to a Healthy Relationship (Alpha Books, 2002)
The Complete Idiot's Guide to Tantric Sex, 2nd Edition (Alpha Books, 2004)

Charles and Caroline Muir, internationally leading experts on tantric sexuality and authors
Tantra: The Art of Concious Loving (Mercury House,1990)
www.sourcetantra.com

CHAPTER 9: INCLUDING YOUR GROOM IN THE WEDDING PLANNING

Ray Bergen, Ph.d., Founder of The HeroGoddess Institute, Creator, *When Hereos and Goddesses Love* and *Turning Tyrants to Heroes and Dragons to Goddesses* audio series
www.herogoddess.com

Gregory J. P. Grodek, romance expert and author
1001 Ways to Be Romantic (Casablanca Press, 2002)
Confession of a True Romantic (Casablanca Press, 2004)
http://www.1001waystoberomantic.com/

Dr Judy Kurianksy (See chapter 8)

CHAPTER 10: THE PAPERWORK THAT MAKES IT LEGAL

Rev. Diane Berke, Spiritual Director of One Spirit Learning Alliance and One Spirit Interfaith Seminary
http://www.onespiritinterfaith.org/

Rev. Vic Fuhrman, MSC, R.M.
Interfaith Minister, Wedding Officiant, and Spiritual Counselor
http://www.enervision.org/

Rabbi Joseph Gelberman, author
Kabbalah As I See It, Zen Judaism, Physician of the Soul (Self-published)
Founder, The New Synagoge, The New Seminary, and All-Faith's Seminary
www.allfaithseminary.org/logo.asp

CHAPTER 11: RELEASE, PREPARE, PURIFY

Shelley Ackerman
Astrologer and Beliefnet.com columnist
www.karmicrelief.com

Ray Bergen (See chapter 9)

Barbara Biziou (See chapter 2)

Debbie Ford, author
Spiritual Divorce
Prayer wall and course information
http://www.spiritualdivorce.com/

Rev. Vic Fuhrman (See chapter 10)

Rev. Paul Michael, creator, The Engaged Couple Class
www.marriagetools.com
paul@marriagetools.com

Roy Anthony Shabala, Ph.D.
California-based healer and founder of BlessTheWorld.com,
creator of Aura Spritz and Karma Cleanse
www.blessthebody.com and www.blesstheworld.com

Karen Weisman, author, with Tami Coyne
Spiritual Chicks Question Everything (Red Wheel/Weiser, 2003)
www.spiritualchicks.com/

Charley Wininger, psychotherapist and dating coach
www.relationshop.com

CHAPTER 14: CHOOSING RITUALS, CUSTOMS, AND RITES

Barbara Biziou (See chapter 2)

Colin Cowie, Colin Cowie Lifestyle, member of The Association of Wedding Consultants and author
For the Bride (Delacorte Press, 2000)
Weddings (Little, Brown; 1st ed edition, 1998)
www.colincowie.com

Family Medallion
Products and Sample Ceremony
http://www.familymedallion.com

CHAPTER 17: TRANSFORMING JITTERS TO JOY

Connie Barrett, flower essence practitioner, teacher, writer, coproprietor
Beyond the Rainbow, resources for well-being and gifts with spirit,
www.rainbowcrystal.com

Michael Edan, Polarity Wellness Educator and essential oils expert, Founder of Healing Touch Services and creator of the soothing "Essential Wedding," aromatherapy blend for brides and "Signature Scents" personal aromatherapy blends.
845-351-4108
meandmy@earthlink.net

Filis Forman, New York–based makeup artist and hairstylist, and beauty coordinator for brides on their wedding day
http://www.filisforman.com

Rev. Vic Fuhrman (see chapter 10)

Goddess Granola
Divinely delicious
and nutritious bridal snack
www.goddessgranola.com

Barbara Kizner, Certified Kripalu Yoga Instructor and founder, Imagine Yoga Works in Queens, New York
646-284-2513

Allison Moir-Smith, founder
Emotionally Engaged—Premarital Counseling and Workshops
www.emotionallyengaged.com

Tony Robbins
http://www.anthonyrobbins.com

CHAPTER 18: THE WALK DOWN THE AISLE

Allison Moir-Smith (See chapter 17)

CHAPTER 20: AFTER THE WEDDING

Rev. Diane Berke (See chapter 10)

Ray Bergen, Ph.D. (See chapter 9)

SUPPORT ASSOCIATIONS

The Bridal Survival Club™
In New York, cofacilitated by Rev. Laurie Sue Brockway
Sponsored by The New York Wedding Group
An association of top wedding professionals in New York City
BridalSurivivalNY@aol.com
www.nywg.org

In Boston, facilitated by Arlene Cronk
Sponsored by The Boston Wedding Group
An associaition of top wedding professional in Boston
bestinvite@rcn.com
www.bostonweddinggroup.com

Association of Bridal Consultants
Gerard J. Monaghan and Eileen P. Monaghan, founders
Bridal Consultants and vendors across the country
56 Danbury Road, Suite 11
New Milford, CT 06776
860-355-0464
Fax: 860-354-1404
http://www.bridalassn.com/

WEDDING OFFICIANTS

WeddingOfficiants.com
Matches you (and your special needs) with the caring, high-quality clergy members across the country
www.weddingofficiants.com

Rev. Laurie Sue Brockway's Creative and Contemporary Ceremonies

Flexible, loving wedding officiants serving couples of all backgrounds with interfaith, intercultural, nondenominational, and nonreligious ceremonies

www.WeddingGoddess.com/www.RevLaurieSue.com

FABULOUS PHOTOS

Jason Groupp www.jasongphotos.com

Arlene Sandler of Lensgirl

Their fabulous photos bless these pages

www.lensgirl.com

weddings@lensgirl.com

BIBLIOGRAPHY

Cheever, Susan. *Looking for Work*, Fawcett Books, New York, 1981.

Cohen, Alan. Daily Quotes from Alan Cohen; to subscribe, info@alancohen.com

Dieda, David. *Finding God Through Sex: A Spiritual Guide to Ecstatic Loving and Deep Passion for Men and Women*, Plexus, 2002.

Ford, Debbie. *Spiritual Divorce: Divorce As a Catalyst for an Extraordinary Life*, HarperSanFrancisco, 2001.

Ford-Grabowsky, Mary. *Womanprayers: Prayers By Women from Throughout History and Around the World*, HarperSanFrancisco, 2003, from Buddhist Vow, page 53.

Handfasting blessing in chapter 14 adapted from a classic pagan prayer.

King James Bible. Canticles (Song of Solomon), from *The Holy Bible*, King James version, Electronic Text Center, University of Virginia Library.

Kingma, Daphne Rose. *Weddings From the Heart: Contemporary and Traditional Ceremonies for An Unforgettable Wedding*, Conari Press, Berkeley, California, 1995.

Kurianksy, Judy. *Complete Idiot's Guide to Tantric Sex*, Second Edition, Alpha Books, New York, 2004.

Latner, Helen. *The Everything Jewish Wedding Book*, Adams Media, Holbrook, MA, 1998. Bal Shem Tov quote.

Moore, Thomas. *Soul Mates: Honoring the Mysteries of Love and Relationship*, HarperPerrenial, 1994.

Muir, Charles and Caroline. *Secrets to Female Sexual Ecstacy*, VHS, Hawaii, 1996.

Mythography: Exploring Greek, Roman and Celtic Myth and Art. Eris in Greek Mythology, www.loggia.com/myth/eris .html.

Newhouse, Flower. *The Symbolic Meaning of Marriage*.

O'Connor, Pauline. "From Tame to Racey, The Bridal Parties," *The New York Times*, Sunday, December 8, 2002. About Caroline Rhea's bridal shower.

Pandya, Meenal Atul. *Vivah: Design a Perfect Hindu Wedding*, MeeRa Publications, Wellesley, MA, 2000.

Russell-Revesz, Heather. *Tying the Knot: The Book of Wedding Trivia*, Barnes & Noble, New York, 2002.

Shakespeare, William. *King Henry the VI*, Viking Press, 1979.

Spangleberg, Lisl. *Timeless Traditions: A Couple's Guide to Wedding Customs Around the World*, Universe Publishing, New York, 2001.

Some of the bridal shower suggestions were adapted from "Plan the Perfect Wedding Shower," article by ARA, copyright-free content, posted at www.PartyMerchant.com and www.aracontent.com.

Thai Wedding Custom, Sai Mokol, adapted from: www.culture.go.th/oncc/knowledge/married/english.htm orchidofsiam.com/orchidofsiam/Thai_Traditional_Weddings, www.thaiworldview.com/bouddha/wed2.htm, www.apmforum.com/columns/thai15.htm and witnessed at The Ninth Annual Asian-Pacific Summit, 2003, hosted by the Association of Bridal Consultants.

Thoele, Sue Patton. *Heart Centered Marriage:Fulfilling Our Natural Desire For Sacred Partnership,* Barnes&Noble, New York, 1996, page 1.

Warner, Diane. *Diane Warner's Complete Book of Wedding Vows: Hundreds of Ways to Say I Do*, Career Press, New Jersey, 1996.

WeddingGazette.com, "The Maid of Honor's Duties," http://www.weddinggazette.com/content/002309.shtml

Wellwood, Ph.D. John, *Journey of the Heart: Intimate Relationships and the Path of Love*, HarperPerennial, New York, 1990.

Williamson, Marianne, *Illuminata: A Return to Prayer*, Riverhead Books, New York, reprint edition, November 1995.

INDEX

ABOUT THE AUTHOR

Rev. Laurie Sue Brockway is an expert in women's empowerment, self-esteem, and spirituality who has long been devoted to helping women access the Goddess within. She helped women discover their divine spark in *A Goddess Is A Girl's Best Friend: A Divine Guide to Finding Love, Success, and Happiness* (Perigee, December 2002) and now offers her sage insights to brides in *Wedding Goddess: A Divine Guide to Transforming Wedding Stress into Wedding Bliss* (Perigee, May 2005).

As an interfaith minister and nondenominational wedding officiant, she has helped hundreds of brides through the challenges and the joys of preparing for their weddings. As co-facilitator of The Bridal Survival Club and creator of The Wedding Goddess Workshop in New York City, she regularly helps brides find empowerment, support, and solutions for challenges as they make that journey to the altar.

Rev. Laurie Sue is a unique and open-minded clergyperson who marries couples of all backgrounds, religions, and cultures in creative, personal, and loving ceremonies, and she's been selected Manhattan's best wedding ceremony provider by the *New York Press*.

She is a member of the Association of Interfaith Ministers, the Association of Bridal Consultants, and she is on the board of the New York Wedding Group. She lives in New York with her husband and son. Visit Rev. Laurie Sue's website at www.WeddingGoddess.com.

BRING OUT THE GODDESS
IN ALL YOUR BRIDAL ATTENDANTS

GIFT THEM WITH A COPY OF:

A Goddess Is a Girl's Best Friend
A Divine Guide to Finding Love, Success, and Happiness
(PERIGEE BOOKS, 2004)

Also by Laurie Sue Brockway